Two Tears on the Window

A True Story

Julia & Kevin Garratt

This is a work of nonfiction.

We have drawn from multiple sources – including personal and family journals and notes, correspondences, media reports, documented consular visits, and meetings with legal advisors. This memoir reflects Kevin and Julia's own recollections and interpretations of the events. All dialogue is recreated from memory. The names of some characters and details have been changed. Chinese Proverbs (author unknown), and all Chinese pinyin used in the book are translated into English by Peter Garratt. Dollar amounts are in Chinese RMB or U.S. currency. Canadian spelling, vocabulary and grammar is used. Scripture quotations are from the ESV® Bible (The Holy Bible, English Standard Version®), copyright © 2001 by Crossway, a publishing ministry of Good News Publishers. Used by permission. All rights reserved. And from The Holy Bible, New International Version®, NIV Copyright © 1973, 1978, 1984, 2011 by Biblica, Inc.® Used by permission. All rights reserved worldwide.

Cover Design by Emilie Stein
Author Photo by Gillian Lo

Printed and bound in Victoria, BC, Canada
by First Choice Books and Victoria Bindery

ISBN: 978-0-2285-0153-4 soft cover
ISBN: 978-0-2285-0154-1 hard cover
ISBN: 978-0-2285-0155-8 electronic book

9 8 7 6 5

For our amazing, resilient children
Simeon, Sarah, Peter & Hannah
&
family and friends around the world
who never stopped praying

Contents

Prologue vii

1.   Ode to Sociology 1
2.   Winds of Change 9
3.   Comrades 15
4.   A Wise Man 18
5.   Laughter 22
6.   Far from Beijing 25
7.   The China/North Korea Border 34
8.   Two Friends 42
9.   Abducted 49
10. Black Cars 56
11. The Compound 61
12. Interrogation 65
13. The Business Woman 72
14. Locked Up 78
15. U.S. Agents 88
16. Canadian Security Intelligence Service 95
17. New Glimpses 103
18. The Bird's Song 112
19. Hope 122
20. Purple Teddy Bears 127
21. Mercy 136
22. Two Tears on the Window 143
23. Dandong Detention Centre 152
24. Bail Pending Trial 161
25. Criminal Detention 169
26. Visitors 176
27. The Tiger Chair 183
28. The Art of Resilience 196
29. The Lawyer 204
30. Undercover 214
31. Surprise 222
32. A Loud Cry 228
33. The Trial 238
34. Hiding in Canada 248
35. Twists & Turns 256
36. Hugging the Bearded Man 263

Epilogue 273

Acknowledgments 274

Prologue

Nobody's family can hang up the sign,
'nothing the matter here'.

—Chinese Proverb

Eighteen plain clothes agents rushed us as we stepped out of a restaurant elevator in Dandong, on the border of China and North Korea. Grabbed, separated and ushered into two waiting black cars we vanished into the night. The Chinese state media broadcast their catch within hours and international news latched on. Alarmed friends called our children and family for information. Knowing nothing, they made a frantic call to Global Affairs Canada then sat glued to worldwide media reports. Kevin and Julia Garratt had disappeared without warning into the dark side of a labyrinth of 1.4 billion people. The Canadian government opened a case file.

The Chinese Ministry of State Security (MSS) orchestrated everything. Two black cars, two different routes in the middle of the night transferred us to an unofficial Chinese jail to extract confessions. No phone call, lawyer visit, or explanation. We were espionage suspects confined in isolation, grappling to comprehend the nightmare.

Canada immediately requested access. Controlled consular visits took place in a different location with heavy surveillance. Strained conversations reflected our captor's threats not to discuss the case or our location. Victims of a tit-for-tat response, we knew nothing about Canada's recent exposure of China's state-sponsored hacking of the Canada's National Research Council which paralyzed its IT department, leaving hundreds of millions of dollars in compromised equipment and data. Nor were we aware that only weeks before, Canada had arrested a Chinese Canadian spy wanted by the United States for stealing military technical data including specifications for F35 and F22 fighter jets.

❖

At 7:02 p.m. on August 4, 2014, time as we knew it, stopped. Hours, minutes and seconds blurred together. A day with variety was six hours of interrogation alone in a room with three uniformed security police. A day without variety was silence. Nothing. Waiting. White walls. Locked in two rooms at opposite ends of a compound, unaware of each other's whereabouts. Two guards' piercing eyes followed each movement until a knock signalled shift change. Meal trays came and left. The breath of despair and the hope of freedom battled within us. Sleep in a guarded light-filled room was a great victory. Waking up in captivity was an even greater disappointment. We interpreted sounds and whispers and patterns. We became face readers, watchers, reviewers, dreamers – disabled, untrained artists peering into the unseen seeking supernatural insight.

Day 183 brought the unusual sound of multiple car doors and footsteps. Freedom? No. Transfer. Thick binders of testimony and confessions filled the trunk of a white Toyota Land Cruiser. No longer held without charge, we became criminal suspects. Arrest and bail documents emerged and vague open-ended timelines. Still separated, we waited for a trial without a date.

Time was both a friend who kept us hoping and an enemy prolonging our suffering. Months passed as the case nudged forward. On paper, we were criminals. In relationship, we were two friends of China caught in an international incident. Trapped in the intricate network of complex diplomatic posturing, what value were two Canadian pawns? We were the wrong bait. Yet chosen. Could we, confined in an information vacuum, carry out our mission to give an answer to everyone for the hope that is in us? Could we give voice to the way isolation, captivity and injustice reveals the capacity and resilience of the human soul and spirit to cling to joy, embrace kindness, and show that love never fails? This is that story.

1

ODE TO SOCIOLOGY

Take care of the seed;
I think it's going to sprout.

—KEVIN

—*Julia*—

I come from a fascinating family. My paternal grandfather left his job as a small-town Alberta principal to train WWII fighter pilots for the British Commonwealth Air Training Plan (BCATP). His wife, a qualified pianist and praying lady, arrived in Canada with ten siblings as a Norwegian immigrant from North Dakota, USA. That meant my father and his two younger sisters had a lot of relatives! And a few famous ones. My Dad's third-cousin, Roald Amundsen, was the first to plant a flag at the South Pole and find a route through the North-West Passage.

Everyone loves my mother's British accent. Born in Cardiff Wales, she and her two sisters grew up in Bristol, England during days of WWII gas mask drills, hiding under Morrison steel shelters and collecting shrapnel from bombs in the blitzes. Her father managed a local bank and had a shelf of medals from competitive rowing. Her mother, a Paris-trained nurse, studied double bass with the BBC Light Orchestra's conductor and inspired me with her passion for music and poetry. Adventure touched down in her family line too. Her great grandfather's brother travelled to Algeria alone on a banana freighter during a student holiday in 1889, and his notebook of adventures remains in our family archives.

My parents were a perfect match when they met in northern Canada on adventures of their own. In 1960, they chose Brentwood, Essex, England to begin their married life because my father's industrial design training landed him a position with Ford. Nine months later, on January 24, 1961, Julia Dawn Gidman, a chubby blue-eyed baby with enough hair to hold a bow, filled one of twelve cots at Brentwood Maternity Home. My first name was the result of a pronunciation test. The name both parents pronounced the same won. The day after my second birthday my sister Deborah arrived and little brother Gregory two years later. My father wanted the family to be in Canada for their education so we boarded the Arkadia and crossed the sea to Montreal, Canada where I joined new classmates flipping lettered cushions in the stadium singing bilingual patriotic Canadian songs for Expo '67.

School bullies targeted my British accent so I stopped speaking in class until I'd mastered Canadian pronunciation. After that I always made friends with classmates struggling to fit in. When not at school or adventurous family picnics and summer camping holidays, I practised piano (often imagining my grandmother in heaven watching to make sure I didn't cheat on my 30 minutes' practice time) or curled up with books, dreaming of places real and imaginary where I longed to go. At ten, on my first day of school, I stood in front of the full-length mirror protesting to my mother I wasn't tall enough for Grade 5.

My junior high dilemmas shifted from height and homework to making moral sense of life. Shy in groups and wrestling with inner fears and deep life questions, I embarked on a personal quest to figure God out. I'd been to church with my family since birth but wanted my own personal relationship with God. Intrigued with the Bible, I underlined passages, asked God questions, and tried to listen to his answers. I kept a prayer journal, ticking off answers to prayers that most people never knew I prayed. At school, I shared my findings with friends but most blew it off so I focussed on studies. I pondered a career as a writer or a musician but my secret dream was to teach in China.

Our home was a revolving door for many needing a friend, a meal or a place to stay. University students away from home, were welcomed around our dinner table as family. Many visiting missionaries sat in our living room telling incredible stories of miraculous work around the world. I soaked up every word, drawn to nations and people I'd never seen.

After my high school graduation, our family relocated to Ontario where I studied English and Communications at the University of

Toronto. Brilliant and challenging professors like Josef Skvorecky, whose powerful first-hand lectures on the role of jazz in suffering during the Nazi occupation of Czechoslovakia, expanded my worldview and fueled my dreams. To cover tuition, I scanned magazines for first usages of new words for the editor of the *New York Times Everyday Dictionary*, taught piano, and ran summer entrepreneurial ventures. When friends and I met, we discussed third world crises and joined local outreaches. As a British-born, Quebec-raised, Ontario-trained Canadian, with a tinge of Norwegian blood, I longed to be part of a bigger story.

—Kevin—

My father was a fourth-generation Canadian raised in Toronto, the son of Torontonians. A Bell telephone employee, he did the same job every day until retirement at 55. After work he renovated the family home and offered his expertise to friends. My mother, the sweet middle daughter of a Canadian Pacific Railroad worker and a hard-working homemaker, was a fun-loving Toronto girl. After a chance meeting on Innisfil beach at 18 and 22, my parents married and settled in the small town of Maple, Ontario. On July 8, 1960, Kevin Ross Garratt arrived. My middle name was a tribute to our family line. Never blessed with a sister, my rambunctious fun-loving younger brother Jeff and cute curly-haired youngest brother Todd and I kept life interesting for my parents!

My Mom remembers me as a calm gentle child with a caring heart and still pictures me at five, gazing at a rainbow through the window saying, "Mommy look! God's not mad at us anymore!" I just remember the pranks we played on her!

At ten, I tried a few seasons of hockey before switching to Boy Scouts. For pocket money, I took a paper route and dog-sitting jobs. My first entrepreneurial venture was growing pumpkins in the backyard which my brothers and I lugged around in a wagon to sell to neighbours. In junior high I visited Norway, Denmark and Sweden for a World Scout Jamboree. What a taste of overseas adventure!

Sadly, at 15, my parents split up and divorced a few years later adding cooking and babysitting to my part-time jobs! But whether I was buying milk or collecting grocery stamps for the family, chopping potatoes in the basement of the local fish and chips shop, or shovelling manure at a mushroom farm, I always had time for friends. In high school, to escape the pressure and confusion from new family dynamics, I tried the partying scene. The downside was my marks dropped and I almost didn't graduate. A caring English teacher intervened. "You can make more of yourself!" she said. It was a wake-up call. At 18, I left a raging party and sat in the park down the street. *My life is pointless. I'm done with the parties, drugs and mindless drinking.* My will power to follow through surprised everyone, but I stuck to my plan and never turned back. I graduated high school and got into the University of Toronto thinking I'd save the world as a doctor or social worker.

After completing two years with my head in books, I was restless for adventure. The picturesque Canadian Rocky Mountains and an opportunity to hone photography skills and meet people from all over the globe lured me west to Chateau Lake Louise. Once, on elevator duty in the middle of the night, Canadian Prime Minister Pierre Elliott Trudeau came through the lobby! I said hello and the Prime Minister returned the greeting before stepping into a nondescript white van that pulled up at the door. *Why did the Prime Minister leave the hotel in this clandestine manner? Perhaps there's an international emergency somewhere!*

After a year at the Chateau, I drove my 1968 VW Beetle back to Toronto to finish my degree in Psychology and Sociology. Armed with new skills and deep compassion for people, at 22, I entered my final year of university watching and waiting for my next challenge.

—Julia—

I arrived late for my Sociology 301 Marxism-Leninism evening class. My usual spot near the front was taken and the only seat left was at the back.

"Did you do the homework?" I asked the guy beside me, flipping open my notebook for the lecture.

"No, can I share yours if the prof asks me a question?"

"Sure."

"I'm Kevin," he said.

For him it was love at first sight. For me it was nothing special. During the break, he invited me to the pub for lunch the next day but I refused. "Then what about Wednesday?" I shook my head. "Thursday?" I was busy. "Friday?" I said I had plans for the weekend. "Then what day are you free?" he asked. Undaunted by my refusals, Kevin followed me to the university entrance after class and chatted while I waited for a ride home. My father was an hour late. In that interlude we became friends.

❖

"Do you ever think about God?" I asked as we sat in my parent's driveway in his light-blue hand-painted Volkswagen Bug.

"Yes, he is the trees and the ground. He is everywhere, in everything."

"Have you ever been to church?" I eyed a fir tree trying to picture God inside.

"Well, I went a few times as a child. The rector was pushing 90 and spoke in Old English!" He laughed. "I went again after my parents split because my Mom wanted company. Maybe I'll come on Sunday and try it again."

He did and one month later, poems appeared. Kevin volunteered as photo editor for the university newspaper *Medium II* and hinted I should read it. I discovered an anonymous poem in the classified section called *Ode to Sociology* that ended with the words *take care of the seed; I think it's going to sprout. Ode to Sociology 2* appeared a week later. Kevin wanted a girlfriend but despite the friendship and love poems, my stance as a Christian meant that without a common faith it couldn't be more.

—*Kevin*—

Julia and her Christian friends who believed in an invisible God, confused me. Frustrated, I went for a walk in the woods one night. Surrounded by evergreen trees, I asked God out loud, "Are you real?" Nothing happened. Determined to get an answer if there was one, I thought I'd give God one more chance and tried the next day. "God, if you are really there, show me."

Suddenly, I felt God. It was like coming out of a dark movie theatre into bright sunshine. That moment and the series of moments following awakened something deep. A few weeks later, November 28, 1982, during an evening church service, the pastor invited anyone who wanted to become a Christian to come forward. *Not me.* I gripped the pew while everyone waited. Then someone or something invisible nudged my hands from the pew and I walked to the front. No one forced me but that prompt encouraged me to do what fear and insecurity prevented me from doing. *God's invisible hand led me forward.* There on the stairs as Pastor Fred talked with me, my beating heart filled with joy and I stopped my search.

—Julia—

I was nervous to risk a deeper relationship with Kevin even after we shared a common faith. After graduation, Kevin worked at a Salvation Army transition house for ex-psychiatric patients in Toronto while I pursued an Education degree at Queen's University three hours away. Every night at 11 p.m. with no cell phones or texting, Kevin's inexpensive *goodnight* was two rings. My answer was the same until one chilly autumn evening when I sat bundled in blankets. Two rings turned to four so I answered. Kevin sounded excited. "I met a man named Dwyatt who taught in China last year and I told him we might be interested."

My heart pounded. Kevin knew nothing of my teenage China dream. "I always planned to teach in China." I said, feeling something amazing birthing.

"Yes, and our destiny is life together," he added. Far from his grin, cute curly hair, and big, blue eyes, I smiled. Life is such a mystery. A marvellous mystery if you let it be that. Soon after, twelve daisy magnets arrived in the mail for Valentine's Day.

❖

In public school, we'd studied this country hidden behind the Bamboo Curtain. We knew little more than chopsticks, fortune cookies, bamboo, and rice paddies. But after Kevin's phone call, discussing a move to China felt normal and there wasn't a shred of fear in either of us. Armed with bachelor degrees, youthful idealism and convinced it was God's idea and not just ours, we wanted to do our part to help a third world country. Raised in the 1970s, we'd cheered with our peers as teams of Canadians mobilised for peacekeeping missions during world crises. We belonged to the first wave of young Canadians influenced by the 1971 multicultural policy. For us, being Canadian and Christian, meant welcoming others to our land and homes and going into the world to help.

❖

Early January, the last day of Christmas break, I waited for Kevin to arrive for a day of cross-country skiing before leaving for school. Dressed in a blue and white striped sweater and jeans, Kevin arrived at the door in a suit and overcoat! His eyes twinkled. "Get your coat and come with me."

What's he up to? We traipsed through the snow to the farthest corner of my parent's field. He stopped and grinned before pulling a red checker tablecloth from inside his overcoat and spreading it on the deep snow. Next came two glasses, grape juice and pistachio nuts. Finally, he reached into his pocket and out came a tiny box. Opening the box to display a delicate diamond ring on a black velvet cushion Kevin proposed, "Will you marry me?"

We still debate how many seconds it took me to say yes. When we returned to announce our news to my parents, they stood by the door with a camera. My mother had watched the whole scene from the window with binoculars!

—Kevin—

In March, Julia surprised me with a visit. As we discussed wedding plans in my Mom's townhouse, Pastor Fred called. "Would you be willing to come in and discuss your August wedding date? I have an opportunity out west and your wedding is my only commitment that month."

"Sure, Julia is back for the weekend. We'll come tomorrow morning." I slipped Julia an envelope. "This came this afternoon. Open it while I order pizza." The letter invited us to come in August to teach English in a Chinese university. We sat stunned! Julia's surprise visit, the phone call about changing our wedding date, and the letter offering us a job in China in August. *Is this a sign?*

The next morning, we showed Pastor Fred the letter. Earlier we'd agreed to his counsel to stay in Canada at least one year after marriage. Today he said, "When God opens a door, let no man shut it."

❖

That settled it. We married on June 23, 1984, with a quiet garden reception at Julia's parents' house and guests donating towards China airfare instead of wedding gifts. I was 24, Julia was 23. I'd chosen our honeymoon destination by writing to three lodges near Toronto and selecting the one with the most personal response. Unfortunately, the owner of the Briarwood Inn was so friendly we spent two evenings in her living room watching slide shows and one afternoon picking strawberries in a mosquito-infested field to sample her strawberry shortcake! Honeymoon humour!

Our final honeymoon days disappeared securing documents and China visas. We leafed through thick encyclopedias from Julia's parents' shelves to familiarize ourselves with the city where we'd teach. Later we realized the dictionary used an old phonetic spelling for Chinese cities and everything we'd read and shared with friends and relatives, was about the wrong city. *Are we too inexperienced and naïve for such a move?*

2

WINDS OF CHANGE

*When the winds of change blow, some people build
walls and others build windmills.*

—CHINESE PROVERB

—Kevin—

M arried for almost one month, we boarded a bus for the 32-hour
ride to Tulsa, Oklahoma to join 15 American teachers for cross-
cultural training. Despite a bout with food poisoning from bologna
and losing a suitcase at the Saint Louis bus depot, we loved each other
and I couldn't wait to spend the rest of my life with Julia. Our lost
suitcase turned up intact and we added one poster to decorate our
new home. *I don't know all the answers, but I know someone who does;* a
reminder for the days we couldn't handle our new lives.

❖

Our invitation to China was daunting. The Beijing Foreign Experts
Bureau invited us as the first foreign English teachers to work in a
Chinese Military university since 1949. China was in transition after
Chairman Mao Zedong's Communist leadership left the country
with both wonderful achievements and devastating failures. After
establishing the People's Republic of China (PRC) in 1949, Mao
replaced traditional Chinese characters with simplified ones improv-
ing literacy for the masses. Women had new rights to work and
equality, and Mao's *Iron Rice Bowl approach* used ration coupons and
strict controls to feed the massive population. Communes or work
units oversaw daily life and the state owned everything. Mao isolated
China from the rest of the world for 17 years while implementing
these changes. Many policies backfired including the Great Leap
Forward where Mao encouraged *backyard furnaces* to industrialize

the nation with people power not mechanization. Filling in lakes with dirt to create more land for rice, disrupted the ecosystem. These initiatives, compounded by three large-scale natural disasters, resulted in over 20,000,000 people dying of starvation. Instead of taking responsibility Mao blamed foreign powers.

A huge ideological struggle resulted, culminating in the tragic Cultural Revolution from 1966 to 1976. As the *Red Guard* youth, red scarves around their necks, rallied to serve their country with revolutionary spirit, it turned violent. These teenagers, and Mao's strong army, carried out mandates to root out and purge the country of its *evils* (imperialist ideas, customs, habits and culture). Generational divides ensued and rebellions spiralled. Many children, radicalized by Mao's thinking, turned in and punished their own parents in public to show party loyalty. Trust disintegrated and secrecy and fear spread. It became taboo to hide family photos or cultural heirlooms and many Chinese historical sites, cultural relics, and associations with religion, western thinking, or luxurious lifestyles, became criminal offences.

Mao died in 1976 leaving his successor, Deng Xiaoping, with great challenges. Chairman Deng's 1978 Open-Door policy reflected a new view that friendship with the world and mechanization was essential for development. In 1982, Deng Xiaoping ushered in a new period of reform, dismantling the controlled state-run system. Foreign trade and joint venture projects sprang up and intellectuals had new hope for the future. Persecuted under Mao, scholars felt Chinese *backwardness* would dissipate as foreigners helped with its Four Modernizations: agriculture, industry, national defence, and science and technology. China recruited and graciously welcomed foreign experts and since English was a key to gaining knowledge and skills, the Beijing Foreign Experts Bureau even invited inexperienced teachers like us.

—Julia—

On August 26, 1984, after a 30-hour milk run flight we landed in Hong Kong. We entered Mainland China by train with four suitcases and less than $20. The train stopped mid-way as Chinese uniformed police replaced Hong Kong attendants. They checked tickets and passports as the train lurched forward past huge barbed wire fences with remnants of ripped clothing conjuring up failed escapes. We rolled to a stop amid a sea of faces in the Guangzhou train station. *God, what are we doing here?* We went through customs and stood bewildered and sweltering in the heat and humidity in the middle of a sweaty huddle of Chinese bodies. Representatives from the Foreign Experts Bureau packed us into vans which honked their way through bicycle-filled roads to the Dong Fang Hotel. Leaving the dirty, crowded, noisy street we entered a pristine hotel courtyard with artistic, Chinese wood-carved doors and magnificent garden pools. The hotel's spacious rooms and empty halls made us nervous. *Are we the only guests?* A dinner of delicacies awaited as we sat in groups of eight with our hosts. The man beside me took food with his chopsticks and placed it on my plate with a greeting. "Welcome to China. This is sea cucumber."

His hospitality was a sign of honour, but my stomach lurched as he placed the spiky slimy sea creature on my plate. I spent the next few minutes contemplating how to slide it into a napkin and under the table unseen! After dinner, a floor attendant who kept all room keys, unlocked our room and handed us a decorated metal thermos flask of hot boiled drinking water. Exhausted, we stretched out on the hard single beds with bright pink embroidered bedspreads. The thin crunchy pillow smelled like hay and Kevin's feet stuck out past the end of the bed, reminding me that in China, Kevin was a tall man.

—*Kevin*—

We awoke the first morning in awe. Peeking through an open window, Guangzhou greeted us with life, noise, and unfamiliar food that gave our nostrils a full workout. Our university hosts appeared wearing traditional Chinese army-green Mao suits. Their English, though limited, was helpful considering our Chinese repertoire was *nǐ hǎo* (hello) and *xièxiè* (thank you). After a quick breakfast of steamed bread and boiled eggs our hosts whisked us to the Guangzhou airport where a Russian propeller plane waited on the tarmac. Our hosts had never flown before. Air travel was a rare privilege in those days and airplanes scarce. We squeezed into well-worn vintage-style uphol-stered seats, exchanging looks about the live chickens in mesh bags that were hand luggage for the couple behind us. Despite watching the cabin fill with steam at take-off, an hour later, battling with teeming rain and poor visibility, our plane touched down safely in Changsha, the capital of Hunan province in south-central China.

—Julia—

Rows of silver military jets and camouflaged buildings hidden between dirt mounds greeted us as we disembarked. After welcome handshakes, we were separated and hurried into two waiting black Russian-made cars, complete with drawstring curtains on the side windows. Waves of terror rippled through me as I watched through the back window. *Is Kevin's car still following?* We later learned our reception was a high honour because the university only had two cars.

"You can rest here and eat in the hotel dining room," said a middle-aged woman in uniform, leading us into the lobby of a small government hotel. "I'm Mrs. Yang, the foreign affairs officer at the National University of Defence Technology (NUDT). We will return later. The attendant will take care of you." She disappeared and the courteous hotel attendant approached. We followed her upstairs and stood with our suitcases as she unlocked a door to a sparse but clean room. With no word from the school the next morning, we cautiously ventured out to explore, returning at set mealtimes as instructed by the attendant. Unannounced, early the third morning two cars returned and drove us to the university.

❖

Our first home in China was a spacious room in a quaint guest house beside the campus. "Dress for a reception tonight. I will return soon," Mrs. Yang said leaving us standing with four suitcases just inside the door. A bed with a heavy white bedspread, two desks facing each other, two chairs, and a small bathroom with two thin towels welcomed us to our first home. A coiled electric hotplate on the desk was both kitchen and heater. Bewildered but excited, we unpacked.

❖

When we arrived at the reception, the complete university staff stood in military array to welcome us to the school, the city, and to China. It wasn't a dinner; it was a full-scale event! Introducing us with great formality the leaders invited us to the front to sing! *In front of everyone?* In shock and desperation, we performed *A Bicycle Built for Two*. They loved it so much they asked for solos! No was not an option so I sang a poor rendition of *My Favourite Things* and Kevin fumbled through *Frere Jacques*. We realized singing was a sign of friendship, like a group handshake. The president sang, followed by the dean, and then an amazing university soldiers' choir, in matching white suits, sang patriotic songs including *Gēchàng Zǔguó* (Ode to the Motherland) and the *Huánghé Dàhéchàng* (Yellow River Cantata). Passionate energy and fervour burst from their united voices. The festivities and warm hospitality surprised us as young and inexperienced newlyweds never expecting such honour for coming to teach. Back in the guest house afterwards we discussed how we already loved these kind-hearted people in their green Mao suits with red stars on their collars and caps.

—*Kevin*—

Every new experience we tucked away for future reference. Changsha, dubbed a half-furnace city, was famous for hot chili peppers and dog meat. The aroma of Chairman Mao Zedong's favourite charred *chòu dòufu* (stinky tofu) cooked on street barbeques filled the air. Mao crafted his Communist ideology while a student in Changsha, staying close to his renowned birthplace–Shaoshan. Our military university's relocation from northern China to Changsha was part of Mao's strategy to centralize power under his banner and escape the perceived threat of proximity to Russia.

We sampled Mao's famous tofu but preferred the guest house fare. Steaming plates of slivered meat, green peppers and overflowing bowls of rice, arrived daily at a small dining room at the end of the hallway. The shock came on payday when the meal bill was 700 RMB ($112), the total of both our monthly salaries!

"You receive first grade meals," Mrs. Yang said. After explaining we needed money to live, we opted for third grade meals with less meat. Our salaries arrived as a thick stack of 10 RMB bills (the highest bank note at the time worth $1.60), along with oil, flour, rice, and pork ration coupons. Most foreigners never got *rénmínbì* (RMB, the people's money) also called Chinese yuan (CNY). They had to use Foreign Exchange Certificates (FEC) only accepted in designated Friendship Stores and Friendship Hotels that locals couldn't enter without special permission. FEC helped China control the flow of western currencies at that time.

RMB gave us access to local markets. We traded oil and pork ration coupons for flour and rice coupons and bought bread or *jiǎozi* (Chinese pork and chive-filled boiled dumplings) from small campus kiosks. Long lines meant food often ran out before we got to the front. Attitudes are choices, so we laughed a lot and learned from our mistakes.

❖

Despite new openness under Deng Xiao Ping, China still reeled from the effects of the Cultural Revolution and a general mistrust and suspicion of everything foreign prevailed. Beyond campus walls, two blonde-haired foreigners were an anomaly and everyone stared. Our clothing stood out because locals wore navy or army green and only children wore colourful clothes made by grandmothers or relatives. Strangers on the street shouted *gwáilóu* (foreign devil) as we passed, showing deep seated prejudices. Our Chinese phrase book failed to help us decipher the strong, local dialect so we smiled, repeated our mispronounced hellos and tried to learn the culture.

State-run shops sold limited amounts of identical items and shop clerks sat behind glass counters with items piled on shelves behind them. I made three attempts to buy an undershirt at Changsha's only department store before the disinterested clerk tore off a small slip of flimsy pink paper and handed it to me. It took ten minutes to find the small booth two floors up, pay, and come back with the paper stamped. After gluing the slip in her hand into a small book, she reached up to the third shelf, and pulled down an undershirt wrapped in cellophane and pink string. It didn't fit but I had to keep it.

3

COMRADES

What you hear about may be false;
what you see is true.

—CHINESE PROVERB

—Julia—

On campus, we worked as *comrades* (friends). Our Sociology 301 book-learning about Communism was quickly dwarfed by what daily life taught us first-hand. From 1984 to 1986 we taught alongside the bravest teachers we've ever met. In 1984, a change in government education policy required Russian language professors switch to English overnight. Our role was teaching them so they could repeat our lessons for students the next day while we taught select students. The older teachers, who'd suffered during the Cultural Revolution for being academics, amazed us with their dedication and resilience as they pored over English sentences to deliver lessons. The younger teachers were equally hard-working and dubbed *The Lost Generation* after Mao closed universities from 1968 to 1975 causing 12,000,000 youth to miss out on high school and university. They were sent to the countryside to understand peasant life away from their entitled lives in the cities. Through self-study years later, they passed nationwide exams to earn university credentials. What an incredible group of dedicated teachers. It was an honour to work with them!

Our classroom students were remarkable too. Shy, eager, diligent students soaked up every word making teaching a joy. Many were the first students from their villages to attend university. Boys outnumbered girls 15 to 1 and lived separate lives even though both received equal educations. They sat in different rows in class and walked on opposite sides of campus lanes. Dating was forbidden though it happened in secret.

The new China had many role models. Campus posters carried slogans promoting local heroes. *Follow Lei Feng's example, love the Party, love socialism, love people.* The Confucian value of honour threaded through everything. Teachers entered class after students, and were greeted with a standing ovation. Our student's names, like *AiGuo* (Love China), *Weihong* (Protect Red), and *XueNong* (learn from the peasants), reflected their parent's patriotism to movements and party initiatives.

Despite our age and inexperience, we were role models as the first foreign teachers on any Chinese military campus since 1949, and as Canadians. During the Japanese occupation in WWII, Dr. Norman Bethune, a Canadian surgeon, saved many Chinese lives and became a national hero. Mao Zedong wrote his eulogy and millions of Chinese memorized a booklet describing his heroism and spreading his fame. Although Dr. Bethune was unknown to us before arriving in China, because of him people trusted us with their stories.

—Kevin—

52-year-old Comrade Fan invited us to his tiny, sparse apartment for dinner and shared his tale. Exiled to a remote countryside region along with most teachers during the Cultural Revolution purges, he survived on corn husks, and saw his own son turn against him after joining the Red Guard. "Suffering strengthened me," he said as he used his full quota of ration coupons to buy flour and meat and make us Chinese dumplings. He even coaxed me into a dumpling eating contest!

We soaked in so much wisdom from our comrades. Everyone was our teacher and we developed deep respect for Chinese in uniforms.

—Julia—

Modernization happened in spurts. Luxury goods were rare in the eighties resulting in *viewings*. English Dean Wang had the first refrigerator in town. We attended the welcome ceremony as staff and students lined the campus streets watching the appliance arrive by three-wheeled bicycle and cheering until it reached her apartment. Invited for a visit a few days later, she took us aside, "Kevin *lǎoshī* (teacher)! Can you help? I think they've sold me a faulty refrigerator. It makes this humming noise and then stops. Then starts again and stops. It keeps happening." Only I noticed Kevin's brief smirk before he explained about motors. Relieved, she opened the refrigerator door. "Why don't you put food in?" I asked surprised it was empty. "Oh no! We like fresh food." I never forgot her words. The refrigerator was a status symbol and she had the only one.

Television was similar. Mrs Yang pointed out her television draped in red velvet with a metre stick on top. With pride, she measured the television as we watched.

"Do you watch it?"

"Not much. There's only one black and white channel with fuzzy reception."

A television was not electronics; it was luxury furniture.

—Kevin—

Each day brimmed with new experiences. We munched dumplings and sweet potatoes doused with canned butter and collected our share of the apples or frozen fish when trucks from the north arrived. Back in our apartment we handwrote lesson plans and sometimes joked the bureau picked us for NUDT because we were young and least likely to be spies.

But deeper than laughter, the country mesmerized us. China's heartbeat started beating in tandem with ours! Every day a new story unfolded around us and we wanted to be part of it.

4

A Wise Man

—Julia—

We felt regal paying two *jiǎo* (four cents) and strolling through Martyr's Park only minutes from the university. The decorated pagodas and tranquil scenic lake with rowboats for hire offered a welcome weekend respite. What we didn't expect to find was a frail elderly Chinese man sitting on a bench speaking fluent English.

"I've been waiting for you," he said. "This morning I prayed and God told me to sit on a bench in this park until two foreigners passed by. I have waited all morning." Captivated, we accepted the mysterious stranger's invitation to share the bench.

"My name is Dr. Wu," he whispered, "I was in prison for seven years during the Cultural Revolution. I am a Christian. My mother was Christian. I learned English from reading the Bible with her. Later, I studied and became a doctor but never gave up my faith. Then the Red Guard came. They beat my wife and I for our beliefs. As they carted my piano away, I informed them it was dedicated for hymns to God and not for revolutionary songs. They laughed in my face. But later, when officers brought me on stage to confess my crimes in public, a common punishment in those days, I saw my piano. A placard sitting on it said *this piano is dedicated to God*. In their mockery was my miracle! The piano sat untouched. After prison, they returned it. But my hands..." he paused, showing withered misshapen hands. "I can't play now. Do you play?"

I nodded.

"I hope you can visit my flat and play while I sing. Come to the park next week and I'll tell you more." Then he got up and walked away leaving us bewildered. *Is he an angel in disguise? Are we dreaming?* All week we discussed the encounter.

The next Saturday we met again. "After prison," Dr. Wu said, "I packed my old medical books into a heavy canvas bag to donate them to the small village hospital where I used to work. I'd sent word ahead to have someone meet me at the bus station. As I stepped off the crowded bus a woman approached and thanked me for saving her life. Perplexed and sure we'd never met, I asked what she meant. Thirty years earlier I'd refused to give her mother an abortion. That baby was her! She works in the hospital now and had always wanted to meet me. What joy! But there was more. After a meal with her family, her uncle doubled over in pain from a debilitating back injury. I had nothing medical to offer but I prayed. Miraculously, his back straightened and he stood up! The whole family believed in Jesus after that."

Dr. Wu told stories as if they were ordinary everyday events. Despite his 65-year-old wrinkles and the scars reminding us he'd been through hard years, his eyes smiled and his face danced with joy. Our chats were short but their impact permanent. We readily agreed to his request to meet the next Saturday at a bus stop in town during lunch hour. "I want to take you somewhere," he said.

❖

The week sped by teaching Longman's English lesson *Puma at Large* to eager students. On Saturday, we paid our fare and squeezed onto the crammed accordion bus that wound around the city. Everyone stared or whispered *foreign devil* and we smiled back. Inching to the exit in time took skill, and we jumped off the packed bus just before the doors snapped shut. Dr. Wu appeared around a corner motioning to us. We wound through narrow alleys to a factory. Stepping through a square opening in the metal back gate, he hurried us into the fourth entranceway of a seven-storey apartment building. We climbed the dimly lit cement stairs to the sixth floor. Dr. Wu knocked and a man peeked out and then opened the door. Behind him, in two dingy rooms, sat 30 elderly Chinese on small wooden stools. Dr. Wu introduced us and they cheered.

They were all blind.

"The light has come as promised," they exclaimed as we greeted them, letting them touch our hands and faces with their worn and wrinkled hands. They offered us stools and leafy green tea in small metal cups. Dr. Wu explained, "A German orphanage mission cared for them as children. When Mao took power 1949, foreign orphanages closed and these blind orphans, teens at the time, were assigned to work at this rubber factory. They've been together ever since."

He pointed to a thin, white-haired lady smiling in the corner. "She's in her nineties and called the walking Bible dictionary because she's memorized the whole Braille Bible. If anyone wants to know something they ask her." The lady nodded as we sat stupefied. Then the group on one side of the room pulled harmonicas from their pockets and played a hymn. The rest sang in German. Peace blanketed the room as music filled every crevice. We wiped tears from our eyes wondering how we'd been chosen to experience such beauty.

After three hymns, Dr. Wu translated for a man whose wrinkles depicted hardness while his face reflected joy. "We have persevered in prayer for years asking God to send a light to Changsha. Every day we call to God for our city. We can only share God's love inside this rubber factory. Now you've come from Canada to Changsha. God has answered our cries. He let us live to see you!"

We are the answer to their prayers? We were ordinary unexperienced youth. They were heroes. One hour in their presence let us touch enough faith for a lifetime. As we sat speechless, stools shuffled closer and these kindhearted caring seniors wept, hugged us, and rubbed our faces with their teary hands. *Gănxiè Shén, gănxiè Shén* (thank you God) they said over and over. We wanted the moment to last forever.

But Dr. Wu was careful not to let a rest-time visit slip into afternoon sirens and the factory kicking back into gear for the last shift of the six-day work week. After prayer and great shouts of celebration, Dr. Wu hurried us to the bus stop. "Thank you for encouraging them."

"Thank you for taking us. They are extraordinary!" we answered, wishing we spoke Chinese and could have understood every word. Dr.

Wu disappeared so fast we wondered if the visit was a dream. We came to teach English. *What story is God writing behind the scenes?*

—*Kevin*—

We had lots of student parties where whole classes crammed into our apartment for games. One night, rooms overflowing with students, a brilliant young student named Paul, the first from his village to enter university, noticed our poster. *I don't know all the answers but I know someone who does.*

"Who does?"

"God." I answered. Paul's inquisitive mind pushed further and he said he planned to test it by talking to God himself to see if anyone answered.

Three days later he returned. "It's true. There is a God." We smiled. *Is this an answer to those blind seniors' prayers?*

The next week, Paul arrived at our door with two classmates. "They're ready."

"For what?" I wondered as three students walked into the apartment.

"Ready to meet the one who knows the answers."

"Oh, you mean God. You don't need us for that. You can talk to him yourselves and invite him to partner in your lives. But if you have questions we know a Chinese Christian with a story to tell. His name is Dr. Wu."

5

LAUGHTER

You will never be punished for
making people die of laughter.

—CHINESE PROVERB

—Kevin—

We stumbled our way through daily life with frequent blunders. Sign language often backfired. On a visit to a state-run restaurant, we fanned our tongues to warn the server we couldn't eat hot peppers. A plate with only hot peppers arrived! Another day, our gate guard burst out laughing when my prized purchase of pink toilet paper turned out to be a roll of 100 firecrackers! We had our turn when we noticed he'd decorated the walls of his guardhouse with Julia's flattened tampon boxes from our garbage.

We laughed a lot and my constant puns resulted in a teacher dubbing me *humour-maker*. The name stuck. Some things were funny; others were embarrassing! We challenged teachers and students to balloon fights, introduced poor renditions of western food, and learned Chinese games. Unaware that in that part of China, losers put things on their heads, Julia ended up wearing a lampshade and I had two steamed buns perched on my head at the end of our first Chinese game night. And a visit to the campus hospital for food poisoning included a free zoo visit since the tiger from the zoo across the street was recovering from surgery on the bed in the next room!

—Julia—

Then I got pregnant. Despite trying to hide it behind a green Mao jacket, everyone gave advice. Don't ride a bicycle downhill while pregnant or the baby will slip out. Don't eat bananas or the baby will slip out. Chinese culture has sayings and warnings for everything!

❖

Teaching contracts completed, we returned to Canada. Simeon arrived six weeks early on November 6, 1986, right after we hosted a Chinese dinner for 20 friends. We joke that when he had to share a space with all the Chinese food I ate he made a quick exit. Unfortunately, it was in the middle of a surprise November snowstorm! 22 months later, on September 15, 1988, his little sister Sarah appeared right as they announced the American election results on hospital TV. We say the whole nation let off red, white and blue balloons to celebrate her arrival!

—Kevin—

While spending time in Canada letting our children get acquainted with grandparents, aunts and uncles, and hoping to work in China long-term, I took seminary courses and completed a Master's of Arts degree in Teaching English as a Second Language (with a child on each knee). When an invitation came after graduation, to base in Hong Kong assisting foreign teachers in China, it was a perfect stepping stone back to the mainland. With a toddler and baby in tow we moved to Kowloon Bay in November, 1988. Things ran smoothly until June 4, 1989 when the Beijing Tiananmen mass student protests and government crackdown attracted unwanted media attention and conflicting reports aroused the sleeping dragon. Fear of foreigners resurfaced and foreign governments recommended citizens leave China until things stabilized. We helped evacuate stranded teachers and respond to panicked parents in North America.

—Julia—

After that crisis subsided we had a few close calls of our own. We almost lost Sarah once in Hong Kong when a lady snatched her from the stroller as I picked Simeon up to help choose vegetables. The seller bolted after the woman shouting and moments later returned with a teary Sarah on her hip. She explained that local gangs target foreign children to traffic them to Europe. I'm forever grateful to that seller. *Thank you, God!*

And Simeon made a name for himself at the local Cantonese preschool where he took pride in finding ways to toss his classmates' shoes into the ball pit when nobody was looking! Since he was always the last out of the school gate at the end of the day, we wondered if he was being punished.

"Simeon, why are you always the last one to come out?"

"Mum, I'm the only one who has to kiss all the teachers before I leave. And there are a lot of them!"

—Kevin—

After our two-year contract in Hong Kong ended in September, 1990, we returned to China as students. Settling into the Beijing Broadcast Institute we felt at home amongst morning loudspeakers, and young broadcasters-in-training reciting, singing and exercising their voices. We loved the sound of Beijing Opera in the nearby park and watching old men hang caged birds in trees by the school fountain. Simeon and Sarah had fun learning Chinese playing on campus while we spent hours memorizing texts and writing tests at the university next door.

❖

In Beijing, development catapulted forward, but less accessible regions struggled. With our language study near an end, I asked the Foreign Experts Bureau which region needed the most help. They advised we move south to Hainan, an undeveloped island at the time. The challenge enticed us. After a trip to scout out the area and lots of prayer, we felt convinced it was God's plan so packed our bags and went south.

6

FAR FROM BEIJING

*When the mountains are high,
the emperor is far away.*

—CHINESE PROVERB

—*Julia*—

Chinese friends warned us Hainan had a mind of its own. A former place of exile, we saw visible signs of its rebellious history. Theft, prostitution and exploitation were rampant. On a local tour to visit Miao and Li villages, we were shocked to see cute children in minority dress offered photos for cash, and teenagers standing by small wooden huts, available for hire. Our colleagues told us that wealthy men from neighbouring countries often had Hainanese mistresses or frequented massage parlours doubling as brothels. The dark side attracted tourists in those days, leaving carnage behind.

"I can't stand the stench behind my house," a worker mentioned one morning at the university where Kevin and I taught English.

"From garbage?" I asked.

"No, from unwanted babies. China's one-child policy stresses farmers who need a boy to work the farm and care for them in their old age. Girls go to their husband's families after marriage so when a girl is born it's a hard decision but…"

I walked away, unable to process her words. *Can I save them?* I opened my Bible to Ezekiel, frustrated and heartbroken at the innocent victims of selfishness. *And I saw them abandoned in the open field, squirming in their own blood… and I said to them, live, live.* (Ezek.16:6 *ESV*) The words *live, live* pierced me. The context was different but the message was clear. *God wants those babies to live!*

❖

Images of the babies haunted me as we searched out the local welfare institute. In a one-storey building, at the end of a row of rooms housing welfare seniors, two young female caregivers sat in a small room full of children. The stench choked us as 24 eyes watched us in the doorway.

"Hello," I said in Chinese. Relieved I spoke their language, the caregivers invited us in. Babies lay on wooden boards around the room. A few of the older children were covered in bedsores and their gaping eyes looked too big for their heads. The children were struggling to live. We sat on the floor singing as a few children inched closer and tried to join in. I wanted to rescue everyone right then but God's whisper was *wait I have something bigger and better in mind.*

The next day I bought sequined hair clips to encourage the workers and that small gift brought an open invitation to visit. Recruited from the countryside, the caregivers worked 24-hour days with no break. New arrivals, especially babies, didn't survive long since they were unable to survive on rice powder. The children craved attention and care and the workers needed relief. Our third child kicked inside me as if trying to voice an opinion. *All children deserve to live!* Welfare unit leader Chen did his rounds drunk, laughing and mocking us for visiting until one afternoon, as Simeon rolled a tiny metal car to a curious child huddled against the wall, he stuck his head in.

"The government allotted money to help these children," he said, "but I don't know what they need. Can you tell me what to buy?" I offered to bring a list next visit. He was desperate. "No, I need it now." If he didn't get the list today, the money might go to others. I took his pen. Milk powder instead of rice powder. Boiled water in flasks. Cribs and cots with pads that wipe clean instead of wooden boards. A mat for the floor instead of cement. As I wrote he smiled and I saw kindness behind his glazed eyes.

Leader Chen had his own story. When the military downsized, those demobilized were reassigned. His new job managing the welfare unit came without training so he drank to cope. As the children's conditions improved, Leader Chen was armed with new purpose. When the government allocated more funds for expansion, he came to us again. "Kevin and Julia, we can take care of the building and the children's daily living now. You know how to take care of the children's hearts. We must work together."

Our joint venture partnership meant hundreds of children lived! Within two years, a full-scale children's home with 100 toddlers and a special needs centre was operational. Many foreign experts assisted and volunteers helped with upgrades and the orphanage received a credential permitting adoptions, enabling many children to find their forever families.

Listening to those small whispers *live* and *wait* made such a difference! When *Little Garden Nursery School* opened to facilitate a smooth transition to primary school for those who weren't adopted, we were exhausted but thankful! From suffering came new hope and marvelous toddler-sized joy!

❖

And adding to our joy, was the birth of our second son, Peter. The main city hospital wasn't licensed for foreign births so we rushed back to Canada for his August 21, 1992, arrival. After six weeks of family reunions and celebration we returned to Hainan. Peter's easy-going personality meant extra cheek pinching and we had to invest in a back carrier to keep him out of reach!

—Kevin—

God's whispers are easy to miss if our story and His don't flow together the way we expect. When two of our university students heard about our orphanage partnership, they asked us to start a bilingual kindergarten. We refused three times before we started to wonder if God was speaking to us. We prayed and visited the potential site. Our hearts pounded. Through the residential compound gate was a magnificent garden with a small cement fish-shaped wading pool and coconut trees surrounding an old stone house. *Perfect!* Friendship English Kindergarten opened in 1993, the first Chinese/English bilingual kindergarten in southern China. Original plans showed the complex belonged to a German Mission before 1949. We loved redeeming a property and filling it with the joy and laughter of children and were glad that whisper came three times!

❖

In 1996, another whisper came. *Beihai.* In Guangxi province, it was an overnight boat ride from Hainan. A small town slated for development, Beihai was eager to boost English education and had limited resources. The timing was good since our Hainan joint ventures were ready to nationalize or hand over. Our biggest concern was our children who loved the island and had good friends. Including them in the decision, they surprised us by sharing our excitement.

"If we did move to Beihai, what would you want the most?" I asked at one of our Friday night family dinners.

"A room of my own," said Simeon who'd shared a bedroom with his siblings since they were born.

"A pink room," said Sarah, following her brother's lead.

"Whatever comes," added Peter.

"Ok, let's pray and ask God if this move is for us," I said. Both Julia and I always loved hearing our children pray and doing it as a family.

The next week we visited Beihai. The only complex that could rent to foreigners, had a four-bedroom apartment – two had a view and one was pink! And there was a green room for Peter. God is in the details!

❖

Beihai, a small coastal fishing town had few foreigners apart from the former mayor of Whitehorse, Canada and his wife, invited to help the local government for a year. Starting in 1996 we established a social enterprise consulting company, taught English and assisted the local government church.

Since we had the only three blonde-haired children in town, they were popular. Eleven-year-old Simeon, annoyed people whisked his brother off for photos on the local beach without asking, started charging. In perfect Chinese he said, "One RMB (16 cents) for me or Sarah, double for Peter, the youngest and cutest." The funny thing was, people paid and perhaps fueled his marketing career! But when two security guards arrived at our door explaining Simeon's firework

(Beihai manufactured fireworks) had landed on a newlywed's bed-spread hanging out to dry on a tenth-floor balcony, we told him all new ideas had to run past us first!

—*Julia*—

Peter made a name for himself in Beihai learning Mandarin Chinese and the local dialect at kindergarten. His fame spread until most of the town called us Peter's parents.

And in Beihai, 9-year-old Sarah had a profound dream. "Mum, you know the little girl from the Hainan orphanage I bought a hair bow for last Christmas? I had a dream last night. I think God wants us to adopt her."

I shared her excitement, "That's amazing! Let's write it down, pray and see what happens. If it's God's idea, he will tell Dad too."

Two weeks later in bed, Kevin looked over.

"What is it?" I asked.

"Nothing." Minutes later he stopped and looked at me again. "I keep feeling we should adopt that little girl from the orphanage in Hainan—Hannah. And call her Hannah Louise after your cousin who came as a volunteer."

My heart leapt! "Kevin, two weeks ago Sarah dreamt we should adopt Hannah! I told her we'd pray and if it was God's plan, he'd tell you. I wrote it here." I picked up the journal beside my bed and flipped back reading aloud, "… and if we adopt Hannah, we should name her Hannah Louise Garratt, after my cousin MaryEllen Louise. I remember walking into the room as MaryEllen held Hannah in her arms singing *Jesus Loves Me* to her and thinking *whoever adopts that little girl will be blessed*. Kevin, I never imagined she'd be ours!"

With miraculous confirmations, we told a super-ecstatic Sarah, and the next day had a family chat with Simeon and Peter who agreed at once. Kevin immediately started the practical steps so Hannah could become a Garratt! Once Kevin starts something he knows is right, he doesn't stop. He phoned Beijing daily to see where her dossier was in the pile as it moved from office to office, stamp to stamp. Kevin joked it took nine months to birth her too!

—Kevin—

A shock awaited in 1999, when we arrived in Hainan to take Hannah home. She had fallen from her crib and compounded by bronchitis had a septic hip joint infection. The orphanage offered another girl. *No!* That moment we knew the reason for such specific guidance–Hannah was *our* daughter! After the local hospital pumped her full of IV medications and tried to pull her dislocated hip into place with bricks attached to the end of a pulley, they released her with no cure. Canadian Embassy officials warned the adoption may not go through as her special needs required different approvals. We prayed all night and due to what Canada called an internal processing error, 48 hours after arriving in Beijing. Hannah received a passport and permission to enter Canada as our adopted daughter.

—Julia—

Back in Canada, the boys bounced a giggling Hannah on the bed and Sarah chose clothes and toys and carried her everywhere. Hannah's journey into our family was miraculous but her special needs meant a change of plans. Specialists in the Calgary Children's Hospital explained that without cartilage in one hip, and with severely damaged nerves, she'd need a wheelchair and ongoing physiotherapy. We'd left Beihai planning to stay in Canada for a year to finalize Hannah's citizenship, but the new diagnosis meant we'd have to leave China permanently.

But Hannah was a dancer. Despite this diagnosis, within a week of the hospital visit she got up from the sofa in my Aunt Janelle's family room and shuffled around the coffee table. *She was healed as we watched!* A later series of x-rays confirmed the cartilage had grown back and only minor damage remained. Within weeks, Hannah ran, climbed, danced and moved like a healthy two-year-old! God saved that miracle for us to see in Canada!

—Kevin—

Hannah's citizenship finalized and a clean bill of health from doctors put China back on our radar. We decided to open a branch of our Beihai company in the larger city of Zhanjiang where there were more resources for our children. In the fall of 2000, armed with suitcases, backpacks and children's CDs we headed to the southernmost tip of Guangdong province, a 14-hour bus ride from Hong Kong. With a skilled staff, we started a Family Center offering theme-based English activities where parents and child could learn together in a drama and story-telling room, a writing room, and an active games room. Families loved it! The centre also offered youth programs and daytime programs for seniors and the local blind school.

—Julia—

In 2004, with the Family Centre running well and ready to hand over, it was time for a break from China. Kevin and I were burnt out and needed a complete change. With our children ages 17, 15, 11, and 6 we returned to Canada hoping to provide a Canadian home for Simeon when he started university in the fall and let our children attend local schools and reintegrate into Canadian culture. A barrage of questions swirled in my brain. *What is next? Where will we live?* As we stopped for a family holiday in Thailand, we prayed for peace. Then, on our last night in Thailand as six of us squeezed into a small hotel room, Peter had an amazing dream.

"Mum, I saw a huge heart running towards a cliff. The heart was me. I ran and then fell off the cliff and went down, down, down. I landed face first in knee-deep water on the ground but wasn't hurt. God was telling me I'd always be ok. Then I saw lots of trees, like a forest, and through the trees in the distance I saw a house. It was burgundy and white, with a few steps up to a porch and a park in front. I tried to walk closer to see it better but couldn't see through the trees. I know it will be our house in Canada." His perfectly timed dream encouraged us all. A reminder that when *we don't know all the answers we know someone who does!*

—Kevin—

Simeon had a scholarship for Trinity Western University, so we found a temporary place to stay in Surrey, British Columbia. When friends recommended a real estate agent, I almost didn't call because we didn't have money for a house. But something prompted me to dial the number.

"I have a house not listed yet but it will sell fast," the agent said. "If we go to see it now and make an offer tonight we might have a chance. It's a beautiful house!" We all went to see. It was a wonderful burgundy *house with white trim*, five bedrooms, and a small yard with a driveway in the back alley. The house fronted on a park *filled with trees and* had *a few steps leading up to the porch*. Our spirits danced inside our bodies. We had no jobs or down-payment but knew we had to make an offer. "What do you suggest?"

The agent gave a number that sounded ridiculous. We said we'd get back to him. "Don't wait, or it will go. We have to make the offer tonight."

An hour later, Ma and Pa Robinson, two dear friends who've been in our lives since they taught English on a summer team in Hainan, called. "We just got some money back from another loan and thought it might make it possible for you to live in a house rather than an apartment." They offered to loan us a down-payment on a house! Perfect timing! *God is always at work!*

That evening we sat outside the house in pouring rain praying while the agent made the offer. He reappeared under a black umbrella and jumped into the back seat. "There is good news and bad news. Which do you want to hear first?"

"The bad news."

"Ok. There were three offers and one was higher than yours. But… they accepted yours because they want a family and don't want their house used as a rental since all the neighbours are friends."

We listened in awe. We had the house from Peter's dream. The next days were a flurry and after one glitch, the mortgage went through. Soon after, a friend called and said she knew the perfect job for me. It was! While Julia tutored, taught courses for visiting Chinese principals, and wrote curriculum for a local school board, I worked for World Vision Canada, enjoying the synergy of an international team.

Three years passed quickly and with our two eldest children settled in university, and our two youngest still missing life in China, we pondered returning. As we prayed about next steps, China and its mysterious neighbor North Korea, kept beating in our hearts and calling us back.

7

THE CHINA/NORTH KOREA BORDER

The best time to plant a tree was 30 years ago;
the second-best time is now.

—CHINESE PROVERB

—Kevin—

Our first introduction to the controlled, secretive country of North Korea came in 1989 when I discovered a book in a guest house library during our first family holiday in Thailand. Intrigued by the history of the united Korea, the Korean war, and the emergence of the Kim dynasty and Democratic People's Republic of Korea (DPRK) in 1948, I devoured each word. As I read, I heard a whisper. *One day you will go there.* Unrealistic and impossible, it entered my heart as a fact. From then on I read books and scanned the news to learn more about this unique and secretive nation. In the summer of 2004, we remembered that whisper. *One day you will go to North Korea.*

—Julia—

We started a bi-weekly Friday night gathering in our home to discuss North Korea and pray for the people. During one of those prayer times words as clear as thoughts dropped directly into my mind. *Go to Dandong and I will meet you there.* We'd never heard of Dandong. When Kevin located it on a map we discovered it was right on the China/North Korea border. The 15-year-old whisper, the imprint of fresh words, and the city's location, put new plans in motion.

Starting in 2005, we took three short scouting trips to Dandong and travelled north along the river border serving as the demarcation line between China and North Korea. First-hand stories of life inside North Korea wrenched our hearts. Border boat trips on the river arranged offered unique opportunities to exchange food and drinks for Korean soldier's buttons with North Korean guards who came down to the river's edge. Dandong was a beautiful and welcoming city. The children loved it too.

—Kevin—

On our third visit, in 2007, we hunted for a rental property. By now we felt certain it was time to give up our jobs in Canada and head overseas again. Dandong was primed for tourism and development and we planned to open a western-style coffee shop, train and mobilize volunteers to invest in local marginalized communities and explore options to facilitate aid and assistance in North Korea. As Julia and I searched for a location near the Yalu river, a *chūzū* (for rent) sign on a small noodle shop caught our attention. We'd hoped for more space and the owner wanted immediate occupants so we left it. But God had written it into our story.

❖

In October 2007, with Peter and Hannah excited about returning to China, and a suitcase full of British Columbia online school curriculum, we moved to Dandong. The noodle shop was still available! In addition, the apartment above was empty so we got the extra space! Two active members of our North Korea nights came too, accepting teaching positions at the local university. And we partnered with a small Vancouver church to set up a Canadian non-government organization (NGO) to facilitate aid and development in North Korea.

In April 2008, with a red carpet and an archway of mauve and white balloons over the door, *Peter's Coffee House* opened with a small but official, ribbon-cutting ceremony. Well-positioned for tourists near the Friendship Bridge, the coffee house sat opposite a beautiful 10-kilometre boardwalk along the Chinese side of the river. The novelty of our shop attracted curious locals and we made instant friends. Dandong's mix of Chinese and Korean cultures, great food, and wonderful people made living there an easy transition. A local historian explained that Andong (Peace of the East) became Dandong

(Red East) on January 20, 1965 to avoid the unpopular connotations of its former name. Eager to acknowledge Dandong's rich heritage, we were thrilled when he provided 1920s and 30s black and white photos from the Dandong historical archives for a feature wall in *Peter's*.

Through lattes and cappuccinos, music and community service projects, Friday night English corners and Wednesday evening business meet-ups, we joined Dandong's landscape. When students called *Peter's* a family we were proud parents. I oversaw the coffee house, networked with overseas partners and local businesses, and forged relationships for North Korea aid initiatives. Julia home schooled Peter and Hannah, taught English for International Trade at East Liaoning University, and coordinated training and volunteer work.

—Julia—

In August 2008, we joined our first DPRK tour. As the train crossed the bridge from Dandong, the atmosphere changed as if passing through a transparent wall into an unfamiliar world. Our *minders,* the assigned tour guides that stayed by our sides, introduced North Korea as the greatest country on earth. Their fervor and passion to promote the country was surreal. Pyongyang, a spotless, uniform city with main roads the width of small airstrips, baffled us as we watched tidy street workers removing stones with bare hands. Every planned tourist stop included opportunities to show respect and worship the leaders. Photos required explicit permission. Unwilling to bow to the large bronze statue of Kim Il Sung, we stood respectfully to one side while others placed flowers and gave three small bows.

At Treasure Mountain, two hours from Pyongyang, we placed covers over our shoes and ankles, passing a guard with a silver-plated gun, to peruse gifts to former leader Kim Il Sung displayed in rooms carved deep into the mountain. When a guard noticed Peter chewing gum, he scowled and Peter swallowed it. The walls and palatial ceilings inside the mountain projected grandeur and majesty and gifts like cars, televisions, and golf clubs filled 150 rooms, divided by countries. We paraded through the Canadian room, passing the Canadian Communist party's carved wooden bear, and viewed a Michael Jordan basketball and white ornate porcelain swan from Billy Graham in the American room. The hallway murals displayed animals, airplanes and other donations too large or awkward to keep indoors.

The final room had special instructions before entry: stay in a line, go forward in groups of three, bow three times at the front, then return in a line to the back of the room. Our minder warned the children to stay silent as we opted to stand at the back. When the massive, two-storey door swung open, an oversized life-like wax form of Kim Il Sung held his arms out to receive us as a god welcoming his children. Dressed in glowing white robes, the lighting gave him an eerie supernatural glow. Observing the rest of our group walk forward in threes, we stood stunned by the scene. The firmly held North Korean belief that Kim Il Sung is the eternal father, perpetuates through these displays. What reverence North Koreans showed as they bowed before this *man*!

The scripted trip with its unique tourist sites and each citizen's attentiveness to praise their leader and country, left us mesmerized. Our minders impressed us with their dedication, sense of humour, and genuine friendship. We went back to Dandong reflecting, praying and longing to do more for this nation struggling to find its place in a much bigger world.

—*Kevin*—

That winter, our formal relationship began. A DPRK welfare charity unit requested winter clothing and supplies for orphans and children and we launched a 2009 *Warm for Winter* initiative. During the follow-up trip to check distribution, we discussed a partnership to upgrade a remote facility for seniors without living relatives and visited the site. With official minders holding our papers, we stopped at checkpoints along the road for permission to proceed. As we drove through the countryside, poverty was reality. Dirt roads wound through large fields and villagers walked long distances to destinations hidden in the hills. The empty roads had occasional sellers with burlap bags of rice or corn and people gathered around for a share.

At one check-point small, thin, barefoot children scampered through discarded scraps searching for food.

As we passed scattered towns, young children raised fists if they caught sight of our faces through van windows, viewing us as the enemy. A quick stop at a local kindergarten brought us face to face with large murals of American soldiers crushed underfoot by brave Koreans. At the nearby primary school, older children bowed their heads and turned away, unwilling to make eye contact.

—*Julia*—

Scenes depicting hatred and violence towards Americans filled banners, posters and murals wherever we went but the people we met showed none of these sentiments towards us as Canadians. They were kind, gracious and welcoming. At the unassuming welfare centre, tucked in the hills far from the nearest village, we sat on the floor with sixteen North Korean seniors, singing and laughing as friends. While touring, a lady with a toothless grin and face covered in wrinkles, peeked through a tiny window in her door and waved. I approached. She invited me in. Clasping my hands in hers with a magnificent smile on her face, she directed me to a worn patch of linoleum on the floor. It was heated! She offered me the best she had—a warm seat on the floor. Although a *minder* called me away seconds later, I had touched the brave, courageous and loving people of North Korea through this woman's kindness. *Father, do not let this older generation die without seeing new hope for their future generations.*

Although we never met again, their smiles, songs, and voices carry forward in us. We left North Korea deeply moved and eager to help and be part of a North Korea whose voice is seldom heard. The trip confirmed our purpose to encourage and provide practical assistance for courageous people who hold on to hope despite hardships most of us never face. God hadn't abandoned them and neither could we.

Kindness is not linked to power or money or race. The poorest person with one act of kindness can impact a human soul forever. After precious encounters in North Korea, we determined to find cost-effective ways to send more practical help to people in crisis.

Living on the border facilitated this and during the next few years, we sent truckloads of aid and supplies across the bridge to help North Koreans suffering from malnutrition or lacking daily necessities. Distribution included thousands of backpacks with school supplies, toiletries, and vitamins along with medicines and daily necessities for the senior's centre. Soybean milk machines and soybeans, rubber shoes and winter clothing reached village orphanages and primary schools. Boxes of hand-wound lights, shipments of seedling trees, and barrels of kimchi (spicy pickled cabbage) for remote villages entered on trucks arranged by trusted local companies. Our Dandong dream was reality.

—Kevin—

On August 21, 2010, Peter's 18th birthday, Dandong flooded. Hannah, returning from a DPRK tourist trip with friends, watched in shock and disbelief as the train crossed the Friendship Bridge. The river almost touched the bottom of the bridge! Along the border, everything was submerged including the coffee shop. Her heart sunk. *God, why?* She heard no answer.

Our shop and small businesses along the river stood in front of the floodwalls built during the Japanese occupation. Chinese SWAT teams rushed in with rescue and evacuation efforts and the waterfront closed to the public. North Korea had no floodwall. Devastated, we sat in our apartment behind the wall watching frantic villagers across the river in North Korea on rooftops waving for help. Others in distress used poles to catch things floating away through their broken windows. A bed floated by along with trees, roofs, and home debris.

As floodwaters subsided, People's Liberation Army (PLA) soldiers allowed business owners back to assess damage. Silt, at least 20 cm deep covered the road and sidewalk so slogging through was hard. A sofa jammed the coffee shop entrance along with furniture and other debris making it difficult to wedge the door open. Stuck in the mud on the top step and under the door were small cards with the word *sorry* face up. Three of them. *Sorry, sorry, sorry.* The cards belonged to a Sorry game that had tumbled from a coffee house shelf and scattered in the water. In the middle of the mess we smiled at the genius of this profound miracle.

At least one metre of water had swirled inside ruining everything under the flood line. We considered closing but local and foreign friends offered to help us reopen so we gutted, fumigated and renovated, removing mold and mushrooms. City water was off for weeks along the waterfront as a precaution so we carted water on three-wheeled bicycles. It took one month and teams of volunteers in rubber boots with buckets to shovel silt and wash and sun-dry our wooden tables and chairs. All our neighbours had their salvageable furniture airing on the sidewalk too, but we were astonished to see the restaurant next door sun-drying their toothpicks!

❖

Business revived. New foods, excellent local ratings, and recognition on a popular travel site brought people flocking back. *Peter's* was once again a hub for locals, tourists and a wide assortment of visitors passing through to gaze first-hand at the mysterious DPRK. It was fascinating to see who dropped in for what we tagged *the best coffee on the border*! EU and Embassy personnel stopped in on weekend shopping trips from Pyongyang, and journalists, swarming to town to cover the latest news along the China/North Korea border, typed articles in our shop. *Peter's* was a hive of interesting conversations and our large wall map, covered with tacks, boasted customers from over 80 countries.

Our internship program in partnership with other NGOs accepted interns from Canada, South Africa, Switzerland, Germany, the United Kingdom and the United States to serve as volunteers and learn about China and North Korea. By 2014, with visas and business licenses renewed every year without a hitch, everything was going well. A talented South African couple had helped build strong ties between *Peter's* and the community, and two young Irish couples full of passion and ideas, had recently joined us. This freed us to focus on North Korea.

—Julia—

In late June 2014, after a brief trip to Canada to celebrate Hannah's high school graduation, we took a productive trip to DPRK. Positive meetings resulted in a memorandum of understanding for ongoing projects and unique opportunities for friendship. Kevin spent July working out logistics to supply equipment to a special needs home, build indoor bathrooms for a village orphanage, provide rooftop solar heating panels for an orphanage school, and prepare emergency aid shipments for North Korean children in crisis.

I helped train volunteers for our third annual camp for a Chinese children's home. Peter, 21, was in Dandong on university summer break working with local Korean youth. Hannah, 17, was in Canada working and preparing for college in the fall. We were excited about the season ahead and had no idea our lives were about to change forever.

8

Two Friends

A faithful friend is hard to find.

—Chinese Proverb

—Kevin—

On, Saturday, August 2, 2014, sipping a latte in my usual corner by the historic photos of Dandong, *Peter's* was humming. A familiar group of high school students drank bubble tea and worked on summer homework. In the back corner two backpackers wolfed down a western breakfast, enjoying our free internet. Our American friend from Minnesota, Jean, sat by the window with her usual Americano, enjoying the river view. It was a spectacular summer afternoon.

Immersed in the details of an indoor plumbing and toilets project for an orphanage in the DPRK, I didn't notice our Chinese friend Glen until he stood beside me, invited me for coffee that evening at seven, waited for my nod and left. I looked forward to a good chat.

After a quick walk-through of the shop, I flung my camera over my shoulder and headed home. Our shop sat in a row beside a seafood restaurant, local police station, upscale bathhouse, and a few shops selling Chinese and DPRK souvenirs. Across the street, the river's picturesque boardwalk offered landscaped parks, cobbled walking paths, and outdoor public exercise equipment. A five-minute walk one way led under the Friendship Bridge which straddled the river, serving as the main trade and travel link between China and the DPRK. This tourist hub offered a myriad of stalls selling DPRK trinkets, and colourful racks of traditional North Korean outfits for staged photos with North Korea and the bridge as a backdrop. Small piers enticed tourists for half hour boat tours boasting close-up views with rental binoculars of North Korean fishermen and soldiers carrying guns. The tours skimmed past navy boats docked along the DPRK side of the river.

Beside the Friendship Bridge stood the broken *half-bridge* built between 1937 and 1943 during the Japanese occupation. It jutted out into the Yalu River, cut off halfway. A 20 RMB ($3.25) ticket gave visitors access and a view of the damaged bridge gears with the remnants of a few pillars stretched across the remainder of the river. On my first visit, a Dandong war veteran sporting medals, explained the bridge's history, detailing America's reckless bombing during the Korean War from 1950 to 1953.

My walk home was in the opposite direction, past a guarded dock for Chinese navy patrol boats and an outdoor stage where children gathered for an afternoon performance. Opposite, beside the number 4 middle school, were the large and prominent pillars of the Dandong Intermediate Court building.

A gentle breeze wafted off the river, and the tide was halfway up a strip of cement stairs serving as the local swimming spot. Only avid swimmers went far due to strong currents and high tides. Swimmers in tight black bathing suits swam daily to North Korea and back. Today, bathers filled the stairs and two ladies crouched on the bottom step scrubbing their window screens while an elderly man washed his wife's stockings. Residential apartment buildings lined the riverside, tucked behind the flood wall.

At our end of town, the DPRK side was a barren island with a row of military homes lining the water's edge. Behind them, a bamboo lattice fence enclosed one of many small commune-style North Korean villages. Soldiers with guns slung over their shoulders patrolled as villagers brought red plastic buckets to wash their clothes in the river. Once or twice a year the waterfront filled with villagers washing and salting cartloads of cabbages to store for winter kimchi.

❖

The Yalu river is a 790-kilometre border and demarcation line between China and North Korea. In Dandong, high tides carrying silt deposits leave shallow water as the river ebbs and flows towards the Yellow Sea. Dredgers, navy patrol boats, and fishermen displaying Chinese and North Korean flags, are free to traverse the river. Professional rowers, kayakers, and occasional windsurfers develop their skills in the strong tidal waters.

The river's source is a 2744m mountain in northeast Jilin province, an active volcano that last erupted in 1903. The mountain, divided in half by the border, is Changbai mountain to Chinese, and Mount Paektu to North Koreans. Official biographies of the former leader Kim Jong Il, claim this mountain with its turquoise volcanic lake was his supernatural birthplace. Visitors to the DPRK side wear special cloth foot coverings to ascend this sacred mountain. The tale declares that over the lake on the night of his birth a new star shone in the sky, the seasons changed from winter to spring, and a double rainbow appeared. Because of this, North Koreans pilgrimage to worship the leader at this sacred site.

The previous summer we'd taken a trip up the Chinese side, popular with South Korean tourists, marveling at the breathtaking views above the clouds. The pristine scene is an artist's dream and decorates walls throughout the DPRK.

❖

The whole border region, with its history of battles and integration with its mysterious neighbor, was a perfect setting for my photography passion. Close to home, I snapped a photo of a wooden fishing boat with a North Korean backdrop. *I'll frame it for our apartment.* I crossed the street, nodded to the gate guard, and climbed to our tenth-floor apartment for a bite before heading for coffee with Glen.

He was there when I arrived. In his usual casual style, despite driving a luxury SUV, he wore a casual t-shirt and jeans. I smiled, reminded of the time he answered his cell phone in the middle of his wedding ceremony. The weather was great, so we sat on the veranda. Things weren't going well for Glen. He had family challenges, business had slowed, and he asked for counsel.

Our chat went from personal challenges to local news, corruption in the city, and President Xi Jinping's nation-wide crackdowns. He mentioned an upcoming arrest of four big fish in the city and the feeling that everyone was under suspicion these days. He laughed and said, "People even think you and Julia are spies."

I joked back. "Maybe spying on other coffee shops!" He smiled but had a point. Paranoia and fear of foreigners in China had been around for centuries. It resurfaced in conjunction with political events then defused until the next provocation.

From politics, the conversation drifted to family and a huge smile filled Glen's face as he boasted about his only child, a coveted son. His pride was typical of parents under the one child policy raising their *little emperors*. He wanted me to see his son and phoned the caregiver to bring him over, but his son was in bed.

"Sorry," he apologized, adding a few cute stories highlighting his son's intelligence.

"I'll see him next time. Let's get together again soon."

"For sure."

"Never give up hope! I'll keep praying for you."

"Take care!" Glen called out as we jumped into taxis heading opposite directions along the river.

—Julia—

The next morning, chatting and sipping coffee on our balcony, Kevin and I watched fishermen toss their nets to catch fish unique to waters where fresh and salt water mix. We loved our apartment with a spectacular North Korea view on one side and a city and mountain view on the other. We'd enjoyed magnificent sunrises and sunsets and feasted on Korean BBQ and other local dishes with Hannah, Peter, and coffee house friends, laughing and doing life together on this balcony.

When the phone rang, I was tempted to ignore it but Susie's name flashed on the screen so I answered. She spoke fluent English having studied abroad before returning to Dandong to work, marry, and live near her parents. Her lovely son was famous at *Peter's,* often arriving with his mother for oven-baked fries and hugs.

"Julia, can I ask you a favour?"

"Sure, what is it?"

"My friend's daughter wants to study at the University of Toronto and her parents want to take you and Kevin to dinner to discuss it. Can I give them your phone number? Her name is Mrs. Shen."

"No problem." Many Chinese parents want their children to study abroad. Mrs. Shen called and we settled on Monday night, August 4, 2014, for dinner at a local restaurant.

❖

Monday was hot and humid and Kevin had errands lined up. I began one week of customer service training for staff at *Peter's*. At 5:30 p.m. I assigned homework and gathered my training materials, glad to have dinner out instead of going home to cook. Kevin texted he was on his way after dropping a painting at home. It was a haunting yet striking watercolor painting by a North Korean child artist portraying three children working in the Wonsan countryside looking much older than their short statures. The inscription *'preparing for the harvest'* had caught my eye during our recent DPRK trip. I convinced Kevin to buy it as a sign of the blessing we hoped would come to the next generation in North Korea. I couldn't wait to hang it in our apartment.

"See you tomorrow," I called to the evening staff as the van pulled up. We drove under the Friendship Bridge past long rows of transport trucks lined up along several city streets waiting for the borders to open the next morning for inspections. Each day, designated trucks transferred goods across the bridge and returned empty at dusk. The Beijing/Pyongyang train crossed each morning and evening and former DPRK leader, Kim Jong Il, and present leader Kim Jong Un, crossed this bridge in a special green armoured train for state visits.

As the van dropped us at the restaurant, Kevin promised to pay the driver next time since we were a few minutes late. Half the city was on the boardwalk enjoying the cooler air after sunset. Exercise groups gathered in matching outfits, toddlers rode tricycles with proud parents alongside, and teens break-danced or tried out new hip-hop moves. Further down, near the large apartment complexes, seniors perfected fan dances, musicians gathered to play Chinese traditional favourites or sing local opera, and couples practiced ballroom dancing in designated areas. The border brimmed with energy, life and lights. On the other side of the river with only a few flickers of light, in virtual silence compared to the noise and excitement of Dandong, sat Sinijiu, North Korea.

We crossed the street. A middle-aged couple by the door stepped towards us. We shook hands and Mr. Shen led us through an empty restaurant lobby. As we got into the elevator he mentioned he'd picked this restaurant for its private dining rooms upstairs.

"Where's your daughter?" Kevin asked getting out on the fourth floor.

"She has a toothache and can't make it but we didn't want to cancel since we know you are so busy."

The Shens seated us in a private room at a table more suited to eight. Chinese parents are eager to secure a successful future for their only child, and this cultural practice of providing a feast for a favour was common. At a table filled with raw oysters, abalone and other specialty dishes, we discussed their daughter's plan to attend the University of Toronto. Having both graduated from there, we knew it well.

"Can you recommend a church for our daughter in Canada?" Mrs. Shen asked changing the topic. "We've heard many Canadians attend church and think it will help her understand Canadian culture."

The question was unusual, but they seemed uncomfortable around foreigners and possibly knew we were Christians. I recommended my sister Deborah, a Public Health nurse as someone who might help their daughter adjust. Mr. Shen looked distracted, kept glancing at a cell phone in his lap and typical of hosted Chinese dinners, insisting we eat more.

"Should I give them the CD now?" Mrs. Shen said.

"After dinner." He turned to us. "Our daughter's resume is on the CD. We hope you can review it."

"Bring her to *Peter's* on Friday night for English Corner and afterwards I'll go over it." They agreed and stood up which in Chinese culture means the end of the meal. Half-eaten dishes sat on the table. Mr. Shen handed Kevin a porcelain vase in a decorative box, thanked us for coming and offered to take us sightseeing when we had time. First get-togethers with people from the Mao generation are often rather formal.

Mrs. Shen handed me the CD in a pink plastic case. "We're sorry for cutting the dinner short but don't want to waste any more of your time and need to get back to check on our daughter," They walked us to the elevator but didn't get in. "We have to settle the bill. Thank you for coming. We'll bring our daughter on Friday."

They waved as the doors closed. We exchanged looks in the empty elevator. The whole dinner was a bit odd.

9

Abducted

*Listen to what a person says
and then watch what is done.*

—Chinese Proverb.

—*Kevin*—

The elevator door opened to a lobby full of people. Men stood up and a crowd approached.

"It must be a wedding. Let's get out of the way," Julia said. I turned to mention how strange the dinner was, when two men rushed me from behind and grabbed my arms. Surrounded and startled, five husky men stood centimetres from my face. One flashed a badge. Oversized video cameras filmed me protesting as they pulled me towards the lobby door.

"What are you doing? Who are you? What's going on?" My eyes darted around for Julia but she'd disappeared through a side door. It was so fast. *The dinner was a set-up.* The rough determined man yanking me by the arms looked familiar. I'd seen him training at the gym I sometimes went to with Peter. Now his huge muscles restrained and escorted me from the building. You never know who your gym-mate will be! I panicked but could do nothing because there were too many of them and no one offered to help. They shoved me into the back seat of a black sedan. Two burly men wedged in beside me and someone gave a signal. The driver pulled away from the curb, right where the van had dropped us an hour earlier.

Through the tinted window I could see the boardwalk, lights, and dancing but everything had morphed into a nightmare. My plan to stroll home with Julia along the river had evaporated. Instead, something terrible and dark was happening in this black car filled with officers. *It's a mistake.* Frustrated no one responded to my protests in the lobby and angry Julia and I were separated and abducted without warning or explanation, I tried to figure things out. My silent prayers streamed upward. Squashed between two scowling Chinese men I noted every street as the car twisted and turned through the city.

Ten terror-filled minutes later the car stopped at the gate of a tall building on the west side of town. The driver rolled down his window. Acknowledging the driver, the guard opened the gate and we drove into a dark back courtyard. Bright headlights announced there were other cars there. A group of officers emerged, forcing me into a stark stone building. Cameras videoed my entry. The entourage escorted me along a dimly lit hallway to a room at the far end on the left. Eight officers encircled me in the small room. I froze. *Where is Julia?*

—Julia—

Grabbed without warning in the lobby, two men in black T-shirts ushered me into a dark car waiting on a side street, cramming in beside me. The driver and a fourth man sat in front. *God, what's happening?* I heard the child lock click after the doors shut and we drove into darkness. My mind spun and body tensed. *Are these Chinese thugs? North Korean traffickers? Kidnappers? Chinese police?* "Who are you?" I asked in desperation, pinned between two men.

Sensing my fear one whispered. "The police. Don't worry. You are safe."

I wasn't safe. Multiple scenarios ran through my mind. *Where am I going? Where's Kevin?* A gate opened revealing a small complex with a circular driveway. A tall grey stone building loomed on one side, reflecting the shadows of a few cars shining headlights into the darkness. Fear gripped me, resonating in every muscle and cell of my body, making it shake involuntarily. Someone jumped out and opened the car door. The blinding light of a video camera blasted into my face. Four men escorted me up several steps into the icy building. I panicked. *Why are they recording? Can't they turn off the cameras?* My body shook and I heard my heart beating out of control as they steered me into the first small room on the right.

Stark and empty, the room bore resemblance to those in movies where prisoners go for questioning. I sat on the hard cot because there was nothing else except a desk. Four men stood guard as I shivered in the yellow floral sleeveless dress I'd bought in Vietnam for a family birthday dinner by the sea. It didn't suit this setting. I burst into tears.

No one spoke so I did. "You have the wrong person. What did I do? Please take me home." I shielded my eyes from the video as another man snapped photos with a still camera. Captive in this small room with bright fluorescent lights and whitewashed walls I felt a sliver better knowing it was a police station. My thoughts raced. *God, is this real?* I comforted myself. *At least it's not thugs. At least I am still in Dandong. At least I'm alive.* These people will figure out soon they have taken the wrong person and let me go. It will be over once they realize their mistake.

—*Kevin*—

Eight officers circled me. Two, still gripping my arms, sat me on a chair in the middle of the room and stood on either side so I couldn't move. No weapons appeared, but the brute force and the number of policemen terrified me. The office had two big wooden desks facing each other against the window and beside them, old bookcases and several tall metal filing cabinets filled with folders. A chilly damp shiver rippled through me as I looked at my beige shorts and short-sleeve shirt. These were not my after-dinner plans.

The man who flashed a badge in the lobby, entered with two officers and spoke as if we would get to the main point. He talked fast with a heavy local accent as I strained to grasp the words. Everything blurred.... If there was a main point, I missed it.

A tall man stepped forward and spoke English. "Sign these papers to agree to be investigated."

"Investigate what? Why?" The answers made no sense, but they insisted I sign. I resisted. They slowed their words and tried to explain the urgency using words like Chinese law, spy, cooperate, and many others. The words ran together. *I am dreaming.* The pressure continued until the intensity, exhaustion, and the sheer number of policemen surrounding me, convinced me they would not stop until I signed.

The officers exchanged muted words. I felt their frustration mounting. The focus was this piece of paper. They attached the camera on a tripod and kept videoing. I knew I had to sign but refused. *Why do I have to agree to be investigated?*

"Sign!" the chief officer yelled, "Do it!" His red face burst with anger and I could tell he wanted to do more but held back.

"What does it mean if I sign?"

"You must!" He lowered his eyebrows and pursed his lips in rage. The agents fidgeted beside him as I stared at the camera and didn't sign.

—Julia—

I turned my head away from the camera, feeling the officer's breath as I clutched my purse, digging through for tissues. Two official-looking men in blue uniforms entered and the shorter one, about Simeon's age, bellowed, *"Nǐ shì jiàndié!"*

"Sorry, can you speak English?" I said, struggling with the vocabulary.

He stepped closer and in the same forceful voice shouted in English. "You are a spy!"

A chill shot through my body and my skin went numb as I swirled in a whirlwind of fear, unable to catch a breath. *God, is this real? This is impossible.* They looked stern and serious. Such a huge, huge mistake. My thoughts scrambled.

"Give us your things to keep safe!"

Safe? The tone made me sound so criminal. I had heard and read stories of false arrests, but never imagined hearing the word *spy* aimed at me. *Is it suddenly my turn?* I handed over everything except my purse, foraging through for four wallet-sized photos of our children: Simeon, Sarah, Peter, and Hannah. I clutched them in my palm. Two officers documented my items as I controlled my sobbing, fingering the photos. Simeon, 27, in Vancouver, co-owner of a new start-up company called Spark, the son whose claim to fame has always been that he was born in a suitcase with an entrepreneurial heart. Sarah, married with two children, Kiana and Joey, and one on the way, living in western Canada and working on her Master's Degree. Peter, on a Canada/China government scholarship completing a Chinese degree in International Business, Economics and Trade. And our youngest, Hannah, 17, just finished high school, adopted at age two from Hainan. I had tickets to return to Canada in a week to help her settle into her first year of college. She was with relatives waiting for me. *Will I get there?*

Fear enveloped me. With nothing to do but wait and watch, my brain scanned everything I'd done recently, searching for an explanation. Nothing. *God, please don't let them take the photos.* I wanted to return to our scenic river-view apartment and jump into bed with Kevin the same as other nights. Instead, I followed instructions as they made handwritten lists of my items. I regretted not going home before dinner to drop off my training materials. Along with a computer, phone, and wallet, I had a thick stack of staff evaluations, two table mats, two sets of kitchen cutlery, scissors, markers, glue sticks, magnets, and photocopied activities related to the seven points of contact between a staff member and the customer. Even paper clips made their list which they copied twice, stretching the time well into the night.

Then one man came towards me. I knew what he wanted and struggling with a new burst of tears, reluctantly handed over my necklace, earrings, and the well-worn wedding rings which had been on my finger since June 23, 1984. Thirty years had passed since that day, most of them in China. I'd learned so much living and working with Chinese people. I remember how one student invited us to his village in the remote countryside outside Xian. Rob, his father and brother, met us at the final bus stop, riding us 10 kilometres on the back of their bikes to their village. His mother prepared a wonderful lunch with eight hand-designed dishes made from dough in different shapes because the family was too poor to afford meat. They borrowed tin cups and plates from neighbours. After dinner, the village leader asked us to sign our names with a special Chinese calligraphy brush on a cave wall to commemorate the visit of the teacher who taught their village's first university student. What an honour! They had so little, had suffered so much, and yet showed incredible courage and kindness. Now I needed an extra dose myself.

The officers finished writing and a tall officer pointed at the four tiny photos in my fist. "Hand them over!"

"Please, let me keep them. They are my children. Please don't take them."

He paused and stepped back. Children are important in Chinese culture. Had this woman begging for photos of her children struck a chord in their hearts? He and the others left to discuss it and returned to inform me I could keep them for now.

"Thank you." I forced a smile. This first act of kindness was a kiss from heaven.

I followed orders to watch as a man with a blank expression rechecked each listed item and placed it in a clear plastic bag. The cameras left us alone for the tedious part of itemizing my things, but returned for the fingerprinting session. An officer opened a sponge-filled red ink tin and told me what finger and where to put it on the papers. "It's standard procedure in China," he said. Asking questions was pointless.

My oral Chinese was adequate, but I never devoted enough time to read or write Chinese well and had no experience with criminal vocabulary or legal processes. I didn't resist, doing everything they asked. Fingerprinting and signing complete, I sat in silence, drained. The men piled the papers, grabbed the plastic bags, and left without a word. *Can I curl up on the cot for the night and go home in the morning? Will they return and take me home? God, please let me go home.*

A young woman entered. "We are taking you somewhere safe," she whispered as the room filled with male officers.

"Please let me stay here. I don't want to go anywhere except home or stay here for the night." Ignoring me the officers gripped my arms so I stood up. Near the exit the woman paused, "Do you have to go to the bathroom?"

"Is it far?"

"No, not very far."

"Ok, then I'm fine." I wasn't fine. Sobbing out of control, I made one final plea to stay but they insisted I go somewhere safer. I pulled away in terror. *Where am I going?* They grabbed me. I cried hysterically, "No, no, no, let me stay here!" *Why don't they see they have the wrong people?* I called one last time for someone to understand. "We only came to help China!" Ignoring my anguish, with cameras still rolling, they dragged me into the back seat of a black sedan. The woman sat on my right. A male officer jammed in on my left.

—*Kevin*—

The pressure to sign increased, but I didn't understand what signing meant. Then, I heard Julia's voice crying and pleading down the hall. *We only came to help China.* I felt helpless. Her cry faded. *They are taking her away!* I panicked and wanted to go too. With Julia's cry echoing in my ears, I took the black pen and guessing she'd already signed, I scribbled my signature on the page. An officer coached me how to dip my right forefinger into the ink and place my fingerprint once on the document and once on my signature. *I guess I've agreed to being investigated.* My body shook. *Wherever they are taking Julia, I want to go too.*

Signature secured, the officers stacked the papers, dumped my wallet and scrutinized everything. They looked excited about several pink prepaid cards for the blind massage salon around the corner from the coffee shop where Julia and I, along with friends in town sometimes went for inexpensive medical massages. They treated the cards as contraband and along with my wallet contents, tablet, and cell phone, dropped them into a plastic bag and sealed it, pressing my fingerprint onto the seal.

When they came for my wedding ring, I pretended to pull it off, insisting it wouldn't budge. They left it. My body ached, my eyes went fuzzy, and officers moving around the room became a spinning blur of images. I caught my breath in a moment of relief as the cameramen left. But before I could exhale two officers grabbed my arms again, and I realized the camera had moved to video my escorted journey back into the waiting car. This time I didn't resist. A row of black cars waited with headlights shining into the darkness. I shivered as three officers shoved me into the back seat of the first car. I sat wedged in the middle of two officers as the doors shut and locked. My body and mind were numb. *God, help me!*

10

BLACK CARS

Don't curse the darkness,
light a candle.

—CHINESE PROVERB

—Julia—

The car wound along the river road and out of town. My sobs subsided, masking my fear as I sat motionless. The city streetlights disappeared in a shroud of darkness as we left Dandong further and further behind. For the first time in my life I felt this could be my last night alive. *Are they taking me out to kill me? Are they passing me over to someone else? Will they execute me? Where is Kevin? Hannah's safe in Canada, but Peter is in China. Will they take him?*

The car seemed to move in slow motion as my mind raced. *What do they do to spies? Would China execute a foreigner?* I'd never heard of it but tonight had thrust me into an unwritten story. *I wonder how long it takes to die from a gunshot in the back of the head? Please, not death by vicious dogs.* Two scenarios played like movie trailers in my mind. One was me waiting and praying as these people figured it out and announced my release and drove me home. The other was me standing terrified ready to die with my eyes scrunched shut hoping it would be quick. Neither stopped my pounding heart and shaking legs as the car plunged forward into darkness.

Persecution and torture horror stories flooded my mind and although I believed China would treat me with respect as a foreigner and that torture was banned in recent years, fear overruled. I'd thought about capture in North Korea where every trip is still a great risk even if you work with approved agencies through legal channels. But abduction in China, our second homeland, I'd never imagined. Chinese were my friends. *Who were these people?*

Small flickers of light caught my eye as we sped by countryside farms. In a moment of courage, I leaned over to the woman and whispered, "Who are you?"

She paused as if thinking and whispered back in English, "Think of us as the Chinese FBI."

FBI? Abducted and driving into the middle of nowhere with the Chinese Ministry of State Security (MSS)? I never even watched spy movies and now I was a main character in one playing out around me. "I'm an ordinary person," I whispered. "This is a huge mistake." I felt a kindness in her, that even though she was an agent doing her job, she didn't enjoy seeing me petrified, fighting with a new stream of tears, fingering four tiny pictures. She didn't answer. I interpreted her silence. *They plan to kill me. I must get a message to my family before they do it.* I tried to press the four photos into her hand as my only hope to carry a message back to my children telling them how much I loved them. I wanted them to know I carried them as far as I could. I tried several times but her hand didn't open to receive them.

"Keep them," she whispered. After a few minutes of complete silence, she reached out and placed her left hand on my right hand. We drove on in darkness but my tsunami of fear was blindsided by this powerful act of kindness. I would never forget it, no matter what happened.

—Kevin—

"What's going on?" I asked, cramped and restricted. The chief officer said nothing as four vehicles jammed full of officers left the complex convoy style. *This does not look good.* My eyes stayed glued to the streets we passed the darkened Friendship Bridge whose coloured strings of lights controlled by China went off at ten. I glimpsed our coffee shop already closed for the night with its neon *Welcome to Peter's* sign advertising summer specials. Few people were on the boardwalk this late and cars and taxis were scarce, unlike the bumper to bumper rush hour traffic.

A cell phone rang beside me. The chief officer yanked a phone from a leather bag strapped over his shoulder. I knew it was his wife because he changed tones. He explained that what she was looking for was in their car. *I wonder if there's a gun hidden in his leather bag.* His last words to his wife, *it will be a long time,* pierced my shaky exhausted body like a dagger. She must have asked when he was coming home. The car stopped at traffic lights near our complex. The chief officer jumped out heading for the local police station. All foreigners working or visiting in China not staying in hotels, register within 24 hours in stations like these. We passed this friendly helpful station daily to and from the market and local shops. Opposite was a small flower shop where I purchased flower bouquets to surprise Julia and our favourite restaurant whose manager always rushed to hug Julia and find us the best seats while I joked with the servers. Tonight, shivering and shaking in a convoy of security bureau cars at midnight, our pleasant neighbourhood looked sinister. The kindergarten on the corner, typical of many new facilities offering quality care, education and facilities for top dollars, looked eerie in darkness without no children laughing in the playground.

Two precinct officers appeared and jumped into the third car back. The chief officer squeezed back beside me. "We are going to your apartment," he said as if pronouncing a criminal sentence.

We passed the closest entrance, stopping further down the road. The cars emptied and cameramen filmed me getting out. Standing shivering in the frigid night air, I counted them. Eighteen. As if in a movie set, everyone took their places to stage my walk to our apartment down the dark backside of a row of residential buildings. The camera rolled and eighteen officers escorted me along a thick wall past three buildings to our entrance. The pitch-black back alley added a shadowy tone to the walk. *Why make a show of it? Why not use the closer, lit entrance? What will the neighbours think?*

Using keys confiscated at the station they unlocked the downstairs metal door and the camera man rushed in first. I squeezed into the elevator with the camera man, the chief officer, and two others, watching the numbers light up to the tenth floor. It took three elevator loads to get everyone up and if it wasn't so serious, it would have been comical. The camera pointed its huge lens at me as I entered our apartment in a fog. Julia's North Korean sketch leaned against the wall. The sun-worn faces of North Korean children looked out of place as the officers marched past, putting on white gloves to ransack the apartment. I looked for Julia but she wasn't there.

I could never have imagined this night, even in my craziest dreams. *Escorted like a criminal? Accused of spying and espionage?* A tall, thin, stern officer took charge and barked out orders while the others followed. He never introduced himself so I dubbed him Boss. As the double bolt locked the door from inside, the officers released their grips.

"Follow me!" Boss yelled. The search started in the kitchen. Flinging open cupboards to intimidate me, he pointed with white gloves at random items, and in steely broken English told me to identify them.

"What's this?" he barked.

"Honey." *Don't you know? It has a Chinese label.*

"What's this?"

"Salt."

"This?"

"A bin of flour." After perusing every cupboard Boss seemed satisfied the kitchen contents were not criminal evidence, and moved to a bookshelf. *This will be a long night.* He picked out books instructing officers to pile them on the living room floor. A few obeyed while others lit cigarettes.

"I don't like smoke," I said walking over to open a window. Three men rushed over to prevent me from jumping out which hadn't crossed my mind. I yanked the tenth-floor window open and stepped away avoiding them. It was well past midnight but Boss intended to search the whole apartment. Shelf-loads of books, including historical novels and memoirs about China and North Korea, teaching materials, music CDs, and family DVDs including one comedy spy series, went into the evidence pile on the floor.

I protested but Boss didn't care, seizing more. In Hannah's room, he removed labeled plastic storage bins from the walk-in closet: winter clothing, Christmas, aid projects, income tax, accounting, personal. He yelled and officers dragged them into the living room. Like a rabid wolf, Boss grabbed random items from shelves or cupboards. The guards like gophers, followed him, transporting his contraband to the piles. Photo albums, Hannah's diaries, holiday trinkets, Peter's telescope, and an electronic game. From a wicker toy box, Boss dumped blocks, children's books, musical instruments, and puppets onto the floor. He lifted an old computer lying at the bottom excited to find stashed goods. *An old, useless computer we haven't tossed yet?* Relentless and controlling he rummaged through everything himself. Boss snatched plastic folders from our bedroom drawers and discovering one with money in each section, gloated. The labels read: Thai baht for family holiday, Canadian dollars for Julia's Canada trip, and U.S. dollars for Wŏnsan, North Korea orphanage project. *Can't he read the English labels?* It was normal for foreigners in smaller Chinese cities to keep more money around since most transactions were cash.

As a detailed person, I kept good records with everything itemized and organized. I hated seeing him mix the money. Even Hannah's coin collection and small amounts of money in other currencies left over from earlier family vacations was dumped on our coffee table. I'd seen similar images on Chinese TV arrests. *Were those set up like this? Were any of them innocent like me?* Explanations made no difference. The evidence, to Boss, was spread out on the coffee table. He made me sit on the couch behind the money; a criminal videoed with his stash.

11

The Compound

Mankind fears an evil man
but heaven does not.

—Chinese Proverb

—Julia—

The car slowed. The woman fidgeted, unsettling me. Fear's icy fingers gripped my shoulders. *God help me.* Two honks. A metal accordion gate opened and we drove in as the gate creaked closed behind us. *At least it's a building.* My tired chilled muscles ached. The woman got out and took my arm. With the four small photos clutched tight in one fist, I climbed four steps and entered the building. *I am a hostage.*

A short thin man nodded as we entered, fiddling with a set of keys. Round wooden tables leaned against the wall on one side and to the left was a derelict reception counter and a locked door leading to another section. Four officers escorted me upstairs to the second floor. A key turned and another door opened. The lock clicked behind us as the woman and three men, led me along the dorm-style hallway to the last door on the left. I didn't want to enter.

Two female guards with plastic tags identifying them as numbers, stood beside me as one locked the door. Footsteps faded as the others left. Two long fluorescent lights hung from the ceiling. The small bare room had a bed, bedside table, one hard chair, and a bathroom with a hole instead of a door handle. Along one white wall was an old worn couch for the guards with a small white clock perched on the back cushion, its ticking punctuating the silence.

The guards eyed me as I flopped on the bed shaking. I comforted myself. *At least it's a room. At least they didn't execute me. At least it's clean.* The guard's piercing eyes met mine with faces exposing their fear. *They are afraid of me? Have they heard I'm a dangerous spy?* Boxed in by whitewashed walls with long, thick burgundy curtains covering the outside wall, hiding the barred windows, I was trapped in my strange cage.

Humiliated, I sat on the toilet with guards at my side then forced myself to wash in the tiny sink. Then, as if white fog filled the room blinding my sight and blocking my judgement, I lost track of my surroundings. My eyes stung and couldn't focus. Midnight had long passed, and in dizzy exhaustion the room seemed only half there. I kicked off my high-heeled shoes in a daze, pulled my hair out of a pony tail and stretched on the bed in my dress. Tucking the four tiny pictures of my children under the straw-filled pillow for safe keeping, I lay motionless. Not moving gave me a few silent seconds to think. The fluorescent lights blazed on my eyelids and the guard's eyes swirled around me until I fell asleep.

Sleep came in waves as the light and movements of the guards kept waking me. Disoriented, I tried to piece my story together. I felt piercing eyes at close range. *How do they know I am awake?* I pulled the cover over my eyes to shield them but the guards yanked it away. *It must be a rule.* I stopped trying and lay listening to the guard's pen writing in a notebook. A rooster crowed in the distance as the lines between sleep and wakefulness blurred.

—Kevin—

They raided everything, leaving me disoriented, watching piles on the floor grow into heaps. *Will this ever end?* A faint glimmer of dawn through the window reminded me I'd been up all night. Boss handed me two small carryon bags from our closet. "Choose a few clothes for you and Julia."

In shock and not thinking straight, I choose Hannah's jeans and shoes for Julia. Boss checked the bags, approving. He scooped the money from the table and counted it twice, listing the total and handing me two documents to sign. After sealing the cash in a plastic bag, Boss yelled at four officers who stuffed everything in the piles and not in bins, into empty suitcases taken from our wardrobe. I rummaged through, searching for our Bibles.

"No! You can't have them!" Boss shouted.

"That's not very nice of you," I answered with a boldness that suddenly came over me. My strong reply surprised him and after a brief discussion he relented and let me put one in each bag.

At 5 a.m. with everything ready to cart off, the chief officer who'd done nothing during the raid took charge of me again. A vehicle was waiting at the closest entrance. I never saw our apartment again.

The car veered left along the river past the university where Julia taught. I strained to stay awake. This familiar road led to the eastern end of the Great Wall 20 minutes from Dandong. Called Tiger Mountain, this stretch of wall ends at the river border. On top are stunning views of the North Korean landscape, small communes with villagers out harvesting or planting, and border guards on patrol. On one visit, we sang a blessing song for North Korea composed by our friend. As melodies floated across, two North Korean guards on the roof of their guard shacks sung a North Korean song back! A remarkable friendship moment.

Today the car sped past Tiger Mountain through the Chinese countryside with its satellite dishes and greenhouses. The tall apartment buildings of the Dandong skyline disappeared. We passed a small dock offering boat excursions along the Yalu River and glimpses of North Koreans on river banks. Guests loved these fascinating tours and sampling local fish at the waterfront restaurant. This road boasted the most scenic views of both sides of the border. But today, no friends joked beside me as we sped on in silence.

Ready to pass out any minute, I hoped to be with Julia soon. We crossed water and entered a local village with seasonal restaurants lining the road and typical countryside houses. The car slowed, honked twice, an accordion gate opened and we drove into a small secure compound. Surveillance cameras, a wall, and a tall communications antenna on the roof, secured the three-storey block style building and courtyard. I scanned uniform rows of windows searching for a clue that Julia was inside. A short pudgy man appeared with a ring of keys as we pulled up and went in. He opened the door to a ground floor hallway and locked it behind us.

"Go in!" A guard flung open the door to a room and shuffled me in. Relieved, I saw a bed. "The bathroom is at the end of the corridor so when you need to go, two guards will escort you."

I winced. Four, bright, fluorescent tube lights glared from the ceiling of this room which appeared to be a modified interrogation room. Red glowing numbers from a digital wall clock at least 80 by 40 centimetres accentuated the ominous atmosphere. Two mounted security cameras, and two thin double student desks pushed together with three chairs behind them filled the rest of the space. Two male guards with numbers hanging around their necks eyed me with suspicion. Thick burgundy curtains concealed the windows. No one spoke so I collapsed on the bed. *This is how shock feels.* In minutes, I fell asleep.

12

INTERROGATION

*Three feet of ice is not the
result of one cold day.*

—CHINESE PROVERB

—Kevin—

M oments later, guards jolted me awake offering breakfast on a
metal tray. Semi-conscious from sleep deprivation, stress and
exhaustion, I attempted a few bites. Three officers in navy blue police
uniforms walked in and faced me. *Am I safe?* Waves of panic returned
and I longed to drift back to sleep.

"I'm Chief Officer Wang," one stated, "in charge of investigating
you." He was the officer whose wife had called in the car. "And he is
Captain Li, the interpreter, and Officer Zhang," he said introducing
the others. I nodded but no words came. Chief rearranged the furniture so the chair faced the desks in full view of the wall cameras. He
motioned me to sit, plunking the small table and a bottle of water
beside me. After double-checking everything lined up, with me in the
center of both cameras, he sat between Captain and Officer Zhang
and reached for a notepad.

I stared in a stupor as three officers leaned on the desks glaring.
Chief's harsh words flew so fast no coherent sentences formed and
my brain refused to focus or produce even the simplest answer. The
specialized vocabulary and absence of context for the brutal interrogation put my muscles in spasms as my stomach knotted. Chief fired
questions like bullets one after another. *This is a mistake.* Waves of
nausea intensified and Chief's facial expressions showed he noticed
but ignored it.

"You are a spy. Confess!" he said. I gave confused answers. The
shock and strain wracking my body obliterated their words. Chief

brought over papers to sign and a red tin for fingerprinting. I must have signed them.

Four hours later the interrogators left and guards returned with a food tray which sat untouched. That afternoon and evening the interrogators left me alone. I recovered enough to be angry and annoyed as the guards scribbled in little notebooks. *What are they writing?* My carryon bag sat by the door. I rummaged through for the Bible. *If they detain me in this room, I will read aloud.* I opened to John and started my English oratory. Ignored by the guards, I continued for an hour. The rest of the day I vacillated between nightmare and reality, anger and fear, confusion and shock. To battle my way through I focused on praying.

—Julia—

My eyes opened to shuffling in the room as the guards unlocked the door from inside, removing the chair wedged against it overnight. A tall strong female guard walked in pulling my carryon suitcase, unzipped it and offered me clean clothes. *How did that get here? How dare someone walk into our apartment, open my bedroom drawers and touch my underwear, bra, and other personal items!* But eager to change from a sleeveless dress, I accepted the offer.

Reaching for jeans and a t-shirt, the horrible thought sunk in. *Someone is intending for me to stay.* The ache in the pit of my stomach reminded me I was in the middle of something unfamiliar and frightening, forced into a crisis without training or precedent. None of the cultural understanding from living 30 years in a country applied.

I was a hostage. My pacing space was limited to a few steps in each direction. I wanted to call and tell my family I'd be home soon and pictured hugging Kevin in our lovely apartment, watching the sunrise and boats out for the daily catch. I wanted to walk to work stopping to chat with toddlers along the way. I longed to test the staff on yesterday's lesson and teach the new one, laughing and brainstorming new ways to improve customer service. My usual Tuesday had been sabotaged.

I hid behind the bathroom door to change. Guard 1 shook her head and approached while Guard 2 made notes. She likely wrote, *Julia tried to hide to dress.* Forced to give up privacy I changed and used the toilet, shielding my eyes from their gaze. My face flushed. "Could I please have a toothbrush?"

Guard 1 returned with a pink plastic cup: a toothbrush, comb, toothpaste, and soap. Solar heated hot water poured into the sink so I celebrated the warmth on my face and hands. Guard 2 stood poised to take the plastic cup the minute I finished brushing my teeth. Guard 1 waited, pen in hand, to write that in her book. I combed my hair into a ponytail and returned the cup.

"Thank you and can I have a drink of water please?" I felt like a child. The clock perched on the sofa behind Guard 1 ticked with the monotony of a metronome as she scribbled notes on my bathroom routine. Outside a rooster crowed, a car honked, and I heard the accordion gate and a car door opening or closing. *It's coming to take me home!*

Guards, the small room and my active imagination created a strange scene. I smiled. Terrified my smile had some hidden meaning, the guards tensed, ready to spring into action if I burst into a fight. Maybe a real spy would overpower them, dash through the hall, break the locks, bolt downstairs and out of the building, and scale the walls. Not me. *How I will do imprisoned in a room?*

The door opened. 7 a.m. Shift change. Notebooks changed hands and Guard 4 brought breakfast on a metal tray with sections. She instructed me to face the wall and eat. I swallowed the bland rice congee so the Guard 5 could write, *Julia ate breakfast.*

I turned my head. A uniformed man entered. "This is your Bible. We have freedom of religion in China so you can have your book."

"Thank you." Surprised, I reached for it. Gratefulness pushed back fear. With the greatest book ever written in my hands, I forgave them for choosing my clothes and making me eat facing the wall. I flipped it open and read. *In the beginning God created the heavens and the earth. And the earth was void and without form and the Spirit of God hovered over the water.* (Gen. 1:1 ESV) I entered the story, letting the words soak into me until I immersed myself in this spirit hovering over the water. I reflected on the profound thought that a creative Spirit moving over the void, gave it form and made beauty. The experience resonated in me. I was in a void, snatched out of my ordered life, my wonderful friends and family, my role as a teacher and trainer and curriculum designer, as wife and mother, into a complete and terrifying unknown. *Can I make form and beauty here? God, please show me how.*

Three strong knocks halted my meditations. Fear recoiled. *What will they do to me?* The guard opened the door a crack. Their words were inaudible.

"They will be ready for you soon. Put shoes on." My body shook. *Who is coming for me?* My valiant thoughts of beauty vaporized as fear engulfed me. I leaned over and slipped on the pink flip flops with yellow smiley faces lying by the door. The guards wore the same ones at night. I smirked at the irony.

Three knocks, then a guard led me a few steps to the adjacent room. My eyes arrived first. My feet shuffled in after them. Coughing from the dense smoke filling the interrogation room, I explained to three confident officers that smoke made me sick. They looked worried. As they drew the heavy curtains to open the barred window, I glanced out. Before they yanked the curtains back into place I glimpsed the reddish orange rooftops of Chinese village houses, and the distant, barren rolling hills of North Korea. *We are on the border.*

My chair faced away from the window towards three interrogators who plunked down at two desks pushed together between me and the door. Frightened and shivering on the seat, the men appeared three times as big as me. The tall lanky officer in glasses sat straight and strong on the left behind a Chinese brand computer and printer with a stack of blank paper and a pen. Although he'd let me keep my four photos the night before, this morning kindness was wiped off his face like muddy shoes at a door. His needle-sharp eyes pierced mine. I flinched, struggling to see the heart behind his gaze but he'd drawn the blinds. Trying to appear in charge when he obviously wasn't, he kept interfering, interrupting and organizing things. The stockier round-faced one in the middle, in his mid-forties, introduced himself as the head investigator. I tried to peer beyond the intimidating navy police uniform into his soul. *I must see in.* On his right, the third and youngest officer wore his toughest demeanor as if not yet comfortable in his role. He waited for a signal to begin as I pushed back the memory of his anger the night before when he called me a spy.

"I am an officer and interpreter," he blurted in Chinese, "but since you speak Chinese try to understand in Chinese first and speak it unless you don't understand." I nodded but worried I'd miss important words or misinterpret. He read from notes. "We work for the Dandong branch of the Ministry of State Security, the agency responsible for counter-intelligence, foreign intelligence and political security in China. You gathered intelligence for foreign agents to harm China's national defense. This is very serious so we expect your full cooperation with our investigation if you want things to go better for you."

Six accusing eyes unnerved me. The interrogators leaned forward and their blue police uniforms, badges, and fierce expressions screamed *criminal* at me. I tried to focus, asking for a woman in the room. They agreed to pass on my request later to higher leaders who observed via cameras from another room.

Fluorescent lights flickered. A huge rectangular 24-hour digital clock attached to the wall displayed the time, date and year in bright red numbers. It was 7:30 a.m. August 5, 2014. Two cameras and microphones hung on the walls, one on my right and one above the door facing me.

"Name? Birthplace? Husband's name? Children's names? Age?" The interrogation started with routine questions then moved on to procedures in technical and formal language. When I faltered, the interpreter tried to help but admitted his English was out of practice. No one brought a dictionary.

"These are your rights under Chinese law," he said, pointing to a paper with numbered items.

"Can I have one in English?"

"No. I will explain it."

"Can you give me an English copy later?"

"No, we don't have one."

The translator's faltering English was difficult to understand, especially since I was shaking and fighting to focus. He referred to humane treatment and human rights and insisted everything followed the rule of law in China. He mentioned the Canadian Embassy in Beijing knew of our detention. That surprised me but sounded hopeful.

"Can I see someone from my Embassy? Who can explain in English?"

"We will ask."

"Can I talk to a lawyer or make a phone call?" I was relying on vague recollections from movie arrests.

"Lawyers aren't permitted during the investigation period. After that you can choose a Chinese one."

"How long is the investigation period?"

"That depends on your cooperation!" interrupted the tall thin one, spitting his words as if he'd had a hard time waiting to speak.

"Who will tell my family? Peter is in Dandong."

"We will inform him," the head investigator assured me, cutting the other man off, "but phone calls and family visits aren't permitted during the investigation period." He spoke as if talking to a criminal. I felt guilty despite my innocence. Three men to one woman. The battle was fierce from the onset. They had notebooks of ammunition but I had the truth.

The interrogators repeated the phrase *full cooperation* multiple times emphasizing that what happened depended on it. "Give full details. We know everything so don't hide information," the head investigator claimed. "We are making sure you tell the truth. Cooperate while we give you a chance to tell us everything." *Confess? Everything?* My brain ran through recent events wondering what I'd done that was considered a criminal act in China.

"What did I do?"

"You stole state secrets and spied on China for your government, the United States and others. It's a serious crime against our country," barked the officer at the computer, typing like a madman.

"You've taken the wrong people. I know nothing about spying."

"You are trained to lie. You used teaching and Christian work to cover up your spy work. The best thing is to cooperate. Tell us everything we ask. If you do, it will help you and Kevin."

"Kevin, where is he?" My heart jumped, glad they let his name slip out. *He's alive!*

"We know nothing about him. China runs by the rule of law so both your cases will follow our laws. Sign this paper to say we've read you your rights." The typing stopped, and out came a small package of tissue and a red tin. "Date it for yesterday."

"But you didn't read them yesterday."

"We paid attention to your safety and arrived late. Do what we tell you."

"You want me to be truthful, don't you? You read these today." I wondered where the boldness came from. *Is it the tangible reinforcement of prayers from far away?*

They mumbled and weren't happy, but let me add the correct date. The tall man handed me a tissue to wipe my finger. *Nice of him.*

13

The Business Woman

Distant water won't help to
put out a fire close at hand.

—Chinese Proverb

—Kevin—

I battled nausea and exhaustion for eighteen hours, losing track of time. The next thing I remember is Chief returning the second morning to inform me a Canadian Embassy representative had come to Dandong to see me.

"Will Julia be there?" I asked, staggering up with new hope.

"We don't know. And don't mention the case or the visit will end." Chief's warning was clear. "And don't tell them where you are or it will force us to make other arrangements for you that won't be as nice. Say we feed and treat you well."

Still disoriented, a glimmer of hope surfaced. *Canada will solve our problems and prevent me from seeing this place again.* The breakfast tray arrived and I forced down a few bites. Chief and two guards returned in street clothes. I requested a notebook and pen but they shook their heads. After checking my clothes and pockets, they unlocked the hallway door. A late model white Toyota Land Cruiser, common in China, pulled up. I sat between Chief and a guard while Captain sat in front with the driver.

Desperate to create order I made mental notes of every detail on our route. When we entered Dandong, I scanned the streets hoping to see familiar people. No one. The wall between me and everything normal was impenetrable.

The car climbed a steep hill and a sign at the gate said City Hotel. The complex reminded me of the government Friendship Hotel in Beijing in the early nineties. Our driver inched towards the main door and kept looking back. Everything was planned and timed to the smallest detail. No one relaxed—least of all me.

After scanning the surroundings, Chief signaled. The car stopped and Captain led me into the hotel. A few men stood or sat in the lobby but no one moved. My mind flashed back to the abduction. *The same set-up.* I felt the MSS agent's eyes locking onto me as we walked past in eerie silence. A short, fierce-looking man in brown leather shoes stood by the elevator checking his watch.

We all got in and the man in leather shoes pushed the button. Third floor. Nothing calmed me as I listened to the thud of our footsteps in the empty hallway. Agents stepped out of the shadows obviously ready to intervene if a crisis erupted. *What excessive formality and security for an ordinary person.*

Two guards entered the room with me. Captain announced his supervisory role, warning me to follow the rules or risk losing all future visits. One guard entered the bathroom and set his phone up to record. He didn't come out. *Does he know I saw him?*

I waited in the clean dated room. Through the sheer white curtains, I discerned trees and nearby buildings. I sat opposite a television and coffee table with an ashtray, tea cups, a thermos flask, and two bottles of water. Paintings of blue and white Chinese vases hung on the wall and the décor was reminiscent of Chinese government hotels in the 1990s. The room felt staged. I fixated on the artwork to crowd out the debilitating anxiety and dizziness vying for control of my mind.

—Julia—

After a restless night, I was reluctant to open my eyes. The head interrogator stepped in. "Get ready. Your Embassy wants to meet you." I burst into tears. I wasn't sad but couldn't handle the shock. My body did strange things and I couldn't stop it. He looked surprised. "It's a good thing. You can talk to them." His tone changed. "But don't mention the case or location."

Valiant efforts to control the tears trickling down my cheeks failed. The guards brought my cup, so I washed in a rush. My legs buckled as the head female guard arrived and checked my pockets. "*Sòng chē láile* (the sending car is here)," the guards said hurrying me downstairs to a waiting burgundy van. The driver extinguished his cigarette as they fastened me in.

Despite uncontrollable shaking, seeing outside was stunning. *Has it only been one day?* I breathed in everything. A child running in the village. A flock of ducks. An old man walking with a cane. Everything reminded me of the China I loved. This is the *real* China, I kept telling myself, *the China I belong to.* As daily life passed by the window, I realized how deep and strong my love for China was. Even as a prisoner my eyes and thoughts were free to celebrate everything China had offered me over the years. I grasped each moment unsure if I would travel this road again. I sang in a muted voice trying to paint a melody on the fears that clutched my heart and made it tremble. *The China I know wouldn't treat me this way.* Thirty years of friendship, kindness, and thank-yous. Even imagining myself as a spy was impossible. China will realize once the Embassy explains.

We entered the city and passed our coffee house. A sign in the window read, *Closed today. See you again soon.* Sadness flooded my heart as I thought of our wonderful staff, the friends I had made, and the incredible moments in that place. Peter and Hannah were 14 and 9 when we first moved to Dandong in 2007, helping us make chair and table-sized paper cut-outs to lay on the floor as we worked out the table and chair arrangements. We'd worked together with locals building this small business to foster friendship and understanding between people of different nations because Dandong was a border city and host to many people.

Our coffee shop name, *Peter's*, was not only our son's name but a reference to the Greek word, Petros, meaning rock. Our logo was a circle mosaic of stones representing how different people and nations working together, are one family. Many talented musicians and bands both local and overseas had performed at *Peter's*. Chinese called our family *eggs*, white on the outside and yellow on the inside. We were.

My thoughts jolted to silence as the car pulled into an old government hotel and agents shuffled me from car to lobby to elevator to room. I sat petrified on a blue and gold floral upholstered chair, staring at a thermos flask and two empty white tea mugs, watching my knees quake and trying to stop them with the weight of my hands. Two guards stood beside me while the interpreter paced back and forth, waiting for a signal. *Why are they so nervous? Is Kevin nearby?*

—Kevin—

Thirty minutes later an official-looking woman carrying a notepad and leather bag entered, shook my hand and showed her name card: Anne, a consular officer from the Canadian Embassy in Beijing. Brushing her skirt under her, Anne sat in the armchair opposite me with a coffee table lengthwise between us. She set her bag on the floor pulling out a pen and notepad. If I wasn't so nervous with Captain perched in a chair next to me, it could have been an interview.

Anne was professional and official. "Pleased to meet you, Mr. Garratt. How are you doing?"

"Ok, I guess, considering I don't know what's going on." I felt sick and confused but couldn't articulate it.

"Yes, we were caught off guard too and scrambled to get here as soon as we received the notification." She scribbled notes as she spoke.

The conversation was an awkward, strained, uncharted experience. She didn't know me. I didn't know her. Anne fulfilled her duties to gather the maximum amount of information in 30 minutes. Time slipped away as she scratched notes on her pad while Captain and my guards watched in silence. *I want to go home.*

"Are you staying here?" she continued, nervous.

"No, an hour from here," I replied, glancing at Captain to make sure I didn't say the wrong thing. He showed no emotion and said nothing. My anxious thoughts blustered into questions. "Why are we here? I am so confused. Can you get us out? Please, help us."

"We have no information but hope for clarity soon. We guarantee visits every three months but this case is different, so I am not sure," she replied.

My heart jolted. *Three months? Can't dialogue sort this out now?* I changed the topic, unable to process her words. "Does our family know?"

"Yes, we informed them. Many people are very concerned. I will see Julia next."

Julia. Right here in this room after me? "Tell her I love her." I blurted, unable to hold back the tears I had controlled until now. Anne's answer scrambled in my brain. With only a few minutes left I tried not waste them. "We have worked in China for years. We run a coffee shop. Julia is a teacher. We love working in this city and have many friends. The coffee house is a hub for students, tourists and the business community. And we provide aid for North Korea."

Anne wrote and looked sympathetic but I felt worlds away from her. The conversation went nowhere. She was going back to her hotel and on to Beijing, her job and her coworkers. *Where am I going?*

Captain stood up. "Time." Anne reached for her leather bag and stood too, maintaining her distance from me.

"Please tell my family I love them," I repeated as they led me out, keeping their strict timetable.

"Try to keep your hope up. Take care of yourself."

I was numb, aching for good news that no one mentioned. Guards whisked me out and the same car returned me to the compound. The shock and disappointment sent ripples of nausea through me. *God, I wasn't expecting this.*

—*Julia*—

The meeting was across the hall. As we entered, the consular representative stood to greet me and introduced herself as Anne.

"Please help us!" Tears streamed out uninvited.

"Nice to meet you, Mrs. Garratt. I just met Kevin and…"

"You did?" I wiped my eyes with my hand. "How is he? What did he say?"

"He said to tell you he loves you." She noticing my legs quaking and asked if I was ok.

"I must be in shock. My body is doing whatever it wants to." Eager to avoid using up the time without learning more I pressed on. "Can you help us? Why did China take us? We have worked in China back and forth for 30 years. We aren't activists. What's happening?"

"Our only information is an official communication from the Ministry of State Security stating that you're in residential surveillance.

But within hours it was international news and picked up by everyone and…"

The tall, serious officer monitoring us in the room interrupted. She stopped mid-sentence aware of the protocol. But I'd heard a sentence that sent my mind reeling. *The world knows. Our disappearance is world news?* Shock waves like earthquake tremors came in rapid succession. *Why?* I got no answers. The conversation turned back to formalities: signing a paper giving Canadian representatives permission to communicate with designated family members and to receive future messages from those listed. My mind faded in and out unable to focus. *This news changes everything.*

Without warning, the meeting ended. Anne's formality fed my fears, not calmed them. The spy accusation was real, not an idle threat from a local police station. The case had moved onto the world stage.

I left dazed, as if anesthetized and stood immobile in the elevator awaiting my fate. As the van pulled up to the lobby door, the hope of going home vanished. People having normal lives were a chasm away. Anyone looking at our car had no inkling that trapped inside was a foreigner being transferred to a secret location. I knew nothing and dreaded everything.

More desperate than before I grabbed scenes along the way, trying to snatch them as we sped past. I gazed at people carrying vegetables and cars overtaking us on the road as if viewing a fictional dream of daily life. Normal had disappeared. As we crossed the final stretch of road, the word *LOVE* three times in large English lettering was attached to bridge railings and a huge heart-shaped carved stone marked a nearby tourist destination. *How odd that Chinese officials approved the message.* Today it was a comforting reminder of God's love in the middle of my nightmare.

Two honks and the gate creaked open. My eyes darted along the row of security cameras on the walls and every corner of the building. Everything prevented escape. I shivered.

Nauseous from the drive and reeling from the news that the world knew, I plunked on the bed while the guards locked up and took their posts. The lunch tray arrived with rice, cabbage and hot peppers. I ate a little. I like hot peppers.

14

LOCKED UP

Captivity can't lock away
the plans of God.

—JULIA GARRATT

—*Kevin*—

I *hope Anne delivered my message.* Back in the room the guards offered
me food, but nausea overpowered me, so they escorted me back and
forth to the toilet to throw up. I tried reading but my head pounded.
I drifted in and out of consciousness. Florescent light stung my eyes as
my mind whirred through recent events with every detail on constant
replay. At least 50 guards, multiple cameras, radar and walls secured
the compound. *For me?* Disappointment that Canada couldn't free us
and the ache that Julia was captive too, added to my pain.

My sickness intensified. That evening while emptying my stomach
of the horrible bile that comes up when nothing else can, a woman
appeared. After seeing only men, this woman in uniform calmed
me. In a caring voice, she asked basic health questions and offered
medication. My mind strayed. *If women are here, maybe Julia is too.*

Night came in a blur and the dinner tray came and went undetected.
I grappled with dehydration, a hard bed, flickering lights, and staring
guards. Through the next 24 hours my body fought back, recuperating
from the initial shock and nausea but my brain never relaxed. As my
thoughts swirled, two gentle complete sentences from heaven flowed
into my battered brain and settled there. *I am with you. I have a plan.*

—*Julia*—

I probed for answers but none came. This wasn't an accident; it was an
international incident. I reassured myself. *This is not a surprise to God.*

I stared at the guards, the walls, covered windows, bed, and locked door. The difference between an enemy and friend is often a choice. Whatever it takes, I will love these MSS guards and interrogators as I love every Chinese person and respect and serve them whatever comes. I asked God for courage and prayed for the guards, investigators, and cooks. I did not know their lives, hardships, struggles, or pain. *Maybe they need me. I must be here for a reason. Chosen.*

To order my days, I studied patterns and schedules. Interrogation happened from 9 to 12 a.m. and 2 to 5 p.m. Six hours a day including weekends. Heavy footsteps in the halls, furniture moving in the next room, then three firm knocks on my door alerted me. Guards brought meal trays at 7 a.m., 12 p.m., and 5:30 p.m. I ate alone facing the wall. My toilet had two small red plastic bowls for bathing and washing clothes and a shower head hung from the wall providing solar heated hot water on sunny days. The guards had to use the communal hallway toilet.

My world was footsteps, whispers, scuffling furniture, honking horns, car doors, or the compound gate creaking open or shut. *Am I the only prisoner?* I sorted footsteps and new ones fed my fears which multiplied like cells in an invasive infection. I had long conversations with God. *How can I survive? How can I serve here?* The answers deposited into my mind and heart were my life support. Prayer was the most joyful communication of all, calming and strengthening me when imagination fed my soul what it didn't want to eat.

❖

On Day 4, I woke with an idea. "Can I teach the guards English during their shifts?" I asked the head guard. She forwarded my request and that evening announced I could start the next morning at 8 a.m. right before interrogation. What favour! I mentioned preparation and she returned with a notebook and short curly pencil too soft to be a weapon.

Teaching lessons dulled the pain and muted the fear. I offered the guards English names to replace numbers. The head guard informed me her English name was Daisy. The rest choose an alphabet letter and picked from names I suggested. The woman who escorted me the first night, chose Celina. My other students were Helen, Vivian and Annie. On Day 6, I added Kylie, Lia, Lisa, Karla, and Bella because off-duty guards asked permission to attend. My podium was a bed and my students were guards but for an hour we stepped out of prison roles. The room transformed as we laughed our way through structured lessons on solitary confinement routines, tongue twisters, and the daily weather. Friendship spilled into the room and during the night shift we chatted about families and life outside.

The leaders noticed relationships forming and decided that the joy from excited, eager students in my room undermined the interrogators intimidation tactics. On Day 10 the lessons stopped. "The leaders have cancelled English classes," Daisy said. "You must concentrate on confessions and the guards have to study material sent by the bureau."

After that, guards had stern warnings not to befriend, talk to, or learn from me. Celina, alone for a moment while the second guard went to the bathroom, whispered that my last lesson on the five love languages was the best and she planned to use what she learned with her husband and future children. She was a newlywed. It was her way of saying thank you. The guards had husbands and children they never saw. Helen missed her daughter's first day of school. Annie's one-year-old daughter cried every night for her mother. They lived at the compound without cell phones or computers, permitted to go to the gatehouse once a day to phone home. We were all isolated.

❖

The lessons ended but the names stuck. I also chose English names for my interrogators, to view them as friends rather than enemies. Two days later, they surprised me by asking for their names. The Chief Investigator I named Stephen, meaning lover of horses and I pictured him running free in the fields. The young officer who interpreted, had a brilliant scientific mind so I called him Benjamin (Benji), and the harsh Officer who typed my testimony, was John because I imagined him turning his strength around for good and doing great things. They liked their names and soon after shouted *Benji* in the hall, laughing because in Chinese it sounded like the word for *foolish chicken*.

❖

No one took my notebook or pencil away since I needed to write confessions. I had other plans. With the pencil tucked behind the Bible, I leaned against the wall, knees up, and wrote the title *Daily Thanks* on a blank page at the back. Under it, I sketched a miniature picture with a number above it. I traced the tiny images I'd scratched with my finger nails since day one.

> *Day 1–four pictures of our children. Day 2–carryon bag with Bible. Day 3–Canadian Embassy visit. Day 4–glimpsed a heart-shaped cloud through the window while guards aired the room. Day 5–notebook and pencil arrived for English lesson. Day 6–first 15-minute outdoor time with 4 guards. Day 7–heard music in the distance. Day 8–I prayed, "Please send a bird to my window, and through the opaque plastic a bird landed on the bars." Day 9–I had a dream of someone holding my hand.*

—Kevin—

I paced to calm myself. Words to a song or a Bible verse like *God is our refuge and strength, an ever-present help in trouble (Psalm 46:1, NIV)* brought reassuring peace. I deduced that if the wall camera's red lights flashed on it signaled the interrogator's imminent arrival. I tried not to look but as the time approached I checked often, growing anxious. I battled to stop my environment from invading my peace.

The criminal accusations intermingled with tiny fragments of truth filled me with guilt and doubt. Laughing with colleagues was an elusive dream replaced by unfamiliar military terms, legal terms, and spy and espionage phrases. No one joked. My mind focused on dates and times and confessions. My puns ceased. That part of me was dying, and I didn't know how to bring it back.

My brain, crammed with collections of remarkable China memories, forced itself along new and unexpected thought trails as the interrogators wanted details about every visitor to the coffee shop, where they worked and what I said to them. Night assignments to confess everything from birth to present kept me as a helpless soldier trapped in underground tunnels hearing, "go this way, go that way," without an exit. It took strength to breathe. Every evening I prayed the interrogation would end, but morning brought more questions. At night, I fell asleep hoping to wake up in another place but there was no other place. I opened my eyes and let the awful truth seep back. The interrogation chair screamed *prisoner, come here,* and I sat wounded in the chair for another six hours.

I never left my room except for the bathroom. Interrogation, sleeping, and eating were in the same room. *Will the Embassy wait three months to come again?* My imagination authored unwelcome narratives that weakened my soul. There was no respite, no information. Tears tumbled out uninvited. My interrogators weren't interested in me or God. My guards focused on getting out to eat or smoke. *Who can I help when I can't help myself?*

❖

On Day 9, the interrogators announced Canada and China negotiated so that I could leave my room for 15 minutes of fresh air daily. To avoid being spotted this happened after dark. When 8 p.m. came and five guards led me around to the back of the compound, I hatched escape plans. Inside, not one plausible plan emerged. Outside with the night sky, walls and river beyond, my imagination took flight. *With an amazing burst of speed and a leap, I conquered the spike-covered gate, ran through the orchard and plunged into the river only ten metres away. I swam 300 metres with the strength of ten swimmers, then clambered up the banks on the other side. I ran along the river road sweating after such a brave escape.* Then reality hit. Would anyone stop to pick up a foreign hitchhiker with no money or ID? I didn't care. The imaginary jump, the bolt, the swim, and the run was worth it because it happened as five guards stood by oblivious to my thrilling escape! Fifteen minutes passed in a moment and heading back in procession to the room, I celebrated my secret accomplishment.

Another night I envisioned a rescue with helicopters overhead, lowering special forces with guns overpowering the guards without resistance. My plot was foiled when I realized the commotion would wake everyone before they landed. But two moments of fantasy was worth it. In winter with the river frozen solid I imagined an even easier escape route, racing across the ice and saving myself the swim. Despite no plausible plan to get a stranded foreigner from the embankment to the airport, the thrill of my incognito escapes strengthened me. *Thank you for 15 minutes to breathe fresh air.*

—Julia—

Excited to leave the room, I didn't complain as four guards marched me to the back of the compound to a small cement pad and stood on four sides of me.

"Walk!" Daisy said. I walked in a circle thinking how absurd it was to pass by three guards standing at attention while a fourth followed two paces behind me. Next to us were walls and beyond that dark shadows from distant trees. A small vegetable garden with eggplant ran along one side of the wall and the guard beside it stooped to pick a few and stuff them into her uniform pocket.

My only freedom was looking straight up. The stars danced overhead and the endless sky shouted freedom to my soul from the place where no guard stood. With each step on the hard cement pad, I imagined myself somewhere else. As my feet moved in circles behind walls, I walked along the street to see horses near my sister's house, by the river in Dandong, or strolled a beach in Thailand with waves splashing over my toes. As I walked I chanted softly, "This land I walk on is yours, is yours." The same rhythm and tune repeated over was my attempt to leave God's blessing with every step. Other nights I stood with tears sprinkling my cheeks, unable to walk. I was just too sad. If I glanced up to the third floor and noticed people watching through the window, I wondered if I was their trophy. *Do they feel sorry for this Canadian hostage?*

❖

On Day 12, Friday, August 15, heavy footsteps put me on high alert. Chairs scuffled in the next room. Before the three knocks came I was ready. Celina came and sat in a corner.

"Thank you for letting her stay," I said, armed for the interrogation with a verse I'd memorized that morning.

"The leaders agreed," Benji answered.

"Who is Omid?" Stephen started, jolting me into the interrogation.

"I don't know anyone named Omid."

"Aha, you are lying," John yelled raising his eyebrows and giving me a fierce glare.

"No, it's true," I insisted.

"It's a code name," he mocked, "confess your contacts. We know everything!"

It is not too hard for you… the word is near you. (Deuteronomy 30:11-14 ESV). As the intensity of their techniques collapsed my defenses, the life-giving words flowed through my mind helping me withstand the pain until courage returned. *It is in your heart and in your mouth so you can do it.*

"I am telling the truth. I don't know Omid."

"You gave him information about North Korea," John continued with a steely voice, "We found it on your computer. How many contacts do you have on your webcam voice and message app?"

"About 15." I guessed. *It is not in heaven that you should say, who will go up to the heavens for us and bring it back to us, that we may hear it and do it?*

"Name them!"

Neither is it beyond the sea, that you should say, who will go over the sea for us and bring it to us, that we may hear it and do it. I listed family members, friends and a few of Hannah's teachers.

"You missed Omid!" Benji added accusing me.

"There is no Omid!"

"Sit and think about it, then confess," John mocked.

The memorized words calmed my brain as it searched for answers but found none. *It is not too hard for you. It is not too hard for you. It is not too hard for you.*

Hours later a CD in a pink plastic case appeared. My mind flashed back to the one at the abduction dinner. *Are all the CD's the MSS use in pink cases?*

"We have your conversations. Confess before we show you."

I said nothing, so they put the CD in the computer and flipped the screen around showing me my chat. *Omid enters the conversation.* As I read, it flooded back. "That was a chat with my nephew Matthew. He and his friend did a school project on North Korea and wanted to ask me a few questions. I guess his friend's screen name was Omid and I added him to the app for one conversation. I never paid attention or talked to him again."

"Lies!" they attacked me with their words. "Children don't study North Korea! Why did you say, 'ask Peter to send him a few pictures for his project'? Why did you say you couldn't answer questions because they were too sensitive to answer from China?"

"Kids do social studies projects on any country and if they know someone in the country, it's more authentic. Peter was in Canada at the time so I suggested they contact him for a few pictures from our North Korea tour."

They didn't believe me. *I can do it.* I tried to focus but kept bursting into tears as they asked what Omid did now and insisted that his school, King's Academy, trained children for espionage from a young age. They were desperate for proof.

I longed for the session to end so I could cry in my room without pressure.

"You didn't cooperate well today," John said as he put me back in my room. Aching and stiff, passing into the sweetness of sleep took no effort.

As I forced my eyes open the next morning, the raging inner battle began at once. Me, Julia, terrified human sitting with guards or interrogators engaged in constant mental warfare, struggling to survive. And me, Julia, on a mysterious love journey, looking for ways to love people in this madness, wondering how this four-walled solitude could somehow be a new and transformational Sabbatical. I wrestled with myself all weekend.

On Monday, dreading a repeat of Friday's pain, I sat ready for another psychological beating.

"Our leaders have accepted your explanation," Stephen said. Relief flooded me. *Thank you!*

❖

Into long monotonous days of interrogation and solitude, laughter found its own way to intervene. On Day 25, heading out in the dark with guards, Celina's high-pitched screams filled the air as she dropped my arms, jumping around petrified. Everyone panicked including me until we realized she'd stepped on a toad! Daisy and the other guards switched gears, grabbed me and we marched to the back as they criticized her. Daisy brought a flashlight after that, but walked backwards and shone it on my feet instead of ahead of me so I still couldn't see where I walked.

On Day 30 the outdoor walk offered another surprise! Tiny lit lanterns dotted the sky with sparkling bursts of luminescent red as they floated off in the distance. *God, did you do that for me?* I spent the whole 15 minutes watching and admiring them, realizing later it was Moon Festival night in China. Red means happiness in Chinese culture and that night it was true!

❖

I continued to scribble tiny images in my Bible and added dots. One to remind me I survived the day's interrogation, and one to note I left the room for 15 minutes. Every day I chose to hope, forcing myself to sing, eat and see the guards and interrogators as people on special assignment, and me on a special assignment of my own. The battle intensified, beating on my psyche the painful rhythm of perpetual uncertainty. I never felt ready.

A month passed, blurring together with similar sounds until a new commotion in the hallway alerted me. Voices called, "The car has come!" I gathered my few belongings grateful for the signal. It was Tuesday and as guards rushed in and out of my room subbing for each other, I pictured what I'd say when they freed me and imagined my first meal. *I'll go to the bathroom alone, shower alone, and get a drink by myself. I am going home! The ordeal is ending.*

Car doors and many honks meant multiple cars. *I'm right! I'm leaving.* I tasted release and waited for a knock on my door. My guards rushed back and forth to the window, opening it a crack then shutting it, preventing me from peeking. I waited in expectation. More steps in the hallway and chattering voices. *Release! The announcement is coming soon.* I was happy.

Then two stiff stern guards walked in and my regulars left. Car doors outside slammed shut, and the gate creaked open and closed. The cars left without me. *Where's my car?* I held onto hope, but no one came. Everything collapsed. That evening when two more unfamiliar guards entered the room, I understood. My old guards, my companions with English names, were replaced.

Everything crashed around me. The guard's icy stares accused me and I had no energy to warm them. Stranded with strangers was a blow to my head, my heart, my soul. I fell under the weight of sorrow from walking a day in the wrong direction and losing sight of the starting point. My thoughts paused. I had no courage to make friends with the new guards or see another metal food tray or ask for a glass of water. I only wanted the pain to stop.

The rhythm of month one I worked so hard to create and maintain, disappeared. The familiar rhythm, like the line on a monitor when the heart stops beating, was one horizontal line with no variation. My weak lips were unable to whisper a prayer. I shut my eyes and lay comatose until sleep swept me away. When morning forced me awake, the disturbing faces of guards who'd invaded my space during the night, unnerved me. The breakfast tray repulsed me. The swimmer floating face down in the water didn't want to hold her breath.

Then, in the awkward debilitating stillness my true companion whispered. *Just turn face up and float.* It was the tone of concern that startled me as if permission to float was all I needed. I turned over, laying still for hours, until a second whisper invited me back to life. Called to a new rhythm, the gentle, calming and recognizable voice wrapped my weary soul in peace.

The next morning, Day 45, I woke up staring at the pattern on the heavy burgundy curtains. Hundreds of faded palm trees, columns of tall then short ones. I noticed the palms were bent down as if kneeling. *Children and adults are praying for me!* I counted them. 900. *I'm surrounded by 900 prayer warriors! I can do more than float!* With new courage, I washed my face, and put on the flip flops ready for the three knocks. I was not alone. Ever.

15

U.S. Agents

*The sheep has no choice when
in the jaws of the wolf.*

—Chinese Proverb

—Kevin—

New guards replaced old ones as I sat for hours a day on a chair with legs crossed, reading their faces and searching for clues to liven my 59 days of sameness. On day 60 the rebellion began. In silence my body screamed for attention. My nerves and muscles complained of neglect. Varicose veins pushed through my skin looking for another way out. My right foot stopped bending at the ankle. When the two red lights flashed, I dragged my numb foot to the chair.

"It's your own fault you damaged your foot. Move around more. Stop sitting with your legs crossed!" Chief barked. Then unexpectedly he softened. "I'll order hot water so you can soak them," he added, then grabbed his pad and charged on with his first question. "Who did you contact on September 10, 2012?"

"Two years ago?" My mind lacked focus, still pondering the foot soak and picturing a comfortable white terrycloth robe and a steamy sauna. "I can't remember."

"You hosted him."

"Can you give me more information?" I forced myself out of the sauna and back to the chair. Sleep deprivation impeded my ability to scan memory archives and reproduce a moment important to him but not me. I had to focus.

"Don't hide one detail. We already know everything. Answer the questions." Chief tapped his pen on the desk in an annoying rhythm.

"I don't know." I shifted to offset the piercing backache and squirmed in prolonged silence. They enjoyed my desperation.

"Stop hampering our investigation!" Captain's accusing voice penetrated through me.

"I don't remember every customer." *Why can't I remember?* A running stream of faces and conversations they claimed happened in the coffee house bounced around my battered mind.

The three of them enjoyed watching me agonize. They never rushed. Captain fiddled with a huge stack of papers while Chief rummaged through the thick file of evidence. Still tapping the pen, he turned a page to face me, pointing to a criminal mugshot. "Does this help? He was no ordinary customer," he taunted. I stared at the unfamiliar face, scrambling to recollect. "Tell us everything. Would you prefer execution?" He leaned forward scowling. I felt so criminal.

"I don't know him. If we talked, he was a customer." Doubting myself, I drifted back to my imaginary sauna. They scoffed. My mind blanked until little by little it filled with tiny details stringing together and filling my brain with possible answers. I wanted to please them. It seemed better than letting them follow through with their threats to extract confessions.

"What did you tell him? Confess you hosted the American Military Attaché," they pushed. "Someone else has confessed."

Who? They paused, and I detested it. When discrediting my answers, silence and waiting was intentional and strategic. My body cringed, forced to think until words formed. I needed an escape from the psychological torture that tore me apart piece by piece, word by word, day by day. Unrelenting pressure and frequent threats for non-compliance weakened my brain, luring me to invent plausible answers to please them and then memorize them for the next time. My confession moved into position, chosen from the medley of possibilities. My lips moved.

"Perhaps I mentioned the darkness in North Korea at night compared to the light in Dandong." *I sound ridiculous.* "And differences on both sides of the river, truckloads of goods crossing the bridge daily and the flow of North Koreans through customs. It might have been that."

"Ahah. You confess meeting him. Good. More detail," Chief continued mocking me as Officer Zhang typed with a smirk.

There was no more detail. If I met him, I didn't know his occupation or purpose. We ran a coffee shop. Locals chatting with native English speakers, backpackers waiting for transit to their next destination, and reporters following brewing North Korea stories, filled the tables at *Peter's*. Asian tourists gawking at North Korea, Embassy personnel from Pyongyang out for shopping breaks, and officers from the U.S. Consulate in Shenyang less than three hours away, frequented our shop while in town. To remember customers by name, occupation and conversation was impossible. The accusations held my brain hostage as my brain and body tensed in tandem. *Will it ever stop?*

"More detail," Captain persisted but I'd given my answer. There was no more detail. Their methodical tactics forced me to wade through and account for seven years of U.S. Embassy and Consulate visits. *Why can't I remember?*

"Which US officials did you host? What did they ask? What information did you give? Were they happy with your answers?"

My mind spun out of control recalling conversations discussing trade across the bridge, North Koreans working in Dandong, and increased local security in response to North Korean nuclear tests. I had showed some customers photos of our recent trips to North Korea. *Was I targeted? Were U.S. agents gathering intelligence? Was I a convenient asset with access to places they could not go?*

"Why were you invited to the July 4th party put on by the Shenyang Consulate? What secret information did they communicate? Explain the assignments they gave and how they transferred money to you."

Shocked, I knew my invitation was a courtesy with no ulterior motive. I picked up coffee house supplies and visited other Shenyang friends, timing my visit to attend. "It was a dinner. A celebration."

"Why did you go and not Julia? You aren't American, so why invite you? Was it an expensive dinner? A *hóngbāo* (lucky red packet with money) for you as payment?"

"No. Julia doesn't enjoy big events with people she doesn't know. That's why she didn't go. No one paid me. It was a party," I said, my stomach churning at their false conclusions and insinuations. Everything was twisted.

—Julia—

"Describe your meetings with U.S. embassy agents," Stephen started the interrogation.

"I didn't have any meetings."

They pushed but got nowhere so switched topics to throw me off guard. "Why did Kevin go to the July 4th party without you, two years in a row? He went to get assignments and his pay."

"That's not true."

"What did he tell you?"

"He told me the meal was delicious."

"What else?

"Nothing, only the food."

"Why do Americans visit your coffee shop so often?"

"Because they enjoy coffee and authentic western food."

"Ha!" John laughed at me, "We know that's not true. They drive three hours for a hamburger?"

"Well, they're in town for their own business. I don't know what. Then they come to eat. That's it. That's the truth."

"Why does Kevin host them?"

"He doesn't, he chats with lots of customers."

"Kevin works for them and CSIS (Canadian Security Intelligence Service). Government spies never tell their wives. You are his accomplice and guilty under Chinese law for helping him spy for the U.S., Canada and England."

The accusations baffled me. *Why do they focus on spying?*

"Did you ever take USBs or CDs or envelopes back to Canada for your friend Chris King?"

"If Kevin gave me something for him, our accountant or our board."

"Did you look at it?"

"No, I didn't care. It was admin stuff. Kevin manages that."

"So you don't know what you carried back for him do you?"

"No, but it wasn't secret information."

"We have copies. It was secret military photos and data undermining Chinese national defense. And you carried the CD!" John raised his eyebrows with a menacing glare.

They built their case with certainty and fired the questions fast. Forceful lies repeated left lingering doubts. *What did I carry back? Were we used? What evil world is it if your own countries put you at great risk for their own gain?* The thought made me sick.

"And explain your cooperation with Global Humanitarian Services Agency (GHSA)," they continued.

"GHSA is a large Christian humanitarian organization based in Colorado. It funds aid projects worldwide and they offered funding for specific projects in North Korea."

"Yes, and the American pastor, Chris King, connected you. More details."

"We only met the CEO in Canada once. I don't remember his name – Tanaka or something. He had wealthy donors that funded their work."

"Yes, he's Japanese! We know him. Why do you work for the Japanese?"

"He's Japanese American and I don't work for him."

"Did you meet his government donors," John mocked, "for your *Warm for Winter* spy project?"

"No, warm clothes for marginalized communities in North Korea. Just hats, boots, scarves, and winter wear for children."

"And coats for the North Korean army?"

"No! Not that!" I answered shocked at the thought.

"Kevin had emails offering containers of warm coats from GHSA," John said, flaunting his knowledge of the contents of private emails.

"We didn't accept them because North Korea refuses American goods. We purchased everything locally in Dandong."

"Tanaka works for the U.S. military. GHSA is his cover. We know their network. We know everything."

Listening to their accusations, I felt danger in a whole new way. "That's not true," I defended GHSA, Chris and our partnerships.

"Why did they call the initiative Middle Kingdom Transformation Project? They want to overthrow China and recruited you to gather information." They flaunted the misconstrued information they claimed came from our computers. I had no defense. *Did they fabricate everything?* They were so detailed and convincing.

John, delighted to boast about China and its accomplishments, added, "Your governments use aid to hide tracking devices and chips to get them into North Korea to spy."

I didn't understand how countries spied on other countries but undermining aid initiatives was evil. The false accusations angered me. Funding starving children to spy for the government? Lies. As I spoke I felt I was convincing myself too. *Are they lies?*

Relishing the momentum, they added, "and you hosted a government delegation in your house. We have proof."

"No U.S. officials ever came to our apartment. They wouldn't. We don't know them and they don't know us."

"Kevin's texts say otherwise," Benji piped in, reading a document with texts from Kevin's phone. "It says: 'Hey Julia, I can't get back in time to meet the U.S. friends. Could you bring them to our apartment to wait for me? Maybe show them the Kim movie while you are waiting.' See, it's right here. You hosted them and showed a secret movie depicting the North Korean leader."

I tried to remember. "The only U.S. visitors to our house were friends. None worked at the Embassy or Consulate or came from the government."

"We saw them come. And why did Kevin ask you to show the Kim movie?

They waited. *Why did he?*

"Think more, it's your homework tonight," they mocked, "and rewrite from scratch your *Warm for Winter* flyer and the complete grant application you wrote for funding. Every detail. Even sketch the pictures you used. You can confess more tomorrow."

❖

After five hours of homework I crashed on the bed. Throughout the night I tried to decipher the text about the Kim movie. *What was it?* My mind pored through every possible visitor, coming up blank. After a restless sleep, I woke at 3 a.m. with the answer. It was crazy.

❖

"Did you remember?" Stephen said the next morning, expecting a confession.

"Yes."

"Good. Confess!" Benji looked pleased as John typed.

"The only movie we showed on North Korea was *Kimjongilia*, named after the leader's flower."

"Ha! A flower? You expect me to believe you?" John mocked.

"Yes, a flower. Each leader has a flower species unique to them and Kim Jong Il's is the Kimjongilia. They decorate hotels and monuments and artists paint them on murals, paintings and mosaics of the leader. We bought the DVD from a popular online retailer in China. It portrays two sides of North Korean life—the cultural arts and the struggles of everyday people. It also gives a good historical overview. That's the movie."

"And the agents who visited your apartment?" John continued, ridiculing my confession.

"None came. Only American friends." They didn't believe me. The more they asked, the more I saw their point. My explanations were true but truth misconstrued sounds false. I pitied Kevin. He networked and had extensive contact lists. *Is he surviving?*

16

CANADIAN SECURITY INTELLIGENCE SERVICE

Once on a tiger's back,
it's hard to alight.

—CHINESE PROVERB

—*Kevin*—

"Today, confess your spying for Canada!" Chief was eager to add charges to my crimes of spying for the United States. "How often did you host Canadian Embassy officials? Hide nothing if you want a better outcome."

"They visited three times I think." Random names and faces encircled me like a swarm of bees. "A lady came from the visa section and Michel LaFleur came, and I have no recollection of the third time.

"Michel LaFleur, good, more details." They jotted notes as I talked.

"He worked in the political department of the Canadian Embassy in Beijing. I received an email from him after a referral by the U.S. Consulate in Shenyang. He arrived in Dandong alone, introduced himself and gave me his card. Interested in local history and how businesses work in North Korea, we discussed China and DPRK. I recommended a few historical places he might enjoy and we had dinner at a North Korean restaurant in town. That's all."

"Who paid for the dinner?"

"I don't remember." *It's always about the money.*

"Was it a fancy dinner? That's how they do it. Pay for dinner so you will talk more."

"No. Most Dandong visitors want to sample North Korean dishes. The next day he hired a car and visited some Jinan historical ruins I recommended." They wrote with great interest.

"Where did you hide his card? We didn't find it in your stuff."

"His business card? I guess I threw it away. I don't keep every card people give me."

"The card used a false name. They do it on purpose. He is a spy known to us," Captain added, glad to have extracted a useful confession. "Tonight rewrite everything you told us. All three visits in detail. First their questions and then your answers. Every word."

It was impossible, the details in my brain were like vacuum packed tea leaves sucked tighter and tighter. I had to guess. As I reconstructed the visits I had more questions than answers. Their visits were casual and friendly. *Was Michel a spy? Was I naïve?* Michel had diplomatic immunity. I didn't. I spent the evening frustrated completing meaningless homework.

The next day they added my *confessions* to their stacks and accused me of working for CSIS. Their proof came from a Canadian cell phone I'd never accessed or used in China.

"Explain your job with CSIS," Captain started.

"It wasn't a job. I met CSIS twice in Canada, a formality. They contacted me by cell phone after our first official aid trip into North Korea in 2009."

"More details."

"We were out for Vietnamese noodles with our children."

"Why were you in Canada?"

"For our daughter's wedding. While we were eating, my cell rang so I stepped out. It was CSIS asking to meet me. Shocked they had my number, I met them a few days later at an Asian restaurant they suggested."

"What restaurant?"

"A Chinese one. We thought it was strange because it was right next to the Vietnamese noodle shop! They asked for a description of our work in DPRK and explained it was standard procedure to contact people working there to make sure they followed international sanctions. I was open and had nothing to hide. I explained we focused on aid, emergency relief and crisis care for orphans, children and welfare seniors. CSIS asked me to keep in touch when I was back in Canada and the lady gave me her card and a business phone number. That was all."

"What was her name?"

"Sue Bradley or something like that."

"When did she give you the next assignment?" Captain continued, glancing down at a notebook.

"There was no assignment. Ever. Back in Canada a year later, she contacted me again and brought a man from the agency to meet me."

"Where?"

"A popular coffee shop in Vancouver."

"More details. Confess everything they asked and your assignment."

"There was no assignment. They asked what we did in both China and North Korea. I discussed our family, the coffee house in Dandong and recent DPRK trips. Routine questions and nothing else. They told me to keep in touch if I noticed interesting changes. That's what I remember." Furious with their insinuations, I glared at them.

"That's how they do it," the interrogators said exchanging glances, "for homework write everything. We need more details. We'll discuss your confession tomorrow so hide nothing."

—Julia—

"Did you ever meet CSIS?" John asked. His accusing tones implied guilt.

"No, never."

"Kevin did," he added and paused to watch me. "He was familiar with them. Did you know he had assignments from them?"

"No, he didn't. Meeting them was a routine thing for people travelling into North Korea for a reason other than tourism. Nothing else."

They produced an email on their computer with Kevin's address at the top. It thanked him for the meeting and asked him to keep in touch if he noticed anything interesting. They let me read it on their computer before questioning me more.

"Is this Kevin's email address?"

"Yes."

"Don't you think this email shows Kevin was familiar with this person? How did she sign her name?"

"Sue," I replied reading from the email.

"Yes, and no last name. They are on a first name basis. They work together."

I didn't know how to answer because although Kevin mentioned meeting a lady from CSIS, I didn't know her name. *Was it Sue? Had they met more often? Did she give him assignments?*

My homework was detailing everything Kevin shared after each meeting with CSIS. I had to produce dates, times, and a map of where we were during that first phone call. They asked me to draw the spot we parked the car, the table we sat at in the restaurant and where everyone sat, and every detail that came to mind.

"And a map to the CSIS office in Vancouver," they added.

"No, I can't do that. I don't know." I spent that night and the rest of the weekend tormented by the homework. Minute case details started to control my mind and I hid the rough drafts to console myself later drawing sketches on the blank backs of the papers.

—Kevin—

On Day 63, while collecting my stack of interrogation assignments, Chief announced that Prime Minister Harper was visiting China. He told me to press Canada harder during the upcoming consular visit. *How can I push a country to act?* I told them Canada had no reason to listen because I was ordinary, without money or influence. I had my own questions for Canada. *Are they telling the world we weren't spies and using every opportunity to free us? What is standing between our countries? Why the CSIS and U.S. military accusations? Have agencies used us?* I squelched my unnerving thoughts as Chief coached me.

"Don't waste time discussing your coffee shop and humanitarian work in China. Tell your government they know what's needed and beg them to act."

En route to the meeting, I imagined the seats that Prime Minister Harper would save for us on his plane. *Canada abhors injustice and will not leave without us. I'm sure they've got a plan.* When I saw Janine, I was pleased because she was kind. She'd been the regular consular officer since Anne came the first visit. I conveyed a message as instructed asking Canada to do more but oblivious to the real reason I was taken, it went nowhere. Janine reiterated that Canada was actively working on the case but offered no hint that a solution was imminent. She showed photos and read family messages before handing them to Captain. I hoped he would give them to me later. "Don't give up," Janine encouraged me, sensing my disappointment.

After the visit, Chief was upset. "You wasted the chance and weren't desperate enough."

"Is this related to economic crimes and China wants our government to trade someone who has fled to Canada because they stole money?" I guessed.

"No, that's different," Captain answered giving no further clues.

❖

For days after that, I sat on the bed with a head full of whirring words and allegations. Plagued with excruciating headaches, backaches and a nerve-damaged foot, I waited for Prime Minister Harper to get me out. Meal trays lacked variety. Eggplant? Eggs and tomato? Rice or steamed bread? Alone with my tray, listening to guards on the other side of the wall enjoying meals at a table was unbearable. Weekend outdoor BBQ's for guards and leaders, laughing and beer-drinking, meant I passed cases of empty bottles against the wall the next day during my walk. *How mean.* Without friends, my trays were an endless sequence of meaningless meals; enemy trays keeping me alive for more interrogations.

I wasted many hours frustrated. *How did they get it so wrong? Is it a punishment? Is this how God treats people?* It was hard to stop the barrage of questions and nighttime was the worst. I feigned sleep at 9:30 p.m. out of boredom, facing the wall away from guards and cameras to hide my tears. Unrelieved sadness, perched in my soul ready to rob joy when it surfaced. I brawled with an unseen enemy, lacking energy to spend time on top. Negative thoughts trampled me and voices told me what I didn't want to hear. The echoes of threats were like bullets from a firing squad targeting my mind. *Will I ever hug my children again?*

I didn't just close my eyes at night, I clamped them tight in a conscious purposeful act to help me sleep faster. Scrunching my eyelids was my only idea to cope, so I did it every night. The best part of sleep was the moment before waking. I had the wonderful feeling I was somewhere else–beside Julia or on a mountain peak with Simeon and Peter, or about to eat a juicy steak. With eyelids shut, I could prolong that feeling for a few more seconds before it evaporated and the room resurfaced.

I hated isolation, forcing myself to get up and dress, fold my pajamas, and toss the bedroll to one side. I didn't make the bed well despite Chief's reminder it was in view of the cameras. The exaggerated effort to save face annoyed me. Even on camera, they needed a tidy bedroll backdrop during interrogation. *Who cares?* I never folded it right and put it on the bed against the wall, instead of in a tidy roll at the foot. It was my small protest, so I laid it that way every day.

I clung to the truth that injustice is God's enemy too. Close to collapse under the weight of accusing voices I pleaded with God to make his voice louder. Instead, it was softer. Someone gentle stood near, close enough to feel his presence, reminding me life wasn't just walking through a minefield in enemy territory. In the middle of my war, the warrior by my side was a loving God. When fear shrieked, love massaged my heart. How surprising a journey through suffering is when the God of the whole universe *loves* me. Heaven tucked inside that thought as my war-torn soul settled and calmed. Even in the darkness, despite my tempted mind following its own path, love restored, balanced, and connected me. Prayer united me with friends and family around the world. Love joined me to thousands of Chinese over 30 years and linked me to orphans and seniors in North Korea. I belonged to a great unfolding love story. I had to choose many times a day, to see or not to see.

❖

The interrogators tactics to make me talk meant that on paper the accumulated testimony screamed guilt. Crafted versions of interactions with reporters and meetings with Embassy staff and visitors from England, Russia, South Korea, Poland, Germany and African nations looked like proof we belonged to an organized network. Each grueling session strengthened their theory that we collected data, disseminating it to overseas authorities in a targeted strategy to undermine China's national security. The political allegations were alarming.

"Fill these in," Chief said, passing me a crisp stack of spreadsheets. "Beside each contact email or entry, name the person, nationality, job, and why and how you connected. We'll collect them after the weekend."

With ten years' worth of Canadian and Chinese email, communications via internet applications and cell phone contacts spread in front of me, I strained to read the tiny spreadsheet columns listing individuals, businesses, organizations, advertising, spam, and travel. Overwhelmed, I struggled to recall each one using an email address for a clue. Hoping it was the final assignment, I worked into the night and all weekend to complete it. On Monday, the interrogators scrutinized my work. Dissatisfied, they handed me another stack of blank paper and told me to rewrite it with more detail.

As my brain rewired in perpetual exhaustion, peaceful rest fell into an abyss. The more I reproduced archived information, the guiltier I appeared as the stack of paper grew on their desks. *Will these pointless assignments ever stop?*

—*Julia*—

The homework watched me like a third pair of eyes. I agonized all weekend, filling in tiny rows on useless spreadsheets. Peter and Hannah's school teachers, business, educational, and personal contacts. *Who cares if my friend is a Japanese Canadian or an American Public Health worker? Does my friend's husband do business with China?* I pored over lists to complete the task, waking throughout the night with sudden recollections of a name. When Monday arrived, a few blanks remained. I was certain they were spam or advertisements since I didn't recognize any part of the addresses. I hoped it was enough.

No one came. At 9 p.m. John called me, glanced at my attempts and demanding more details, sent me away miserable. On Tuesday, chairs shuffled above me as leaders gathered. On Wednesday, nothing. I scribbled in my Bible small things to be thankful for as I slipped into hopelessness as if it were a comfy chair luring me with billowy cushions. Drained in a hazy stupor, I ignored the dinner tray and fell asleep at 7 p.m. The next morning, Day 66, I drew a black rectangle to remember the darkness yet celebrate a twelve-hour sleep. Every long sleep was a miracle. On Day 68 I scribbled. *True confessions are saying the same thing God says about something.*

17

New Glimpses

When you drink the water,
remember the spring.

—Chinese Proverb

—Kevin—

F reedom teased and upset me. When guards left the room, or returned to the city every second week, their escapes stung. They did as they pleased while I remained a caged and wounded man unable to help my family. From embassy-relayed messages I heard my father had mini-strokes, sensed the agony in my mother's messages and ached that 17-year-old Hannah had no parents to text or call or cook her dinner. From fragments and phrases, I pieced together their lives, dissecting messages, imagining everything.

I missed day-to-day texts with the kids. The normal things. I prayed by name, struggling to express my love and take part with a silenced voice. Heaven was the courier of my messages when I couldn't be a father to my children or a son to my parents. I promised to spend every possible minute with family when I got out, feeding hope by setting goals. I searched for Bible prison stories, found one and scribbled a date, determined to arrive home in time for upcoming holidays, birthdays or special events. As Canadian Thanksgiving approached, I imagined walking in on the family just in time for a big turkey dinner. When dates passed, I overcame disappointment with a new date. I never stopped imagining ways home.

The permanent ache in my heart to hear their voices or laughter grew stronger. My greatest joy was imagining them near; my greatest sorrow was knowing they weren't. *God, is this your will?*

—*Julia*—

Thanksgiving weekend. My Saturday task was turning confession paper scraps into small thank-you notes for the leaders, guards, investigators and cooks. I was determined to write something personal for each person. I asked Daisy to talk to the leaders for permission to distribute them, explaining it was Thanksgiving holiday. They gave it! Daisy handed them out but said I could give the guard's notes when they did their shifts. Viola held her note tight as she read how much happiness her lavender sneakers brought, adding colour to the room. Tears appeared as Annie read my thank-you for bringing cups of water and caring for me. Joy filled my room as I watched them with their notes. I doubt anyone thought I was a typical prisoner after that! When the leaders told the cooks to make chicken and peanuts for dinner as a treat for my festival, I ate every bite.

—*Kevin*—

Chicken and peanuts appeared on my tray on Day 71. While wolfing it down, I realized it was Thanksgiving Day and wondered how they knew and what had earned us such favour.

—*Julia*—

The next day the investigators thanked me for the notes and stood them on their desks.

—*Kevin*—

On Day 73, special interrogators from Beijing arrived with new confession techniques. Their mind games produced false proof leaving me hopeless, frustrated and unable to prove my innocence. The 24/7 light produced darting black spots in front of my eyes that impeded my vision and confinement for 23.75 hours a day or more had reduced me to a suffering caged animal. Throbbing headaches impeded lucid answers to questions and the unrepaired nerve damage in my foot accentuated my depleted state. Despair almost triumphed. Home was a faint and remote dream.

I guessed Julia was near but hadn't seen her. Women at the top of the stairs and random noises overhead kept me hoping. *God, I need a sign.*

The next morning Chief appeared earlier than usual. "You're having breakfast with Julia this morning. Don't allude to the case. This is a special privilege," he said.

The dormant joy in my soul flooded back, but I stopped it. *Is this a trick?*

—Julia—

"You're having breakfast downstairs today," Daisy announced. I'd prayed to have a meal with my captors as a sign of reconciliation before freedom. *This is my answer! I will have breakfast and they'll tell me I'm going home.* In excitement and anticipation, I asked for a hairbrush and minutes later Daisy and two guards led me downstairs to a meeting room. Curtains covered windows facing the back court-yard and a large round folding table was set for six but big enough for twelve. The short thin man with the keys spoke.

"Who do you think you are eating with today?"

His game terrified me and I suspected my celebration was premature. "Peter?" I guessed, thinking it unlikely in this secluded remote compound.

"No," he said, "Guess again." The teasing intensified my fear. "I guess you must wait," he provoked, standing in the doorway.

—Kevin—

As I entered Julia fainted. Two guards held onto her. Coming to, she sobbed out of control, looking thin and apprehensive as if her thoughts matched mine. *Why this sudden meeting?* We sat immobile beside each other as she tried to stop crying.

"You have 20 minutes. If you behave well and don't mention the case you might meet again," the short man said and left.

"Eat breakfast," my guard spoke as if it was a typical morning. A special meal–yogurt, eggs, sliced apples and oatmeal waited in our places while the four guards had steamed bread on their plates. They chewed as Julia and I maneuvered the precious minutes. I wanted to wrap my arms around her and never let go but didn't dare.

"What's wrong with your foot?" she asked, struggling for a topic.

"I damaged the nerve in the back of my knee from crossing my legs too much on the chair. They are treating it, which helps."

"I will pray." Tears formed in Julia's eyes as she spoke. "Is it difficult? Do you cry all the time?"

"Yes, whatever you feel, I feel too." I covered her hand with mine. No one spoke, so I left it there, relishing the comfort and warmth of our skin connecting. "It won't be much longer. I've been told…" I tried to convey something positive from deep inside instead of empty words. I switched subjects. "I read, pray, hope and pace. What do you do?"

"The same. And look at family photos and messages word by word. It's been a long three months."

We strained and struggled, choosing non-sensitive topics and forcing ourselves to eat a few bites to acknowledge the kitchen had provided a special breakfast. The clock ticked beside us. I gazed into her sad, blue eyes. "We will make it. And after we get out, we'll do everything together. Even grocery shopping. Everything."

"Time," announced a guard, standing.

The short, thin man returned. "If you cooperate with our investigation, you may have breakfast again in the future."

I stepped towards Julia to hug her but guards blocked me. Led away, I glanced back at her sitting helpless on the chair. Hearing the words *in the future* disturbed me, crushing my hope we'd leave soon. But I had seen her, touched her. God answered my desperate prayer. *She is near.* My new mission to decipher her schedule and glimpse or get messages to her began at once.

❖

I had a hunch her walk followed mine. My bathroom, shared with male guards, had a window overlooking the back courtyard. After my walk, I stood at the urinal and peeked out. A rush of joy filled me.

I'm right! Julia walked in circles with three guards posted around and one following. I ducked away, careful not to be seen.

Glimpsing games filled my day with challenge. When her eyes darted in my direction, I smiled because she'd seen me! It was worth it. The *good* guards pretended not to notice, the *bad* guards shut the door forcing me to use the stall. Glimpses healed me for hours.

❖

The darker side to breakfast was a shift in interrogator tactics.

"Confess you were on assignment for CSIS. Julia confessed yesterday," threatened Captain, and taking my hesitation as a lack of cooperation added, "Maybe you prefer eight years in prison, or execution? Or transfer to North Korea? Your treatment there will be far worse."

Threats had power, echoing in my aching heart, and fear latched on like a tiger's teeth sinking into its' prey, shaking it without mercy. *Prison for eight years without my family? Execution?* I shivered, wondering how they did it. *Gunshots? Am I ready to die? Trade me to North Korea? Could China do that?* My pummeled mind spiraled into darkness. "I'm telling the truth. I don't know what CSIS does in China. We love this country." My courage diminished with each word.

"You had expert training!" Captain continued, confident and cocky. "Julia has confessed… and your encounters with U.S. government agents. She disclosed everything."

I knew Julia hadn't and I loathed them bringing her into it. *I hate how they deceive and distort the truth!* The red numbers on the clock reminded me the session ended soon. I waited.

"Bad cooperation today," Chief declared as the clock hit the six-hour mark. They always gave a report card and today I flunked but didn't care.

—Julia—

The interrogators staggered their hours. Their new techniques to summon me day or night, forced me back on guard when I had calmed myself. They offered desirable food for good behavior and punished poor cooperation with long hours of sitting still. Topics jumped without logic from threats of executions to beheadings in Afghanistan and why I didn't go there. I picked out Americans on their wanted list from 32 criminal mugshots, verified printouts of photos I'd seen on Kevin's computer, and denied accusations that Peter's Chinese studies were for a CSIS job after graduation.

"We will take Peter if you don't confess your CSIS connection," John said.

He's trying to break me. My heart stung and throbbed. "Then you'll have to take him...because you won't believe the truth."

❖

My testimony produced at least ten pages a day to fingerprint and sign. At night, Benji read summaries as I scanned Chinese characters for my name, fingerprinting whenever it appeared. At the bottom of each page I added a signature, date, and fingerprint and wrote an English sentence I'd insisted on since the first day since the testimony was in Chinese. *These words, as far as understood, are exactly what I said.* I thought adding a disclaimer might help if I ever had a lawyer or trial. The pile of summaries grew and I focused on catching mistakes as they rephrased my words to match their agenda. I *met* a U.S. Embassy delegate at the coffee house became I *hosted him.* I *told* him turned into I *informed him.* I *talked to* my university students was I *gathered secret information* from them. Hundreds of words appearing as minor translation issues gave a criminal slant to everyday work and interactions. *I'm getting framed by my own testimony.* They changed the ones I caught, but it was exhausting and I'm sure I missed or misunderstood many since it was all in Chinese.

❖

Every guard that moved through my door, reinforced my captivity. The case consumed me. The flickering, florescent light with its incessant hum day and night, tortured me. The plastic covered, barred windows were thieves stealing the outside world from my gaze. I grasped relief in moments not minutes.

Alone, I thought of the lonely. I imagined the terror of people in a coma on a bed, aware of surroundings but unable to change or control them. I pictured refugees in sinking boats trying to grasp lifejackets thrown their way but just out of reach. The isolated, elderly confined to beds, those floating on scraps of carnage in a vast ocean and children caught in war—were in my room. Those without freedom to ask for comfort or choose it. I felt the loneliness of a 90-year-old woman in a nursing home forever hoping someone is coming to visit, and her overwhelming disappointment when she hears footsteps in the hallway or doors open but no one comes in. I wondered why I'd never cared so deeply and realized I owed half the world an apology.

❖

Creativity helped as days blurred together. One evening, after interrogation assignments, I begged for a page of my rough copy and folded it into tiny rectangles forming a set of miniature playing cards smaller than my thumb. Amazed guards watched a whole deck appear from half a sheet of paper and a short curly unsharpened pencil! I played Solitaire, the only game I knew. A week later, Daisy arrived smiling. "I have a gift," she said handing me a packet of playing cards.

She was the gift giver who'd given me the notebook and pencil that first week, and an eraser when she noticed me sketching on leftover confession paper. With playing cards, I invented at least five new games for solo players and figured out a way to tell the whole Bible narrative using every card in the deck. Next, I invented one using every card to tell the New Testament narrative. I practiced until I had both memorized. Then I started using them as *praying cards*. Every night before bed I sat with the deck of cards, pulled out the top card and prayed for what came to mind. I flipped through the whole deck, saving the final card. *Ok God, this last card is for you to speak before I go to sleep.* I held it tight in my hyper-attentive state, waiting for insight and listening to God's encouraging, intimate and personal whisper. *Julia, I love you. Julia, trust me.*

The longer I prayed through the deck, the more I wanted to peek at the last card! How selfish I was even in isolation! Furious, I hid the last card under the covers for later. Some evenings I spread the cards on the bed to visualize stories I read in the Bible, or grouped them in countries or families and prayed over them. Wasting my deck of cards was not an option!

—*Kevin*—

Monotonous days flowed into each other in an endless stream of sameness. On Day 99, Canadian Remembrance Day, the interrogators informed me that Prime Minister Harper had left China. We weren't on his plane. Chief was annoyed and so was I. *Why did he leave us behind?*

A photographer arrived to set up a video camera on a tripod. "We'll make a video for your government," Chief said. "We want you to plead for help. Be emotional so they want to respond." I sat motionless against a blank white wall after Chief and Officer Zhang yanked off a picture to remove identifying information. Confused, I'd seen hostage videos on television and this was similar so I followed their instructions.

"Add more emotion!" Captain scolded. "Sound needier, more desperate so they will act." I tried as hard as I could but conjuring up emotion wasn't natural.

"Canada, please help us return to our family, our children, our country. Find a way, any way, to get us back to Canada." I emphasized the words but felt ridiculous. *Will Canada do more because of this video? What's the real reason I'm here?* The contrived video proved this was geopolitics but I had no idea what had provoked China. I determined to push harder at the next visit.

—*Julia*—

As captivity turned 100, fragments of information played havoc with my mind, forming a swirling mixture while I drifted in and out of sleep. At times, I awoke immobile, unable to find calm. *Did Simeon die in a horrific crash riding his bike? Is my dream true?* I asked the interrogators if they'd tell me if a family member died. Their evasive answer terrified me. I persecuted myself but couldn't stop. I was the enemy of my own careworn soul.

On Day 106, I scrawled this note in my Bible.

I was having this rush of sadness—no matter what I tried it was trying to burst out until suddenly it did. Tears poured down my cheeks. I tried to stop but as soon as one tear left, another had already formed—my heart was just too sad. Then a question dropped into my mind. "Julia, can you walk on water?" Surprised I reflected and then I heard it again. "Julia, can you walk on water?" No, I answered, but you can. "Yes, Julia, I did—even in a raging storm." Only that morning I'd asked him to increase my faith and here he was when I was sobbing out of control, asking me if I could walk on water. I got it. Humanly I was not capable of escaping this storm of sadness. I had to walk by faith and not by sight through it.

18

THE BIRD'S SONG

A bird does not sing because it has an answer,
it sings because it has a song.

—CHINESE PROVERB

—*Julia*—

Songs and melodies, patterns and whispers, sounds and glimpses were the building materials of hope. I often woke with a song and it became a banner for my day. As songs came to mind, I listed them and sang for 30 minutes each morning and evening. In November, I had an idea to convey at the consular visit.

"Janine, please tell my sister to ask friends and family to sing carols with me twice a day at 7 a.m. and 7 p.m." She noted my request. I never met the rest of this long-distance choir but felt connected to a journey bigger than me. Music brought its symphonic peace into chaos and made melodies of the suffering.

❖

After a morning declaration of song, I worked on puzzles. Unlike traditional crosswords or word searches, these involved figuring out and predicting from sounds, facial expressions and behaviours. I discerned and drew conclusions. At 7:30 p.m. chairs shuffled on the floor above me. *Daily meetings.* When Daisy came at eight adding new instructions for my care in the back of the notebook, I proved my hunch. I took note of cars in the compound as I passed by for my walk. On Tuesday nights–black sedans. *Leader meetings.* An expensive car with a cover. *Top official here.* Pickup truck. *Supplies arrived.* Maroon Van and Toyota Land Cruiser. *Consular visit tomorrow.* Mini Bus. *Weekly guard exchange.* I tested and revised my theories. Guards wearing their number tags and no outdoor walks. *Leaders on site.* Guards very strict and better food. *Top official here.* There were always puzzles.

Consular visits were never announced but predictable. Our transport cars took specific, timed routes to the city hotel and back. The thud of car doors announced Kevin's departure, and I knew I'd follow 15 minutes later. Once by mistake, the maroon van caught the Land Cruiser. The nervous driver slowed to a crawl and I acted oblivious while watching Kevin's car turn right passing the back gate of my university, skirting the town. Mine followed the river road past the coffee house. Solving this puzzle brought unexpected joy.

❖

Since books were a rare treat for cooperation, my novels were the eight-hour non-verbal stories my guards told each shift. My guards were characters—active and inactive, kind and unkind, authoritarian and indifferent. Celina sat by the door not moving or looking up for eight hours, fiddling with her black pen but seldom making notes. She couldn't look me in the eye. Old Bossy loved control. With a self-righteous air, she flipped the cushions on the guard couch when she entered, complaining and commanding when there was nothing to control. Glamorous Janie wore makeup to sit in the room and when leaders were offsite, wore casual shirts with English phrases like *Bounce the Baby* in bold black letters. Always cold, Helen sat and shivered with her arms around her pulled up knees. City girl Annie complained about the bugs, the suffocating room, and the oppressive heavy ugly curtains. One morning her face was smeared with tears because her one year old had a fever and she couldn't go home to care for her.

Daisy hated her hips and wished they were smaller like the other guards. Raised in the countryside, her skin revealed she'd worked hard. Daisy loved smacking mosquitos and flies, cheering as they splattered on my walls. Tall, thin Kayla, smuggled snacks for herself during the late shift, keeping them tucked behind her as she sat. I know she wanted to offer me a bite but didn't dare. Kylie, the tall strong leader of the military guard volleyball team, did pushups late at night if leaders were offsite. Arlene stood against the wall for 30 minutes after eating to improve posture and digestion. She believed westerners large backsides came from sitting instead of standing after eating. I tried it too.

Vivian, one of the youngest and strictest never broke the rules or gave me a perk. She wanted a boyfriend and beat her thighs with fisted hands to get rid of excess thigh fat. The noise grated on me. Gentle Lia, had a two-year-old son and was always sad to come back on the Tuesday minibus every second week. One Tuesday, Lia ducked into my room to show me her dress before changing into the uniform. I cried. The nicest guards made me cry most. At first I didn't know why but later realized it was the unexpected kindness. I stopped crying from intimidation, shock and harsh words early on, but kindness revived feelings and tears came.

Linda was kind too. She politely looked away when I changed and once, when Vivian ducked away to the bathroom, she smuggled me a chocolate bar from her pocket. Fear enveloped me. *How will I eat it without getting caught by Vivian?* I hid it until after shift change and occupied my day hatching plans. My safest option was in the bathroom with the tap running. But the wrapper? It was too risky to flush it down the toilet. That night, tucking the treat inside folded pajamas, I entered the bathroom like a criminal about to commit a crime. Pajamas balanced on the sink, I requested the toiletries cup and as Kayla left to get it; I turned on the tap, bent over the sink, slipped out the chocolate bar and ripped it open with my teeth. With it safely hidden in the folded pajama layers before the cup arrived, I waited. Then I turned the tap on full, stood with my back to Kayla and Lia, washed one hand and ate the chocolate with the other—in three large chunk bites. Chewing and swallowing so fast left no time to enjoy the flavour, but I planned to relive each taste in my mind after going to bed.

My foolproof plan succeeded but shredding the wrapper needed two hands. My face reddened and filled with beads of sweat as I managed to tear it while changing into pajamas. I swallowed the pieces with gulps of water from the cup as I brushed my teeth. I flopped onto my bed triumphant but convinced that sneaking chocolate to the prisoner was a bad idea. When Linda didn't return the next Tuesday, I asked why and Daisy said she had a new assignment.

❖

On Day 106, two apples arrived in a small, flat metal bowl as a treat for good cooperation. I begged to keep the bowl. Intrigued, the guards watched me crumple used confession paper into a ball. A metallic clang rang out as I batted the ball against the wall with the bowl. My goal to hit it 100 times without touching the ground meant I broke into a sweat, rejuvenating my body. The guards controlled the bowl for night use only and I improved at my sport for a week before Old Bossy snatched everything and returned it to the kitchen.

I switched to piano exercises on the desk or in the air. Old Bossy stood close enough to breathe on me as I practiced Hanon finger exercises, Chopin's waltzes, Schumann's Scenes from Childhood, and other songs from memory. Then I started quiet, vocal practice. A-a-a-a-e-e-e-e-i-i-i-i covering scales and vowels. I even formulated a doctoral thesis outline based on my own theory of voiceless articulation to diagnose pronunciation errors and remove second language accents. On good days, I survived. On bad days, I collapsed on the bed and cried myself to sleep.

❖

I accepted non-negotiables like 24/7 lights, guards, meal routines, interrogations, assignments, and leaving the room. But inside the room, some negotiations helped.

"I can't live without daylight," I told Stephen. The curtains had to stay shut because the leaders worried local villagers might see me. I didn't give up. The next day I returned from my walk and found him in the room covering the windows with sticky opaque plastic. He pulled back the curtains.

"Can you leave a crack at the top, so I can see the sky," I pleaded. With a knife, he cut a strip away. "I'm shorter than you. Can you peel back a few centimetres more?"

Surprised at my logic, Stephen carved off one more strip. "No more," he said.

"Thank you." I flopped on the bed gazing through the crack at the blue sky. On Saturday, I spent hours watching the clouds. *No annoying advertisements in God's movie!* Animals leapt, robed elders passed with gifts, and youngsters on motorcycles did daring acts before their motorcycles evaporated into thin layers. Every time I watched, new cloud and light shows excited me in majestic shades of grey, with occasional rays of peeping sunshine, and sometimes the full eye of God.

❖

Little by little, the guards and interrogators became my temporary family. I spoke first when entering the interrogation room to diffuse my fear and show genuine concern, treating them as friends coming for dinner, despite the dread in my heart as I sat in their presence. Over time I learned their habits and moods, their strengths and vulnerabilities. On Day 109 Stephen writhed in discomfort in his interrogator's chair.

"What's wrong?"

"Chronic back trouble." I looked straight at him saying nothing.

"Are you doing that praying thing?" he asked, watching me. My lips weren't moving but he felt it. The next day I asked for an update and thanking me, he said it was better. I smiled and said if he noticed a change to thank God, not me.

Two days later I commented on Benji's droopy eyes. He shared he'd had horrific nightmares since coming to the compound. I prayed quietly. The next day he told me they'd stopped. *God is good!*

My inner strength puzzled them. Although fear and threats affected me, friendliness and baffling inner peace made intimidation difficult. Stephen admitted at the start he knew nothing about Christians. Amazed at this woman captive who could change an interrogation room into a prayer room, he commented, "You have good character but what would happen to Communism if everyone in China was a Christian?"

"That would be amazing!" I said. Stephen said nothing as I imagined the leaders watching the recordings.

John piped in. "What's your strategy?"

"It's not a strategy. I'm a Christian by choice and it's not my job to make anyone else one. I introduce God by being myself. If others ask why I'm helpful or joyful or how I get through my struggles, then I tell them the good news."

"How? More detail."

"Well, I might walk along the river in Dandong, see a Mum with a toddler and stop to chat. They notice I have a Chinese daughter and ask questions. Then I tell them she was a special needs child and they ask why she looks fine. I explain God healed her and they ask me to share the story. After I do they might invite me to their home to pray for a family member. It's just normal life stuff. There is no law in China against answering questions or praying for people is there?"

"No," said Stephen, "But do you knock on everyone's door to give them pamphlets or something?"

"That's illegal in China. I try to follow Chinese law like you. Christianity and Communism agree on many things. It's just that Christians have God helping them to serve others, live honestly, avoid corruption, and those things in your Chinese laws. Our work as Christians is to give an answer to everyone who asks for the hope we have. Our life manual is the stories of other people who've lived with God as a supernatural partner. The Bible is God's resume.

Stephen, John, and Benji squirmed when I gave those answers. They did not understand what being a Christian meant. In the interrogator's quest to prove my criminality they came face to face with truth they'd never considered. I had to recover daily from the intensity of spy accusations and isolation; they had to recover from my answers to questions of faith and the way I lived my life in the compound.

❖

On Day 110 John produced a thick binder. "See this binder of evidence against you? If you will sign to say Kevin is a spy, you can go free tomorrow and we'll throw this away."

"He's not a spy."

"Why toss away your chance for freedom?"

"You want me to tell the truth and that's the truth."

"Trust China," Stephen interjected. Although I couldn't, I knew he was offering a way out.

"I can't lie to save myself even though I want to go home. I'm trusting you to do the right thing because I'm innocent." My words shot into the atmosphere, penetrating their minds heading straight for the heart. Truth does that. The interrogators knew by now I was innocent but had to prove my guilt for their authorities who might reward them with status and money. *Is it harder now they know me?* Stephen reached into his desk and handed me a photo of Hannah in Canada by a lake.

"You've cooperated well today," he said kindly.

"Thank you." I spent the next three hours in my room appreciating every detail of the photo.

❖

My new after dinner game was leaning against the second-floor window straining to listen, as guards, leaders and the interrogators passed by below, chatting as they circled the compound for evening exercise. If my name or an interesting phrase reached me, I waited until they passed again, hoping for more clues. The muffled voices didn't stop me and sometimes I grabbed phrases every five minutes for half an hour. I was desperate for hope in any form. At shift change when the door opened briefly I heard wisps of conversation. Once I overheard a guard say she loved our coffee house spaghetti. I grinned for hours.

Birds sometimes flitted passed the window or stopped to rest on the bars and sing. I drew each melody into my room and celebrated. But the best noise was children. Rules dictated I stood one metre back when guards aired the room but I didn't mind. The open window brought a symphonic blast of squealing children running on the village road and dogs barking. Every second Friday, a boisterous street market operated outside the gate and I visualized shoppers with bags of fresh vegetables. Twice the screams of a pig being slaughtered pierced the air as I sat captive within whitewashed walls just 50 metres away.

❖

After dinner, I ran tap water drip by drip to enjoy it trickle into the sink, watching it seep towards the drain and disappear. I washed each finger instead of the whole hand at once, to enjoy the flowing liquid. I discovered if I caught the hot water in the two red plastic bowls for washing clothes, I could keep the warmth longer. I sat wedged into one bowl with my feet in the other, preferring this modified bath to having the water fall all at once from the shower head, touch me, and disappear into the drain wasting half its heat. From the first trickle of water, to the last drop, I used up 90 minutes.

Imagination and boredom turned my bland room into a miniature world filled with travel destinations. I tried each one, taking small steps and pausing, imagining each small chunk of wall as a new country to visit with a new culture and different things to see. I interpreted every fuzzy dot and the tiny particles that appeared between me and the wall. *What diverse populations my countries have!* Exhausted with travels, I watched flies choose hundreds of landing spots within minutes and realized no two mosquito splatters look the same. When tired of standing, my bed became an invisible checkerboard with 100 seating options and the premium spots were facing the wall with my back to the staring guards.

I sat with my notebook and wrote.

November 2014. Who am I in isolation? The interpreter of a car door closing, able to infuse that simple sound with both exhilarating hope or exhausting disappointment. The reader of faces, translating them into possibility or despair. The reviewer of all imaginings of the human soul and heart, lining them up, rearranging, tossing, over-ruling, editing in a stream of consciousness pattern without end. The watcher of clouds, stars, birds—a sign of closeness and distance, companionship and separateness, never knowing which will pass my window and lodge in my soul. The dreamer, the poet, the untrained artist. The one peering into the hole of solitude and seeing myself, as if a shadow, groping the sides from within the hole, peering into the light of my own gaze. The one waiting for knocks on the door, the signals of chats. The one piecing my own family's life together from fragments passed on second hand. The grateful recipient of kindness and favour too numerous to count. The disabled one searching for a meaningful vocation of service. The shareholder in a new community. The lover of sunshine. The called, the blessed, and the blesser.

—*Kevin*—

The days got longer and colder. On November 25, Day 114, Janine confirmed Prime Minister Harper raised our case at the Asia-Pacific Economic Cooperation (APEC) meetings and talks were ongoing. "Maybe you could trade us for someone. Do you need to send someone home from the Embassy? China wants respect and to save face. Maybe Canada should write an apology for using us," I suggested.

Janine made notes but said little. She mentioned having lots of family messages and needing time to get through them. The wall between me and the government had no door.

❖

As the case dragged into winter, the leaders installed a large coal furnace next to the compound kitchen and ran pipes through my room, hiding me during installation so workers didn't see a foreigner in the building. A truckload of coal arrived every few weeks. Since temperatures dipped below zero, the interrogators cancelled outdoor walks. They must have reconsidered because within a week they reinstated them, thrilling me because they were in daylight instead of darkness. I feasted my eyes on guard's clothes strung on lines to dry or paw prints from a wandering stray cat. And looking up, I tasted freedom. It was huge and blue.

Winter brought increased silence. Interrogations were sporadic at odd hours making them unsettling and hard to predict. Only the digital numbers moving forward one after another reminded me time moved. *God, take this pain.* As silence screamed in an incessant hum I waited for answers. I stretched out my hands with nothing to offer God but suffering. He didn't remove it but peace came. I felt him close. The more I offered him the more he filled my nightmare with himself. He entered my fear, despair, and loneliness. In his presence, the size of my suffering was incomparable to the size of his love.

—Julia—

I thanked winter for daylight walks. The giant canopy overhead expressed itself in shades of blue as cloud tufts chased each other in playful dances. Tree branches beyond the wall rustled and shook off their final obstinate leaves while birds unafraid of the winter perched on the stark branches to sing. Four guards in thick navy police coats with embroidered crests stood near but crisp breaths of air filled my lungs with hope.

We traipsed inside after 15 minutes, stamping off snow on the outdoor steps. Back in the room, I draped my coat on the chair and shut my eyes, rocking back and forth on the bed until dinner, remembering what I'd seen. *A tree doesn't try to be anything yet it is a refuge and a feast for many. A bird sings because it has a song.* After coping with another food tray, I braided my hair, rolled the brush up and down my legs to massage them as if I'd always done that, then picked up my playing cards for my nighttime chat with God.

I flipped them one by one and let the thoughts that came guide my prayers. *God, give my parents strength. Father, give Hannah courage. God, bless Deborah and Kevin's brothers and show them what to do to help.* The final card, like a specialty chocolate at the end of a dinner, I saved for myself. God often spoke precious words to me as I held that last card. Tonight, it was a six. I stared at the six red diamonds. Then I heard a whisper. *You can go home on December 6th.* I jumped and the guards did too though they heard nothing. *Yes, Julia. December 6th.* There it was again. That voice I knew and loved. I did not doubt. My mind shifted gear as I added a tiny six to my rows of images at the back of my Bible. A plane from Beijing on the 6th would land in Canada in time for my nephew Andrew's birthday on the 7th. I imagined holding Kevin's hand and rushing into the arms of our children for an incredible Christmas. For gifts, I had my captivity sketches. *Only eleven days more!* Bursting with courage I fell asleep thankful.

19

HOPE

Keep a green tree in your heart
and perhaps the singing bird will come.

—CHINESE PROVERB

—Julia—

The next consular visit, I expected good news. When none came, I comforted myself knowing China does everything without warning. During outdoor time a flock of magpies, called *happiness birds* in China, landed in a tree and sat chirping over the wall. I overhead Celina mutter to Vivian that if happiness birds come in a group and chirp three times at once, good news is coming. They too, waited for release from the middle of nowhere, longing to return to families and MSS jobs in town.

I prepared to leave, washing my clothes, tidying the room and scrubbing the bathroom, determined to leave things as clean as possible. On Monday, December 1, 2014, my last prayer card was a six again. I shut my eyes and saw a six flown carried away by a bird in flight. *Another confirmation.* On Wednesday, December 3, I woke with a song. *Count Your blessings, name them one by one.* I spent the day naming my blessings–each child, each parent, each aunt, uncle, cousin, niece and nephew, each friend. On Thursday and Friday, I waited, envisioning the announcement and excitement. Every knock I expected good news. By Friday night, December 5, Day 124, the room was clean and everything prepared for departure. I picked up the cards and prayed still holding onto the promise and pausing at the last card. The six of diamonds again! Exploding with joy I heard God speak. *Julia, I could get you out tomorrow but have a question. Will you exchange the 6ᵗʰ for my greater glory?*

I burst into tears. *What? God, how unfair! Why did you string me along to the last day and then ask that?* Then a song came. *Trust and obey, for there is no other way.* I looked to heaven bewildered and said *yes* when everything in me screamed *no.* His ways are higher than mine. His plans are bigger. No matter how disappointed I was after 124 days in the room and how ready to leave, I was curious to see the greater glory.

Tears streamed down my face. I looked at the clean room, the well-packed bag, the guards, the curtains–everything. I had to keep trusting. *For God's greater glory.* Many times, I had taught that God makes good exchanges and encouraged others to exchange what was hurting them–fear, pain, unforgiveness, shame–for God's good gifts. *What are they now?* With no answers, I cried myself to sleep.

❖

On Saturday, Stephen walked in smiling. "We are taking you to see Peter. You can have 30 minutes. Get ready."

Shocked yet excited I grabbed my coat. *Is this the first gift?* They drove me to the stone building I'd not seen since the first night. As I walked past the first room on the right my mind flooded with images of me shaking, crying, and shivering. We entered a room at the end of the hall. Peter, nervous yet calm, sat with a plastic bag in his lap. My love overflowed. A few strained minutes facing my son with a small table between us felt wrong. A mother should comfort her children. Today my son sat in pain I could not take away. I reached for the plastic bag but the interrogator took it. Neither of us reacted but our eyes spoke the messages our lips could not voice. With my hopes of imminent freedom dashed, I pushed back fear and quietly prayed. The room filled with peace tangible enough to soak in. Guards and investigators stood near, affected by this calm presence. *God is here.*

I extracted a memorized personal poem from my mind, asking Peter to write as I dictated and send it as my Christmas gift to family and friends. As he wrote each line, tears dropped from my eyes uninvited as the words opened a window into my isolated world. Peter, warned not to mention the case or make me cry, avoided my eyes as he wrote. Mine searched his peaceful face, his long eyelashes, his strong frame and blue clothes, grasping a stream of images for the days ahead.

Every moment was precious yet painful as he masked his suffering with a deep love and desire to care for me. I was so proud. As he sat there, Simeon, Sarah, and Hannah were there too. Each one suffering yet strong in weakness. No one wills this on their child or knows what they will do with such pain. The investigator had a daughter Peter's age, and I imagined he thought of her as he said,

"You can hug before we go."

"Are you ok Mum?" Peter whispered into my ear and I gave him a tighter hug. "Love you Mum."

"Love you Peter. Tell Simeon, Sarah and Hannah I love them so much. We *will* have a family hug again. A huge one!"

Whisked off, I relived every detail. That evening the investigator gave me a white knit winter hat, a white sweatshirt, and cozy navy sweat pants. It comforted me to know they came from Peter's favourite street corner discount shop where *seconds* sat in piles and there was only enough room to squeeze in between the stacks of clothes. We once cleaned out the shop buying several hundred sets of winter jackets and padded trousers for five dollars a set. After carting everything to our apartment, we sorted and labeled each outfit before sending it across the river to help North Korean children survive the icy winter.

The warmth of the new clothes encouraged me even though I wished that tucked in the sweatpants pocket was a ticket home. Two days later Stephen returned with a bag. *Chocolates?*

"A gift from Peter," he said, handing me a thick red cashmere wool scarf in a plastic bag. I could tell they liked that it was red and from Peter. I did too. After dinner, knees tucked up on the bed, I draped the soft comforting wrap over my shoulders. Basking in the peaceful warmth, something caught my eye. Stitched in red thread in the bottom corner, barely visible and the same colour as the wrap, were the words *Love U*. A message! I flipped the wrap to hide it from the guard's gaze. This was not from Peter; it was from my best Chinese friend Lily!

❖

The greater glory was so unexpected and delightful, a treasure chest stashed for days of suffering. God had saved this for me. On Tuesday, Day 128, after reading and fingerprinting summaries, the interrogators praised me for good cooperation and John reached into his desk.

"Your Embassy sent this stolen magazine for you. It says do not remove from the airplane. Can't they afford to buy you one without stealing?" he mocked. I ignored him, eager to feast on the Canadian magazine full of seasonal articles and pictures, holiday destinations and festive food. Stephen pointed to the magazine's front cover, a pork roast dinner.

"Can you cook that?" he asked.

"Maybe I can make you one if you let me out." I carried this treasure back to my room and read every word, even the tiny print of the ads. When Saturday arrived, I checked both sides of each page, choosing the best images to decorate my room. Palms, oceans, fir trees and anything green I tore out and folded into a 3D Christmas tree. Next, without scissors I punched out circles with my pencil and turned the back cover into a large cardboard circle. With rice as glue, I stuck the mosaic of circles together forming a Christmas wreath. I found an ad for a decorative pillow with the word *home sweet home* on it and pasted it at the bottom.

The curious guards, intrigued by my creations watched me complete one task and start the next, pressing out family faces from photos and making tiny ornaments hung by red threads meticulously extracted from the fringe on my wrap. Determined to celebrate Christmas even if my guards were the only guests, I tied the wrap into a huge red bow, found a *let there be light* advertisement for seasonal candles, and made myself a Christmas card. On Sunday, noticing a guard use thick tape to remove lint from her uniform, I asked for some. Daisy brought me a whole roll. With added fervor and unlimited tape, I made the rest of the magazine into glossy picture frames for my family pictures and taped them to the wall. Everyone, including the investigators who arrived back Sunday night, dropped in to see my decorated room. What delight to host everyone for Christmas!

The more I normalized captivity, the better I coped. Later that week the interrogators took photos in the room to send my family at Christmas to show I was ok. The MSS photographer directed several poses on the bed near my decorations. I took that chance to hand

Stephen a detailed request and plan for two hours with Kevin on Christmas Day.

—Kevin—

The posed shots with a hidden agenda infuriated me! When the MSS photographer brought in a comfy chair and took shots from different angles, I felt violated. After explaining they were for my parents and children, it made sense but the interruption in routine still aroused my suspicion. I liked to keep days moving. Routines created meaning.

When it snowed and the guards wanted to cancel outdoor time I insisted it was my right because both countries had agreed. Bundled up, I marched back and forth showing five guards my determination. I paused now and then to make boot-print hearts in the snow or bent over and carved a 'K' with my finger. Marks mattered. If I noticed a 'J' beside my 'K' when I checked the next day, I felt pleased for the rest of the walk. Small victories and love messages were my survival kit.

As snow piled up in December our messages intensified. The moment I turned the corner and saw Julia's first snow sculpture, I cried. She and I sat on a couch with our children and grandchildren standing near. *How did Julia carve it in 15 minutes?* Another day she carved a saxophone with musical notes around it, and a few days later the pile became a slide with a lion's head at the top! *Did she slide down? Probably!* The next day the bushes inside the compound wall had blossomed snowballs! Were the skies aware that snow kept us close? *Did someone pray for more snow this year?*

I got bolder and wrote Bible references in the snow. Grumpy guards stamped them out but sympathetic ones found fresh snow for my markings. We were children making sense of suffering, playing games in the snow. On Christmas Eve, I discovered a whole Christmas dinner carved in a snow cave. My mouth watered at the snow turkey on a plate beside a plate of rolls, a dish of veggies and a pie at a snowy table set for two.

20

PURPLE TEDDY BEARS

Fragrance clings to the hand
that gives flowers.

—CHINESE PROVERB

—*Julia*—

The leaders approved my Christmas Day request and offered me the interrogation room. I couldn't wait! Interrogations, anger and accusation melted into kindness in extraordinary ways. But Christmas Eve held another surprise.

"We don't want Peter to be alone for Christmas so we've arranged a dinner tonight. Tell no one," Stephen said. "It's a special privilege. Get ready."

A well-timed car door kept me hoping the invitation included Kevin. My transport car drove to town, pulling up to a dark deserted building at the far end of the complex where consular meetings took place. Ushered upstairs through dim light and past dark empty rooms, I realized the building was deserted. Lights glimmered at the end of the second-floor hallway. Benji led me into a room. *I'm dreaming!* A table set for dinner with Christmas Santa hats at each place and a lit Christmas tree with purple teddy bear decorations! Kevin sat smiling yet bewildered at the round table set for eight. Daisy pointed and I sat one empty chair away from Kevin. This explosion of thoughtfulness was extraordinary. I imagined God smiling in heaven as Peter walked in and sat between us. Invited at the last minute he had cancelled Christmas Eve dinner with Stuart and Leslie, to be ready when the MSS picked him up.

With two interrogators and two guards, we feasted on huge chunks of meat, fresh vegetables, tofu, rice, and a whole steamed fish. Food never tasted that good before. We savoured every morsel, enamored by the flavours, colours and textures of this unexpected spread. Such kindness is not random; it's deep. I thanked everyone. Benji reminded us to wear Santa hats, and we laughed because they were too small and sat perched on our heads. The hour flew. Our encounter was awkward but wonderful, strange but magnificent. Peter handed us a Christmas card which no one confiscated. The MSS gave him an envelope.

"This photo is only for family. Keep it out of the media," they warned and he promised.

—Kevin—

I ate as much meat as possible. This room in an empty building; this amazing dinner and Peter sitting between us, was a dream I wanted to keep. Before leaving, I asked to go to the bathroom and as if Peter knew my thoughts, he asked to go too. A friend once told us real meetings in North Korea don't happen at the table; they happen in the bathroom. A guard followed us along the deserted unlit hallway to an icy bathroom. He entered a cubicle giving me a moment to whisper a message to Peter as we stood by the urinals. "Tell Chris I hope he gets the chance to stay home with his family," I whispered along with a warning for another friend. We retraced our steps with the guard and minutes later Chief led Peter away and my transport car returned me to the compound. Julia had already left. That night I closed my eyes and fell asleep happy.

❖

On Christmas Day the joy continued. The leaders gave Julia and me a 15-minute walk together and I could choose pizza or chicken and they'd bring it from town for dinner. I wanted both but said pizza as I dressed for our walk like an excited teenager going on a date. Strict warnings to keep our conversation off the case didn't dampen my joy as I reached for her hand and walked her in a large circle. Oblivious to nine guards surrounding us, her hand nestled in mine and we walked as if the compound was our own.

—Julia—

In a dreamy daze after the walk, the guards arrived excited, telling me we could move my room decorations to the interrogation room. They smiled and laughed as I hadn't seen them do since the week of English lessons. The investigation tables transformed into a dining room table with chairs on each side. I made a family photo tree on the wall, and a homemade paper chess game and card for Kevin from the leftovers of the magazine. The investigators added the purple teddy bear tree carted back from town. Only wall cameras and memories reminded me of interrogation.

Kevin came as scheduled with interrogators carrying pizza, snacks, coke and grape juice. The biggest surprise was permission to stay in the room alone with the door open while four guards waited on chairs in the hallway. Trust was a powerful gift! I followed the approved plan, and as we sang carols, heaven stepped into the room. *Emmanuel, God with us, is true.* We spoke words of blessing over our children and family members, read the Christmas story, and ate. Christmas in the compound was a delicious taste of the greater glory!

—Kevin—

As we joined with Christmas bells and songs around the world, peace sprinted through our weary bodies, hope nestled in our hearts, and joy sprang from our lips. Two hours felt longer than two days and every part was pure ecstasy. *Are the angels in heaven clapping for the God who arranged such a party?*

Although the celebration ended and the guard's giant eraser removed decorations and rearranged furniture back into interrogation position, the China I had always known, the kindness and hospitality experienced throughout 30 years, had returned this Christmas. *Thank-you leaders. Thank-you friends and family who prayed for this. Thank-you God for thinking of this day long before we did.*

❖

After a peaceful sleep where pizza dreams replaced interrogation nightmares, I awoke on December 26 to flashing red lights. The interrogators arrived with a stack of papers, waited until I rushed into the chair, and asked if I'd enjoyed the holiday. They smiled as gratitude poured out.

"Good. Now, please cooperate with the investigation," Chief said, jolting me back to reality. I had feasted and now they wanted their favour. My brain heaved as its internal fire alarm pierced my mind. I wanted to scream. *I need more time to relive yesterday's joy.* I hated the case. My brain had no more details. Fragments of conversations, dates and times, photos and meetings, like tiny broken glass splinters I'd ignored for two days, rushed back into view.

They read summaries of my crimes as if I'd agreed to them. I was a spy and Julia, my accomplice. On paper, after five months, it was there in black and white, enough to put us both on trial. Today our Christmas Dinner together felt more like the Last Supper.

"Don't worry. We must do this," they insisted. "The prosecutors are waiting for the final copy and need these condensed versions. We know that CSIS, your government, and American agents, used you. Because it wasn't intentional and since you confessed, it will be better for you. Don't worry about signing."

My head throbbed with jabbing pain and yesterday's feast faded from memory. I wanted to go home so I signed. After 40 minutes, signatures and red fingerprints, all mine, covered the pages. Captain put the stack aside.

"And now, what would you like to say to China?" he asked. "This is your chance to apologize for your actions."

I sat up straight and took a deep breath. I was ready. "I'm sorry if I hurt China. I had no intention to hurt China. We only came to help. I'm sorry if my actions caused any pain or harm to China. I am sorry if any communications with the US or Canadian Embassy, CSIS, or other government visitors or journalists at *Peter's* Coffee House, hurt China. I apologize for taking pictures considered sensitive to China's national security. I had no intention of harming China. We love working in China and our family loves China. Chinese are our friends. Please forgive me for hurting China." I summarized my handwritten confessions.

"Use stronger emotion," they coaxed as I let someone put strings on my voice so it did what the puppeteer wanted. Contrived and unnatural, it pleased them.

"Good job," they said, offering me a book. I wasn't 54 anymore. This game of rewards for behavior turned time back. I was a five-year-old who wanted the book, took it, and read the whole thing at once. And after I finished, I kept it as close as a teddy bear, hoping it was mine.

—Julia—

The day after Christmas, on the desk we'd feasted on, Stephen piled a stack of papers and copies of confessions.

"Today, you can apologize to China," he said, "and then we have special paper and instructions so you can rewrite your confession following Chinese regulations. Apologizing wasn't hard because I had done nothing on purpose to hurt China. I expressed my love for China and Chinese people and deep regret if my words or actions had hurt China. I went back to my room with a new black ink pen, and instructions about keeping fixed margins and writing official confessions. Despite the tedious task, I felt sure this final copy meant celebrating the new year in freedom. *This is the end!*

❖

Days of silence followed. No one came for the confession and the guards gave no clues. Thinking of worst case scenarios that didn't happen made the waiting more manageable. *No one executed me. No one beat or tortured me.* I opened my Bible to a page where I'd recorded my feelings month by month and read them out loud.

What do you feel? Month 1. Awareness of your own unrighteousness. How holy God is. Your own pride. The value of connection. Open book but safe. Month 2. Love for all around you, compassion. Month 3. The human part of you starts to despair and you have to keep renewing it with the word and spirit. Renewed appreciation for tiny acts of kindness. Month 4. How proud and arrogant we can be. how wrong it is to feel entitled. anger then guilt. Month

5. Hopelessness. Longing for heaven. Restless with the Bible – it seems to say everything. wait...now...tomorrow...at hand...ups and downs more frequent. Constantly leaning on God, sustained by his word over and over.

❖

On Tuesday, December 30, Day 149, Annie pulled Swiss cheese from her pocket. "I saw this in your magazine," she said, "and went online last week in town and ordered it. It's been outside my window keeping cold. Today I tasted it but think it's bad. Could you check since I've never tasted cheese?"

I hid my excitement as she broke off a chunk and popped it in my mouth. "It's fine. Swiss cheese tastes strong so you may not like it," I added hoping she might offer me the rest.

"Oh good. I didn't want to get sick." She disappeared with the cheese, leaving me smiling that God's glory came in a hunk of Swiss cheese–my favourite.

❖

Day 150. Wednesday. New Year's Eve 2014. The outdoor walk coincided with coal deliveries, and the big, blue coal truck blocked my usual route to the back forcing us to walk past Kevin's window on the ground floor. Open a few centimetres, I strained to peek in and glimpsed him sitting in the back of his room. Proud of my success yet longing for more, the guards hurried me past to the back courtyard where I stomped my feet to keep warm and jogged on the spot, fixated on whether I'd get another look on the way back. I did. He stood by an open barred window holding a book and a cup, smiling in his light blue shirt–almost close enough to touch. He mouthed *I love you* as the guards rushed me past. Our New Year's moment was brief but I carried it to my room as a sparkling diamond no one could steal.

I never stopped trying to see him. In one corner of my window, the plastic had curled back from condensation, and when I timed things right, I watched the top of Kevin's grey wool hat moving back and forth below. Saw it. Missed it. Missed it. Missed it. Saw it. Some days, wisps of hummed songs of courage, valiance, bravery and victory reached me. The melodies were faint but when I recognized the song and drew it into my soul, we were one.

Every day, as the guards stood wiggling their freezing toes outside for 15 minutes, I hunted for signs of his presence. No icy wind or hard, cold cement surface deterred me from my only chance to see the sky, search for a snow heart, or leave my mark for Kevin the next morning.

—Kevin—

With Chinese Spring Festival, the six-month mark, less than four weeks away my guards rebelled. Tired and frustrated realizing they had a babysitting job instead of the prestigious spy-guarding job they'd expected, when the leaders left the compound at night they brought in comfortable chairs. The head guard defiantly brought in his tablet, watching things he'd downloaded in town the week before. Other guards brought snacks and one ate chips, so I told him I liked chips. After a nod from the other guard he went to the village and bought me some. I ate the whole bag at once.

With guarding downgraded to a boring bother, they ignored me and followed their own routines. One threw fake punches in the air, practicing his boxing skills. Another guy always ate instant spicy noodles right after dinner. They went outside or into the hallway to smoke and sub for each other during night shifts and scribbled fewer notes in the books. *It must be a sign of imminent release.*

After the apology taping, interrogations tapered off. *They do this before releasing people so they say good things about detention.* My conclusions brought new flickers of hope. The guards chatted and sometimes discussed their families. One night a guard brought an IKEA catalogue and we pored over each page, choosing things we wanted like children choosing a new bike or toy.

The interrogators rewarded my cooperation by hooking up a TV for 30 minutes of Chinese news at 7 p.m. I negotiated for an extra minute to watch the weather and gloated because I got two full-colour advertisements and then the weather! Small victories mattered. A few weeks later, restrictions lifted, and guards put on earphones after I fell asleep, watching violent historical TV series for most of the night. But I couldn't leave the room or escape my crazy one-man daycare.

❖

In this more relaxed atmosphere, I sat in the interrogation chair whenever I wanted, not because I had to, and moved it to different parts of the room as I liked. Successful, I took one of the empty investigator's chairs to put my feet up. No one stopped me. For five months, when the guards put my food tray on the interrogation desk, I'd eaten with my legs banging into the front of the desk. Now, I slid my tray over and sat in Chief's seat on his side of the desk. I felt great and ate all my meals in his chair. Chair by chair, I took ownership of everything until the whole room was mine.

On Day 150 I woke up in the middle of the night. *There's only one guard and he's sleeping.* Determined to sneak to the bathroom undetected, in a rush of power, I walked out of the room into the locked hallway. The second guard sat smoking in another room as I walked by exhilarated by my daring escape. I was returning to my room, when the first guard rushed to the door in a panic.

"I went to the bathroom," I announced enjoying his terrified look. It was worth it and I went back to sleep gloating.

❖

I never got up asking, "What should I do today?" The clock was my reliable assistant as I kept my self-imposed schedule to frame the hours and keep time moving. I created tasks to complete, fixed hours to read the Bible, to pace, to sing, and to pray. Routines broke time into manageable chunks. One guard mocked my singing and praying making comical hand motions and shouting "la, la, la, la!" *How dare he mock me in my room!* After that, I noticed him in severe back pain and he refused my offers to pray for him. Days later he couldn't sit due to pain. He agonized for weeks. I shouldn't have gloated but I did.

I plastered my family photos on the wall instead of leaving them in a pile. My niece and nephew, Aniela and Tristan wearing reindeer hats at the Santa Claus parade, Ma and Pa beaming from the wall during a

Chinese restaurant outing, and my brother and brother-in-law cutting trees. *If I can't leave, the interrogators have to deal with all of us!*

Desperation swallowed eloquence as I prayed. *God, get me out of here. God, get me out of here. God, get me out of here.*

21

Mercy

*You cannot prevent the birds of sadness
from passing over your head,
but you can prevent their
making a nest in your hair.*

—Chinese Proverb

—*Julia*—

Since November, I'd fasted on Tuesdays and forced myself to take a Sabbath rest on Sundays, a conscious choice not to think about the case. Fasting from food was easy; resting from thoughts was hard. I often caught myself working on details of questions and had to interrupt programmed thought patterns built up from five months of interrogation. I diverted my mind from the case by singing or reading the Bible or rehearsing memorized verses.

Frustration took new forms. In August, windows kept the world out. In January, windows offered privacy from the guard's stares and the shame that I still cried. Every afternoon at 4 p.m. I stood staring at the changing reflections of soft, pale colour on the opaque plastic as the sun set. From start to finish it used up 60 minutes. The guards ignored me.

When Friday arrived, I agonized to push each hour into the next. The harder I tried the more each minute weighed as I forced it forwards. Collapsing on the bed in tears, "God, I'm too lonely. I can't make it through the weekend!"

"The three of us will come for the weekend." This was not a whisper; it was a clear voice!

"Three?"

"Yes, the Father, Son, and Holy Spirit. We will come."

My strange conversation was not a debated doctoral study for theology students–it was a practical revelation of the Trinity bringing heaven to my room. The Holy Spirit rested on my right shoulder, perched without form but present. On my left sat a man who I knew by the gentleness and kindness in his face was Jesus. Above me, the whole ceiling filled with the face of a great and caring Father bending down from heaven. As heaven squeezed into my room, earth became a shadow. *I have friends for the weekend.*

The harder survival was, the closer heaven came until the line between heaven and earth disappeared altogether. On Day 153, after a Saturday of silent staring, the compound walls disappeared as if transparent. The courtyard filled with brightness and there stood a huge angel wrapped in a magnificent bright white robe. As tall as the building, its two large hands cradled a huge golden bowl filled to the brim with golden bubbly liquid. The angel stepped towards me. *God sent an angel to rescue me! I am going home.*

A strong yet quiet voice spoke into the silence, "These are the prayers of my people gathered into bowls. This is a bowl of mercy to pour over your building." I watched amazed as the angel approached and with both hands, lifted the bowl until it was over the compound roof.

"Join us," spoke the voice.

Peace enveloped me. *Is this the greater glory? God stepping into my reality and speaking to me about the things of heaven?* Thoughts of rescue evaporated as I contemplated the invitation. I started to pray. At that same moment, the angel tipped the bowl and liquid poured over the building, seeping through the roof into the third floor and then down to mine and through my floor to the ground. It soaked the entire compound. In awe, I prayed for the guards, the investigators, the officials and leaders in charge of the case. I prayed for the leaders in Beijing and Ottawa. *I want everyone to know what mercy feels like.*

God's invitation to join this powerful partnership of heaven and earth surpassed comprehension. *Do my guards feel this?* Chairs moved above me as the leaders held meetings. *They don't usually hold meetings on Saturdays.* Annie paced. Bella took off her sweater. When I saw the English words on the t-shirt underneath I couldn't believe it! The words *Go Forth* in large bold print covered the front. She had no idea what it said but to me it was a sign. Even my weak prison prayers mattered. I was a participant in a supernatural event in progress. God had pulled back the veil, letting me peek at his great love. *Was that why Jesus often said the kingdom of heaven is at hand?* My skin tingled as I sat in awe, covered in God's presence, soaking until I fell asleep.

❖

The greater glory moments continued. The next morning God revealed things hidden in the words of the Bible. Peace flooded me and I felt full. Of God. He gently mentioned that if I got too exhausted making minutes pass on earth, I could come up to heaven for a look. Excited, I closed my eyes as he led me to a fragrant garden and cabin for rest. *It's yours. Come and go as you like.* There was no barrier. Heaven was near enough to touch and see and hear. My true Father had saved these gifts for this time. How perfect his care-plan for suffering was–his supernatural presence and heaven at hand.

❖

Earth struggled to lure me back to hopelessness with one meal tray after another and the next weekend everything turned so black I couldn't move for hours. I lay on the floor beside my bed as if the ground was further away from the darkness. No interrogators came. *Have they abandoned me?* The nervous guards made prayer gestures hoping I would take their hints. Instead of praying, I visited my cabin.

❖

On Day 156, January 6, 2015, I expected a consular visit but no one came. With the rhythm interrupted, I panicked and feared the worst. *They usually come on Tuesdays. Kevin died. One of our parents died and they are trying to decide how to tell us we can't go to the funeral.* Preoccupied with fear and devoid of energy, I forced myself to accept the daily outdoor walk. The taped apology to China spun in my brain and interrogator's binders full of confessions flashed before my eyes. *Why no news?* Stepping slowly, each leg carried the full weight of my disappointment and grief. I glanced at the snow sprinkled over the vegetable patch. *Much, much, love.* Kevin wrote in the snow! I breathed his love into my weary heart. *I can wait another day.*

❖

"Weather caused the delay," Janine said at the rescheduled meeting. *Did it?* I trusted Janine but at the six-month mark, I was fragile and anxious.

"Please tell Canada to apologize or send someone or something. The people here can't solve it," I said. The interrogators insisted Canada had to act and that Prime Minister Harper came for APEC not us. The interrogation period was near an end and criminal arrest and detention in a larger prison came next.

"Were you told to give us this message?"

"Not directly, but I'm told you know what needs to happen. I don't so I'm guessing." I glanced at Captain to be sure I wasn't saying too much. He said nothing.

Janine explained the Chinese lawyer requested bail but the outcome was unclear. I didn't even know my lawyer's name and had never seen him. She switched topics. "Try to focus on the idea that something will happen soon. There are a few possibilities. Some people prefer prison to isolation because you are with others, you can talk and have more routines and more space." Terror gripped me as she spread a rough timeline of Chinese criminal proceedings on the table.

"Can't you get me out?" I said frustrated. "What about this six months? Haven't I started the criminal timeline yet?" My mind had no space for timelines or managed expectations. I wanted hope.

Janine slipped the timeline into her folder and smiled as she did at the end of every visit. "I hope I don't see you next time," she said then stood and gave me a hug. She always tried her best to calm me.

—*Kevin*—

Will Julia and I meet again on earth or in heaven? When a painless heaven held out its arms, I longed to wrap us both inside. Official formatted handwritten confessions and interrogation testimony filled a book at least 10 centimetres thick. *Why am I still here?*

Recent sporadic interrogations produced nothing new as Captain and Chief dug like frantic miners searching for gold in the wrong places, leaving me trapped in the mine. They disappeared for days leaving me thousands of disconnected details. *Did I say things I didn't mean?* Alone, I lashed myself. The trial, and even a sentence seemed preferable to endless silent waiting. Everything ahead was blank. *Will this last years?* Language misunderstandings made it easier to craft a criminal story. I'd heard of coerced testimonies but never imagined its daily pathways were so deep and dark and confusing.

I devoured the Bible. Prison stories like Joseph sold into slavery and imprisoned for years became quests for details. *What did he eat? Could he chat? Was he interrogated? Could friends visit?* I questioned Joseph's words, *you intended to harm me but God meant it for good. (Gen. 50:20 NIV) What good?* I knew imprisonment saved his family from famine, and later his whole nation. I believed my story was part of a bigger plan too, but living it in millions of seconds was so different from reading the story in a chapter.

Yesterday's reward for cooperation, perhaps pulled from our coffee house shelves in the raid, was Esther Kim's memoir, *If I Perish.* I disappeared into her far-worse prison in Korea during the harsh Japanese occupation. Offered freedom, she remained in prison six years to encourage others. *Could I stay for some greater good? God, whatever comes, I choose to encourage others.* I spoke the words but didn't want to live them.

❖

Friday, January 23, Day 173, the guards let me write *K+J 24* in the snow. I'd asked permission to see her on her birthday the next day and hoped they would allow it. I hadn't seen her since Christmas and with each step back to my room, I pictured the upcoming 20-minute reunion.

"Did you hear the good news?" Chief said as I tossed my winter jacket on the bed. *Good news?* He never said that. The band inside me played a home-going song as I waited for more. "Julia might get out on bail." Yes! Awesome! The band kept playing as I listened for my name. It didn't come. "But you are going to the Dandong Detention Center because the longest we can keep you is six months. The case is not finished," he said explaining it wasn't his fault.

A different prison? With other inmates? My muscles tensed. How could he speak as if it were a simple relocation? It's a mistake. A frantic conversation began. *God, how can this be good? It must be your plan but why? Are you sending me to encourage others? Can't you choose someone else?* I switched gears. *Is this a test? God, you can save me. You can release me at the last minute. Yes, that's what you are planning.*

The interrogator's focus shifted to my transfer. They moved on. I couldn't. The guards made me separate my possessions removing clothing with strings or buttons. Chief assured me the prison officials were instructed to treat me well.

"Have you been inside?" I asked. They shook their heads. I expected a miraculous release. Big prisons were for criminals or movies, not me. As Saturday ticked past without a birthday visit, I felt hopeless. *Why can't I see her?* After dinner, guards told me I could have ten minutes in her interrogation room.

When I walked in and sat opposite her, she smiled, "I heard we might be out on bail if we can get the 1,000,000 RMB ($161,290) bail money each."

"I am going to prison."

The look on her face switched to one of terror. "No! it can't be. I thought the option of bail was for both of us. I thought we'd wait in our apartment for the trial together."

"I can't do it." Courage drained out of me. I looked helplessly into her sad blue eyes.

"Yes you can, and you will!" she stated with confidence, recovering from the initial shock enough to encourage me. "We will pray every day until then that it won't happen, but if it does, you will do it. We are in this together, whatever comes, we will do it."

Her words penetrated my heart with hope. As she spoke I slipped off my wedding ring under the desk, clutched it in my right hand and slid my cupped hand onto the table. It was my only chance to give it to her as I knew they'd force it off in prison. "At least in prison you can see me every ten days and we can write back and forth. They will put me in the medical wing–better than other cells," I rambled on repeating things I'd heard, but later found out weren't true. As I talked I reached across the desk, clasped Julia's hands in mine and slipped the ring into her left hand. "They said I should watch everyone else, obey everything I am asked to do, and it should be ok."

We jerked our hands back as I glanced at the guards. Nothing. Victory. Julia had my ring. I handed her a card made with scrap confession paper and pictures from my only magazine. I titled it *Epic Birthday Card*, filling it with things to do and places to go when we got out. Julia's eyes sparkled. We focused on making our last few minutes together happy. It was always a choice. Today was her birthday and we'd celebrate no matter where we were or how little time we had. We'd keep our love journey strong.

"I love you so much," I spoke in a gentle voice, "I think about you all the time and it keeps me going. About our future. About the kids."

"Me too."

I reached over to hug her but time was up.

22

Two Tears on the Window

You have kept count of my tossings;
put my tears in your bottle.

—Psalm 56:8 ESV

—Julia—

I clutched the card on top of the ring. *What was Kevin thinking? I must hide it.* Heart pounding, I searched the bag for long underwear. As one hand pulled out long-johns, the other hand unzipped the side pocket dropping the ring in undetected. I put on long underwear under my jeans and plunked on the bed with the weight of our conversation. *Why didn't I see this coming?*

John had mentioned bail just before I met Kevin. My imaginings of us together in the apartment became splintered logs tossed into the flames. *Prison for Kevin?* I will call down the armies of heaven to stop this. I will pray without ceasing. I will fast and somehow stop this from happening. The thoughts ran in circles as my brain shifted into full gear. I didn't repeat the same request over and over. Instead, I reasoned with God, explaining why this was the worst option and why we needed to be together. I told him we had done what we could and our family needed us home. I filled my prayer with plausible suggestions for God, willing to wait until the last day for a sudden change if that was his plan. I suggested ways to keep Kevin out of prison and reminded him how the rejoicing that would come from release would influence everyone.

❖

Janine visited two days later in a new location, a hotel opposite the university. Wedding fireworks from the hotel gate had often interrupted my classes minutes before lunch and many of my tourism students had interned there. Today, MSS agents staked the hotel. I waited in a third-floor room with Benji and two guards, looking from the window at the snow-covered ground and the tall university building across the street. *I should be over there.*

Benji, happy to access texts in town, scrolled through his phone messages, pausing to show me a picture. His three-year-old son had mastered chopsticks! When it was just him and guards, we were friends and I talked to him as if he were my son.

Chief shoved the door open. "Push your Embassy hard. You need 1,000,000 RMB within three days so we can let you out on bail with restricted freedom pending trial. If they won't help, ask them to recommend a guarantor in China. If they can't, insist they ask Peter to tell your family to get the money ready."

"It's impossible. The Embassy doesn't give bail money to ordinary people like me and my family doesn't have that kind of money. Even if my family could gather it, three days is too short. Banks don't work like that."

"It's the only way. Otherwise you will go to the big prison too," he said looking worried.

I passed the messages to Janine who said the request was unusual. She didn't sound hopeful or make promises. "I'll pass it along to those who make decisions," she said and started talking about prison. "People say it's better than isolation. There are more things to do and you can talk to people. If they give you work, it helps pass the time. At least it's a change, and change is better than continuing like this."

When the Canadian government's approximate timeline for criminal cases in China appeared, I stopped her. "I don't want to see it," I said. She put it away, mentioning she was transferring to Shanghai soon so this might be her last visit. After apologizing for the bad timing, she promised to stay informed and brief her replacement, Adele. I didn't want a new case manager. I was not a case; I was a captive. Janine had been my stability for six months; the English voice that passed on family messages and encouragement. Despite Janine's assurances that Adele would be wonderful, I felt abandoned to a stranger.

As Janine left, Chief looked worried, "You weren't desperate enough," he said and dialed a number. "I'm calling Peter. Talk to him.

Tell him your family must gather the 1,000,000 RMB. If they can't get it all at once, maybe we can work out installments. It's the only way." He handed me the phone.

Shock reverberated in Peter's voice as he heard mine. I felt awful, responsible and unwilling to give him any more pressure. But I had to follow through. "They need 1,000,000 RMB in three days. Call Simeon," I said, "He will know what's best. Most of all, pray. Don't worry. Something will work out. I love you!"

Chief Wang took the phone back worried. "Can he get the money?"

"He will try, but three days is not much time."

"It's important."

❖

For three days, I waited in my room listening to the clock. *Am I going to the big prison?* I asked Daisy to request a final visit with Kevin and sent a list of questions about medication and finances in case I got out. She took the list and the leaders permitted a brief exchange. Kevin handed me the paper and they whisked him off. He'd answered the questions and at the bottom in his own handwriting he'd written, *I can't take much with me. It will be hard but I can do it. I miss you so much. I love you. Keep praying. Never stop. Kevin.*

No language has words for the excruciating, piercing pain we felt torn away from each other again. I braced for the worst, hoped for the best, and prayed for a miracle. There was always the possibility of last minute release. I stood by the window, hiding my tears.

Something moved on the wall beside me. The sun had cast a shadow of two raindrops trickling down one after the other. I turned to find their origin. Outside my plastic-covered barred window two drops of water followed a slow and steady pathway down the glass pane. *Why only two? How can this be, it's a sunny day?* Then I heard a whisper. *Julia, I'm sorry.* My eyes followed until the drops reached the ledge out of sight. My miracle wasn't release. It was seeing God's sorrow. Two tears on the window. I took my pencil and scribbled the image in the back of my Bible. Day 182 *I saw God cry.*

❖

Our suffering is personal to God. The image of two tears comforted me through the night and I awoke extra early listening for noises, signs that Kevin was leaving. About 6 a.m. car doors and trunks opened and shut and I stood peeking through the small hole in the plastic. A bus. More cars gathering. Old Bossy placed my breakfast tray down without a word. Footsteps scurried back and forth in the hallway. A car engine started. I couldn't see his car but in my soul, I felt it. *They are taking Kevin away.* The accordion gate creaked closed and I imagined his car twisting through the village and winding along the river. *Then where?*

Footsteps got louder so I shoved my Bible under a few clothes. Old Bossy burst in and Violet and Panda jumped up and left.

"What's happening?"

"Pack your bag. You're the last to leave."

In less than a minute, I was ready. Old Bossy was in such a rush she forgot to check my bag. She zipped it up and tugged it away, calling me to follow and leaving the door to my room open. *It has never been left open.* In disbelief, I took a final glance at the room and walked alone down the deserted hallway. *The door at the end is wide open too.* I went downstairs unguarded, scanning the area. No one.

The white Toyota Land Cruiser waited by the door. I got in and no one checked my seatbelt. Freedom felt uncomfortable. I was in a daze as if this was the dream and reality was back in the room. Stephen sat behind the wheel next to Benji. Old Bossy threw my bag in the back and jumped in beside me. The bus and cars had left and one guard remained to close the accordion gate after we passed through. I glanced back at the greyish white building covered in security cameras–the place that held me captive for 184 days. *Will I miss it?*

We passed the village, crossed the bridge, and took the river road. I wasn't in the van used for consular visits. This MSS car felt different. Benji turned the radio to a music channel and asked if I liked it. The car chatter was friendly as if it was a day of victory for everyone. The hour-long drive ended at the gate of my apartment building. Stephen lifted my bag out of the trunk, setting it down on the sidewalk.

"You are on bail with restricted freedom pending trial," Benji said in Chinese from the front seat as I waited for instructions. "Don't talk to any media, don't meet anyone without telling us, and stay inside except for essentials. The media will try to find you so don't tell anyone where you are or there will be trouble. They are not your friends. We will contact you through Peter if we have questions or news about the case. He knows you are coming. Report everything to us at least once a week and if you meet anyone, give us their name and phone number and all the details so we can ensure your safety. Your bail period is one year and the trial should be within that time. Stick to the conditions and things should be ok. We'll bring documents later for you to sign. Do you understand?"

I nodded. That was it. I was on bail. The Land Cruiser pulled away as I stood by the gatehouse in shock with no key to my apartment, no ID, and no money. I smiled at the guard, who nodded as if I was back from a holiday, then rolled my bag to our building and rang the buzzer. When I heard Peter's voice I started shaking. The outer door clicked open and the elevator took me to the tenth floor. When I got out, the door was wide open. Peter wrapped his arms around me, holding tight.

"Can I make you a coffee?" he said as we walked in. Peter and his best friend Jimmy had moved in and rearranged things. The discarded white nylon gloves and masks used in the raid sat on a shelf by the door. The walls and most shelves and cupboards were empty.

"What happened to the apartment?"

"They raided it. They took almost everything except furniture. The few things left I tidied because there were cigarette butts everywhere. But I couldn't touch the nylon gloves because I felt too sad that they took all our stuff."

Broken wall sockets, empty bookshelves and picture frames, and a few scattered leftover possessions made the apartment look more like a war zone than home. I peered into Hannah's bedroom which doubled as Peter's. I missed her zest for life as she walked around with earphones dangling from her ears. *How is she?* My heart broke imagining it. I opened her cupboard. Empty.

"Wow Peter! No wonder you couldn't find my winter clothes. I gave the specific bin location and they always told me you were a kid and couldn't find it."

"Nope, they took it. I had to buy the stuff they wanted me to get for you."

We sat down with coffee. Everything was new. I went to the bathroom in private with no notebooks recording every move. I sipped hot coffee and stood by the window. The beautiful Yalu river and North Korea on the other side with guards patrolling in thick olive green military coats. I was back with my son beside me.

"Mum, there is so much to tell you!" Peter went on, "I haven't had anyone to talk to these six months. I heard you disappeared when Stuart texted me the next morning saying I didn't need to go to work at *Peter's*. When I asked why, he told me to check the news. I searched Chinese news sites and a headline popped up. *Canadian Spies Arrested in Dandong*. I didn't believe it. I tried texting and calling Dad but his phone was off. It's never off so I knew something was wrong. The last thing he'd said to me the night before was he'd text me pictures of the dinner. Then a text came from Simeon who'd heard something from a Chinese friend. Within the hour it came out on all the major news networks. I didn't think much about it until that news erupted.

"Simeon was inundated with media calls and told the family to direct all calls to him to protect them. I didn't know what to do. Nothing made sense. The next day Chief called me to the Public Security Bureau (PSB) main office. I asked Jimmy to come because I didn't want to go alone. Jimmy was so upset at the news he took time off to stay with me. Chief made me sign and fingerprint a paper saying they'd notified next of kin within 24 hours. It was a blur and more than 24 hours but I signed. They only asked one question. *Do you know if your Dad does anything else other than run a café?* I said aid work in NK. Then they told me to go home, hang out with friends, try not to think about it and they'd contact me if they needed something.

"It took days for the truth to set in. My body felt numb. I didn't know where to turn so I cried out to God and spent lots of time alone, listening to music and praying. Songs helped. I sang some over and over. My heart had to keep choosing to trust and not just look at the circumstances! The next weeks were rough. Jimmy and Danielle from the coffee house were amazing! We tried to make ourselves feel better by talking lightheartedly about the situation to distract ourselves from the truth and reality that was slowly sinking in. And to cheer ourselves up.

"A lot of things happened in six months. Taxi drivers who knew me asked about you. Other drivers, finding out I was from Canada said, 'Oh yeah we caught some Canadian spies recently running an undercover coffee shop.' It was a real mix. My entire world changed. In my usual internet café, the cleaning lady said, 'Hey, I saw you on TV. They said your parents are spies. Is it true?' I told her it wasn't and she said, 'Yeah, I thought it was fake. You can't believe everything you see on TV these days.' But after that, every time I went to the café she called me Xiǎo Jiàndié (Little Spy).

"I stayed away from the apartment because it made me too sad and brought up emotions and feelings I couldn't handle. At times the MSS asked me to get things so I had to go. It annoyed me because most things they asked me to find were taken in the raid. I searched and searched. The first time I walked in I couldn't stop bawling or go into your room.

"A lot of people knew the news but no one said much. I decided to go back to school to keep things as normal as possible. Back in Dalian a few weeks after you disappeared, I went for training for the Dalian city foreign university student speech contest and my coach said, 'Some teachers said you might not want to enter the speech contest this year because of something going on with your parents.' She didn't know. When I explained, she burst into tears and felt so sorry for me.

"Sometimes I read articles on Chinese chat sites – people's comments were all over the place. I remember one sarcastic comment, 'Yeah the Canadian spies are here to see how we make our scallion pancakes out of plastic.' Some people thought it was fake news but some said, 'Ahhh we got them!' No one in Canada understood why I stayed in China. I had to. I didn't want to leave you and Dad here. I wanted to finish my last year of school and be here for our Chinese friends and all our team."

"Peter, thank you for everything," I said, tears covering my face. I was only beginning to comprehend how hard those days had been for him and the rest of the family.

"Mum, what about you? What did they do to you? Where were you?"

"Peter, I can't tell you anything. They gave me clear instructions not to talk about the case. I can't. It's not over. They are everywhere. Getting out on bail is a privilege. The trial is still ahead, and no one knows what will happen. I thought Dad was getting out like me but they took him to prison. He is strong and we will get through this, but until it's over, I can't talk about anything."

Peter saw how jumpy and nervous I was, always looking behind me to see if someone was listening, even in the apartment. "We are never alone. China is trusting me and I don't want to break that trust. They are watching." The case had been my whole existence for six months. Adjusting to partial freedom was a huge burden.

"Mum, you're home. It's ok to talk now." Peter coaxed me.

"Peter, no, don't ask me anything. I can't talk or I will go to prison too."

"Well, it will be all over the media soon and…"

"I can't talk to anyone. The media don't care about the truth. I have to follow all the terms which means no media conversations at all."

"Mum, a few reporters have been fantastic through this whole thing. And within days they will be all around Dandong looking for you."

When I heard the word reporter my body shook. "Well, they told me to stay inside and I'm going to."

"Mum, they won't do anything to you."

"They might." I thought it would be easy to be out. It wasn't.

That night Peter arranged for a few co-workers to meet for dinner in a small restaurant a short walk from the apartment. I was terrified others would be monitored because of me but Peter insisted. He said it would be good for me. Hiding my fear in his promise to stay by my side, I went through a door for the first time because I chose to.

I half expected someone to grab us. We entered a small private room in the restaurant. My friends were there. Our two Irish colleagues, Stuart and Leslie, who'd managed *Peter's* the previous year. Jimmy, like a son to us, and Danielle, like a daughter. I sat at the round table and Leslie moved to the empty seat beside me. I was overwhelmed. I belonged. I could breathe. Love was all around me and I was part of the circle.

I don't remember if we spoke. The words are erased from my memory by the calm of belonging. The food burst with flavour and colour: bright green vegetables, bright orange sweet and sour pork, and bright red spices on eggplant. In those moments, I forgot I was part of a case leading to trial. But when I opened the door to head for the bathroom, someone jumped out of the way. Fear seized me with an all too familiar feeling. An MSS agent had been listening at the door. We'd done nothing wrong but it cast a dark shadow on the dinner and I wanted to leave.

As Peter and I walked back, I soaked in everything. With him by my side the buildings stood strong and tall. The lights on the alley to our apartment twinkled. Above me the open starry sky smiled. I enjoyed watching Peter open the downstairs gate and noticed every detail of the elevator ride. It was fun to see our apartment door open and walk in.

That night I got into my own bed for the first time in six months and turned the lights off. The streetlights shone dimly on the curtains which I left open. I wasn't ready for complete darkness. I looked over to Kevin's side of the huge queen bed and told myself to be brave. Laying my head on the soft pillow of freedom, I drifted off not needing sleep or a dream to take me from captivity. It was sweet and a bit scary.

23

DANDONG DETENTION CENTRE

Kill one to warn a hundred.

—CHINESE PROVERB

—Kevin—

From wisps of conversations I knew the Dandong Detention Centre housed 900 criminals. *Who are they?* I panicked. I had adapted to isolation. My isolation room had grown safe and predictable. As we sped through Dandong, we passed our favourite Sichuan restaurant decorated with red lanterns. Many birthdays and special events we enjoyed their flavourful spicy dishes, telling stories and laughing. *I miss everything.* Families on the street carried children bundled up like warm cozy balls. Even the old man taking slow and painful steps with his cane along a bumpy sidewalk was choosing his steps. *I can't choose where my feet step. Someone always leads me.* The car slowed and stopped at a local hospital. I recognized security agents waiting there from the way they stood with legs spread apart, plain clothes soldiers standing at ease, blending in but vigilant.

The old grey cement building reminded me of a pre-WWII hospital. Friends often said no one in Dandong goes to Dandong hospitals if they can afford something in another city. Chief and two guards led me in, glancing in both directions. More plain clothes agents waited inside the smoky dirty hospital. I felt satisfaction I could identify them. Chief did the paperwork for a prison entry health check. I broke into a nervous sweat. *Had these doctors and nurses heard a Canadian foreigner was going to prison today?* In the first doctor's office, patients crowded his desk in droves. No privacy. When it was my turn, the doctor wrapped the blood pressure armband over my thick, navy pullover sweater.

"Don't you need to roll up his sleeve?" questioned Chief, masking his annoyance.

"It doesn't matter," the doctor replied scribbling on a form.

160/100 through a sweater didn't sound good. I shuffled from room to room through whitewashed hallways jammed with people. A blood test, a chest x-ray, a urine sample, complete in half an hour with all boxes on the form initialed. It was a formality, not an assessment.

"Often they do the check at the prison but we asked to do it in a hospital because it's better," Chief announced putting me back into the car. He was nervous handing me over to the prison. That alarmed me. He didn't trust it. "Don't worry," he said, "We have explained your case and asked them to give you the best room and care. But after the transfer we can't do much because the prison has its own rules and policies."

With everything timed and planned we drove past Dandong Airport turning right on a countryside road. Beyond open fields, near hills on the horizon loomed a huge dark grey prison. My heart pounded releasing a poisonous dread which stung as it oozed through every vein. A thick metal accordion gate opened and closed behind us. I stared up at thick solid cement walls at least two storeys high where military soldiers with rifles patrolled the perimeter and stood in glass towers on each corner. This dark hopeless place fed my fear. My body involuntarily shook. Horrible images flooded my mind. *Will they beat me? Will I come out alive? God, I need a miracle. Do something!*

The car pulled up at a door and Chief entered with a small plastic bag while I took mental notes from the car. He chatted with a lady in the reception area–the prison warden. She examined the handful of warm clothes, my Bible, and a few family photos. Everything required special approval, and I saw her nod and motion to me.

The clean reception area reminded me of Chinese banks with a row of seats, small windows with signs, and small openings to hand documents through. My information passed through the *new inmate's* window beside the *lawyer's* window. A guard introduced himself as Guard Deng, took the plastic bag from Chief and motioned me to follow. Chief followed too, taking care of me. Guard Deng opened a thick secure door with his fingerprint. I entered, waiting in disbelief between that door and a large barred revolving door restricting entry to a single person at a time. A soldier with a rifle strapped over his shoulder stood by a small reception window while other soldiers milled around behind him carrying large weapons. *There is no turning back.* The window slid open and Guard Deng signed in. About to unlock the revolving door, he noticed my shoes.

"You can't have those here," he said making me take them off and hand them to him.

I can't even keep a pair of shoes? He passed them to Chief, pressed a button, and I passed though in sock feet. Waiting for a third door to open, I glanced back. *Chief is leaving.* I felt sad and wanted him to stay but he left without a word. Guard Deng unlocked the third door with his fingerprint and we entered a place I didn't belong.

The finality of the heavy door clanging shut ushered in my new prison life. No longer a hostage, I was a criminal. A duty guard took my height, mug shot, weight and blood pressure in a small room while Guard Deng found an old pair of plastic army green flip flops lying around and tossed them my way. *No new shoes? What criminals have worn these before me? I'm glad I wore socks.*

Formalities complete, Guard Deng handcuffed and led me past a narrow empty cage, enough for several prisoners to stand but not move, and we descended into a tunnel of bright lights and cameras. Dotted along the walls, posed photos of inmates doing prison activities reminded me of my first night behind money spread out on our table, and the posed picture of Julia and I on comfortable chairs for a Christmas photo. In a haze, I passed photos of prisoners holding books in a library, getting haircuts in a prison salon, playing billiards, and singing in a karaoke room. I'd seen similar displays before in Chinese government buildings, painting a harmonious picture when reality tells a different tale.

The tunnel ended with stairs. We climbed up and Guard Deng tapped a card, opening a gate into a caged landing. After securing gate one, he opened gate two and stepped up to a window. "Kevin Gao," he announced to a sleepy guard who checked his computer.

"Cell 318," came the reply as a third gate clicked open giving us access to a hallway with wings on the left and right. Cells lined the halls and down the 100s wing, prisoners in red and blue striped uniforms with white and red patches on the shoulders delivered food on metal carts.

Around the corner the main prison corridor stretched the length of the prison with wings on both sides. Guard Deng paused at a window behind the guard room to grab a set of keys lying on the ledge with other sets. Across the hall through a window three guards monitored 15 to 18 large TV screens mounted on the wall. *Is one of them cell 318?* On the screens, prisoners in grey uniforms with big orange shoulder patches and grey pants with thick orange stripes sat crammed together back to back on small stools facing a long platform style bed running the length of the cell on each side. *They are making sanitary paper toilet seat covers.*

The glimpse haunted me as Guard Deng hurried me along the main corridor past doorways with English and Chinese signs: Duty Room, Meeting Room, Hair Salon, Electronic Education Room, and Library. *Really? It looks so modern but are any of them used?* Section 2 had signs pointing to wings on the right and left. We stopped at Section 3 beside another control room with TV monitors manned by women guards. The sign pointing left said *Women's Section.* I tried to see but Guard Deng steered me away and we went right. The sign said *Hospital.*

He shoved open an unlocked gate, and I peeked into a room where several doctors in white lab coats with stethoscopes around their necks examined prisoners. Next was a guard's office, a medical equipment room, and a medical room for women prisoners. Room 317 had thick barred doors and IV bags hung on wall hooks while well-guarded prisoners sat on wooden cots or small plastic stools receiving treatments. Then I saw the black numbers on a white plaque mounted above a heavy cell door. Cell 318.

I shivered as Guard Deng fumbled for the key and the inner barred cell door creaked open. Twelve inmates sat on stools, staring in fright as if I was a foreign devil. Two rows of cots lined up side by side took most of the space, leaving a narrow aisle in the center to stand or pace. A skinny prisoner waved me over to an empty cot in the middle on the left side in direct view of two wall-mounted cameras. This wooden board on a metal frame had a black plastic bag on it. Two thin, army green cotton pads sat folded on the end—one to cover the board and one to cover me at night. Beside them were two well-worn white sheets. No one moved or spoke so I rummaged through the bag pulling out a toothbrush six centimetres tall, toothpaste, and a bar of soap in a cheap yellow, plastic wrapper. The label said *Sulphur Soap* in English and my first thought was *this is hell*. I pulled out a thin opaque plastic bowl, a plastic Chinese soup spoon, and a small thin hand towel. Guard Deng told me the bedding was special for hospital cell rooms and I later learned the starter kit was only for me.

"Thank you," I said. He locked the cell door and left me inside. I held up the green pillow case looking for the pillow but Skinny shook his head. No pillows. Everyone stored clothes in the pillow case and slept on them.

The twelve Chinese inmates in the medical wing cell looked healthy. *Are they privileged prisoners?* The cell had cots and fewer inmates than the rooms on the monitors. I knew Chief had done his best and sent a silent thank you his way. Half the inmates with me wore royal blue vests with large white numbers. The other half wore faded blue and white striped pajamas like I'd seen in movies. Shivers shot through me as a duty guard appeared, tossing me a similar set through the bars. I buttoned the top over my sweater and noticing a few others weren't wearing the trousers, tucked them into my pillow case. The plastic bag with my Bible and few clothes was already under my bed. Comforted, I fumbled through for the Bible. I wanted to read but tears formed. Not ready to cry I shoved it back and sat gasping for breath. Six months of isolation and interrogation in one room. *Now this? Is this God's plan?* I had many questions and few answers.

Lunch arrived on a metal cart in a bowl too big to wrap your arms around. A nondescript man in the hallway slopped it through a hole in the cell door using a large ladle. As he tipped the ladle, food fell into a red plastic bowl held up to the hole by Skinny who then placed the bowl under his bed. Several other prisoners followed suit, passing plastic cards back and forth through the bars. *Are they paying? Why don't they eat? Why doesn't everyone get food?* Thirty minutes later a piercing bell rang and bare hands dropped steamed bread through the same opening into a second plastic bowl held at the door. As bowls appeared from under the cots, cellmates gathered around the bowls and ate in groups of three or four. My hunger dissipated as the spoons dipped in and out of communal bowls. I didn't want to join in and no one invited me. Slurping down lukewarm food no one talked or showed emotion. I cautiously took a steamed bun from a bowl on the floor and nibbled. Disgusting. *I can't eat like this. I can't live like this.* A few inmates peeled off the bun's outer rubbery layer. They must not like buns tossed in with bare hands either. I stopped eating. It was enough for my first meal.

Rest time came next so after cleaning up, everyone lay on their cots uncovered. I found it odd until I learned we could only use covers at night. As my cellmates napped, I stared at the high ceilings covered by four sets of long fluorescent tube lights. Cameras positioned near the ceiling at opposite corners of the room kept watch. A TV screen hung above the cell door. Pasted on whitewashed walls across from me was a daily schedule, a well-worn menu, and foam core posters listing prison rules in bold print. Everyone slept with their feet to the wall and head to the aisle. My exhausted eyelids finally covered my eyes and sleep spared me painful thoughts until a bell rang and everyone scrambled to straighten their beds. Skinny muttered instructions under his breath to help me conform to the rules.

The afternoon activity was sitting doing nothing. The back of the cell had a solid door and a metal caged-in screen door leading to an outdoor cage: two cement walls, a concrete floor, with bars on top and at the far end from knee height up, the same width, but shorter than the cell. *I guess that's where we go out to play.* The cage faced a narrow dirt yard separating our wing from the windowed hallway of the 400s wing. A battery-operated clock hung out of reach above the door to the outdoor cage.

"Do we ever go out?" I asked Skinny. I wasn't ready to talk to anyone else because I didn't know their crimes or dispositions.

"Sometimes, but only into the attached cage. It's supposed to be open twice a day, but not on weekends, holidays, or when the guards are busy. Not during inspections. Not if it's too hot or too cold, or raining or snowing." His depressed looks gave more answers than his words and I could tell he wasn't in the mood for more questions.

At 2:30 p.m. the dinner cart rolled down the hall carrying four large metal bowls. Two cellmates rushed to the door to announce what the one dish was so others could decide if they wanted it. Smashed cucumbers! Five inmates grabbed large red communal serving bowls and held them out as scoops of cucumbers seasoned with vinegar were ladled through the opening. The filled bowls were stashed under cots.

I had been avoiding the bathroom but finally had to use it. Wishing I'd gone during nap time, I approached the glassed-in enclosure with a *hole in the floor 'squatty'* toilet in the corner of the cell with barred windows facing the hallway. Relieving myself in view of twelve others, cameras, and the hallway where a female nurse was walking by, humiliated me. *I won't do this again!* I determined to do it when others slept. *I can't risk people brushing their teeth with me squatting over the toilet!* Revolted, I returned to my cot and another prisoner went in. He turned on the knob under the shower head hanging directly over the toilet.

"Showers?" I asked Skinny.

"Yes, someone turns it on around 3:45 p.m. so we see when the hot water comes on. We get 30 minutes of hot water every afternoon if it's sunny since it's solar heated. If not, it's ice cold."

Fifteen minutes later someone yelled, "Water's on!" and three inmates stripped to their underwear and rushed in. They flung their underwear over the bars separating the bathroom from the hallway and stood packed like sardines around the edge of the squatty. One stood directly under the water and then rotated so the other two could have turns. Get wet, shift, lather, shift, lather, shift, wash off, shift and out. As they grabbed their underwear, the second group of three rushed in. This assembly line shower was both comical and appalling. One man dropped his soap and retrieved it from the toilet hole. The last group stood lathered with soap when the hot water stopped and cursing under their breath, they washed off in icy water. Skinny muttered that newcomers shower last. I stared in disbelief as twelve half-naked men holding tiny thin towels scrambled back into their clothes half-wet. Thirty minutes wasn't enough.

As everyone except me dressed, a guard arrived to take me to the prison shop. "I'm Guard Yang," he said in a gentle voice and I guessed him to be near retirement. "Whatever you want to buy after this, tell

Old Ding your cell leader and he will tell the guards and they'll keep track of what you owe."

I followed him. Everything in prison cost money, even soap and water. I had no money. Overwhelmed and trying to understand the system, I accepted his offer and chose peanuts divided into small bags, packaged sweet rice cakes and breakfast morning biscuits. No one explained I'd only have one trip to the shop or I would have bought more. Later I realized that privilege was just for me.

Pleased with my stash, I munched biscuits when the 5 p.m. dinner bell rang, ignoring the steamed buns tossed them through the opening with a bare hand. The cucumbers appeared from under the beds and my cellmates ate in groups. *Will every meal be like this? I'm not looking forward to breakfast!*

The evening activity began at 6:40 p.m. We sat on our uncomfortable short plastic stools at the end of our cots facing the TV monitor while a designated prisoner climbed up the cell door, reached up and switched it on. With straight backs, sitting in perfect rows, we waited for 20 minutes. It was a rule. At seven, CCTV state-run news flashed on the monitor and we stared motionless at 25 minutes of monotonous meetings in the great Hall of the People or other prominent meeting halls. Xi Jinping or another top leader read out plans, strategies, laws and other official announcements to rows of well-dressed stone-faced people feigning interest and scribbling notes. No one paid attention but we couldn't move until it ended.

After meetings came sordid excerpts from criminal trials where criminals in bright orange vests bowed heads in shame to receive sentences from three stern judges. Important criminals wore street clothes. I hated watching trials while waiting for mine. The last few minutes, international news flashed on, and I paid attention with interest to this brief Chinese sketch of current world events. The moment it ended, we jumped up. Some prisoners prepared for bed while others chatted in hushed tones or read well-used books left by transferred prisoners.

I stowed the stool under my cot and gazed from cellmate to cellmate wondering about their crimes. *Are any innocent like me?* None looked criminal. Their faces resembled people I could have met anywhere. It was eerie locked together knowing nothing of each other's lives yet sleeping less than an arm's reach apart. *What will happen at night? Am I safe? Lord, let me wake up beside Julia. Any place but here.* Two night-monitors, prisoners from our cell, paced the aisle brushing past our heads, or stood at each end of the aisle until their three-hour shifts ended. *Why can't I have my head near the wall?* My overactive and overstimulated mind refused to cooperate with my body despite exhaustion. It was difficult to sleep.

At 10 p.m. I lay in a room of snoring men and one teeth-grinder, realizing I was the only one awake. The hard board and thin pad hurt my back. I pictured Julia in our bed for the first times in six months and tried to imagine myself with her. *How can we glimpse each other now? Did they clean up after the raid?* I bunched up the cotton prison pajamas, socks, and underwear, stuffing them inside the pillow case, squeezed my eyes shut, said a quick prayer and fell asleep.

24

BAIL PENDING TRIAL

*There are always ears on
the other side of the wall.*

—CHINESE PROVERB

—*Julia*—

A phone rang. "Peter," the investigator said, "tell your mother to stay in the flat. We're coming."

"Why? What did I do wrong?" Dread filled me.

"Mum, it's probably nothing. Don't think about it."

I couldn't help it. The call took me back into the interrogation room. "Please stay with me."

"I will Mum, don't worry, I'm sure it's nothing." He did his best to calm me but the interrogator's voice on the other end of a cell phone triggered fear, and unwelcome patterns of threats and interrogation from isolation and captivity resurfaced. I froze in the wake of fear.

The buzzer rang. Stephen and Benji strode into the room dropping documents on the coffee table. Peter gave a rough translation.

Decision of Dandong State Security Bureau on Bail. No. 1. Suspect Julia Dawn Garratt, due to suspicion on crime of endangering national security, is determined to be on bail with restricted freedom from February 4, 2015 per Article 65 of the Criminal Procedure Law of the People's Republic of China. The Suspect should be monitored, comply with the following requirements during bail and shall take related legal responsibility for any violations.

The requirements included not leaving Dandong without approval from the enforcement authority, appearing any time when summoned, not destroying or falsifying evidence or colluding with others regarding confessions, not disclosing the case to anybody, nor meeting with lawyers or accepting interviews by domestic media, and getting prior approval to meet with Canadian Embassy officials. The official security bureau seal was stamped at the bottom of this disturbing document. I signed and fingerprinted both Chinese copies.

"But how do I live with no money, documents or work visa?"

"This is a hardship time for you. We will ask our leaders." Stephen turned to Peter. "Help your mother as much as you can." Peter nodded. Stephen turned back to me. "We'll contact you for regular reporting sessions. Peter will arrange a phone for you with our number and other approved numbers. Keep it on and charged. We may need to reach you for other reasons too. Stay away from public places and follow the conditions. Stay inside for your safety." I nodded.

"What about my Dad?" Peter asked.

"We don't know. He'll be ok. The prison has instructions to take care of him." Stephen and Benji stood, exchanged our guest flip flops for their shoes, and left with a parting word. "Have a good Chinese New Year!"

"You too!" I replied.

The door shut and Peter handed me a small blue analog phone. "Mum, here's a phone for you with Stephen's number and mine and here's the charger." I plugged it in.

When someone knocked minutes later, we expected the MSS. Peter opened the door as I crept out of the bedroom and stood behind him. Huge smiles greeted us. Our landlord held out a colourful bouquet.

"I wanted to make you feel better so I brought these. None of us know how to comfort you. We are so sorry this happened. How is Kevin?"

"Ok, but not home yet," I answered mindful not to disclose information and amazed that instead of being angry her tenants were involved in a complex criminal case, she showed incredible compassion.

"Well I hope he'll be home soon and you'll reopen the coffee shop and rent this apartment for many years."

She spoke with such kindness that my heart burst with joy. "Thank you. I'm so sorry the rent is late and that agents damaged your residence during the raid."

"Don't worry about us; we worried about you! You have helped so many Chinese people. Peter was a good son and explained you needed a three-month extension. We knew you would pay."

We thanked her again for her patience and understanding. Still smiling, she excused herself and headed upstairs. I arranged the flowers on the coffee table. Their pinks, reds, and yellows were a healing balm and released gentle fragrance into the room, a pleasant contrast to the frosty Dandong winter lurking outside the balcony door. *I love flowers!* My mind went back to early years in China when Sarah bought magnificent bouquets for Christmas and my birthday, including one heart-shaped basket of roses. Chinese florists are master designers of gorgeous, yet modestly priced floral arrangements. Today's exquisite bouquet reminded me of goodness.

—*Kevin*—

Wednesday, Day 184. My twelve cellmates were asleep and the hallway quiet. I crept to the bathroom with my tiny toothbrush, soap, and facecloth. *No morning showers in prison.* I prayed for courage and wondered about Julia's first day on bail. A loud bell at 6 a.m. got everyone scrambling. *I'm glad I missed the bathroom rush.* Skinny gave me a lesson in folding my cotton pad military style and placing it in a neat square at the foot of my cot.

A cart rolled along the hall. *Breakfast?* Half the prisoners bolted for the door. Someone yelled my name so I went too. *Not breakfast.* A nurse dropped pills through the bars into my hands. *Are they mine?* I swallowed them. Diabetics got insulin needles and a cotton swab dipped in antiseptic to use before giving themselves injections by the cell door. A guard watched everyone take their medicine and collected used needles.

When this unusual medley of cellmates prepared for breakfast I took my plastic bowl and spoon, folded back the thin pad on my bed to expose the board as a makeshift table, and positioned my stool. We sat in two neat rows back-to-back in the aisle, facing the end of our cots waiting. At 6:30 a.m. the clang of cart wheels set things in motion. A prisoner set a red plastic bucket under a small opening in the cell door. He lifted the bucket just in time as a large metal square funnel designed to fit through the hole poked in and thin, watery corn congee slopped into the bowl. Someone yelled, "How many steamed buns?" Skinny yelled a number. A bare hand came in and out through the hole, dropping them in handfuls of two or three, into a basin.

We served ourselves from the bucket of watery corn congee using a communal plastic serving cup and took steamed bread from the bowl on the floor. I sat on my short plastic stool forcing myself to swallow. Everyone slurped. In Asia, noisy eating is the norm but in cell 318 the magnified sound disgusted me. My cellmates sounded like overgrown toddlers whose parents never trained them how to eat. The bland glutinous congee and tasteless steamed bread was free so most people ate it. Later I ordered dried soya milk and brown sugar from the prison store to help me swallow it. After a while I stopped eating it altogether.

After breakfast, everyone cleaned up and a balding inmate with a comb over that kept falling over his eyes, inspected the cots and assigned tasks. New prisoners got the worst jobs and slept closest to the bathroom stench. A burly, heavyset man washed the floor with a wet cloth while a thin, lanky prisoner swished a tattered rag around the bathroom. A short man, his face frozen in sadness, washed the communal dishes. Skinny's duty was piling garbage by the cell door to be squeezed back through the food slot onto the hallway floor every evening after dinner. *It sits there all day?*

By 8 a.m. we sat with backs straight on small stools until the duty guard passed by, changed into his uniform, and returned for roll call, inspections, and announcements. Prisoners stood and said "Here" as he called names but no one called mine. After roll call, a thin man a few cots away introduced himself. My first real connection in the cell.

"My name is Wang Ting. I'm 46," he said as I wondered about his crime. He continued, "Doctors rounds begin at 9 a.m. Lawyer meetings are 9 to 11 a.m. or 1:30 to 4:30 p.m. but most days no one has one. They're expensive and not helpful because the court has influence over lawyers. Outdoor time in the cage is 9:30 a.m. and 2 p.m. on weekdays if conditions are right. Guard Yang picks cell leaders and cell leaders pick prisoner duties. That bald guy, Old Ding, is the cell leader. He and his wife cheated a business partner out of lots of money.

She is at the other end of this wing but they have no contact. Old Ding's appealing his sentence so he's still here. We never leave the cell except for lawyer meetings, trials, or verdict hearings or once a week to clean the halls. Lights stay on. We can't use blankets during the day. Each prisoner gets tested on the rules hanging on the wall over there. And the other schedules and menus are for show, replaced for official inspections. There is not much to do on weekdays since we can't leave the cell. On the weekends, we play cards. We order them from the store but Guard Yang keeps them during the week. But," Wang Ting added smiling, "there is no restriction on chatting." *That's good news.*

He continued, "We eat in groups and take turns paying. Do you want to join our group? The other member is Joe Gang." He pointed to a young man of medium height and build with a unique brush cut.

"Sure," I said.

❖

Guard Yang called my name. I tensed. *What's wrong? What did I do?* Without a word, he led me past two cells to his office. Two chairs, a table, and two desks faced each other beside an old metal filing cabinet. A camera hung in the top left-hand corner of the wall. An adult high chair with a chain on a hook in the middle to latch handcuffs and a place to attach leg irons sat alone. I shivered as Guard Yang offered me a seat at the desk facing an ashtray full of cigarette butts. He sat opposite with his own ashtray. *No wonder the room smells smoky.*

A short old guard with thick outdated glasses entered with a handmade wooden box. He grunted as he took out ink pads and paper.

"He wants your fingerprints," Guard Yang explained.

Silent and focused, the man grabbed my right hand, pressing my palm into the black ink then onto the form. *Shouldn't my name be on the page?* It didn't seem to matter. I was a piece of routine work. After finishing the left hand, he grabbed my fingers, pressing them into the proper boxes. Then he packed his box and disappeared. Guard Yang handed me a tissue. The meeting was over.

❖

Joe Gang, Wang Ting and I ate lunch from a common bowl. Winter melon. Wang Ting, a former policeman, was caught stealing. "I want to see my wife and daughter so much. I'm appealing and hope to get 18 months knocked off my five-year sentence. I haven't told my father. He'd be so ashamed. My wife says I'm away on business but we can't keep the lie going if I'm transferred to the provincial prison. Everyone goes to *the big house* for sentences over two years. Otherwise they stay here. Five or six thousand prisoners are locked up there and spend the first month learning rules. Inmates might return to home town prisons after that, but I won't because I know too many people in prison who might help me."

Joe Gang interrupted in broken English, introducing himself through a mouth full of steamed bread. "Call me Joe. Nice to meet you." He continued in Chinese, "I'm waiting for my trial. My wife and I and eight drivers got caught mixing inferior gas with cooking gas and selling it as pure cooking gas. We made a huge profit! I have an infant son and a teenage daughter from my first marriage. I did it to make money!" He boasted without remorse. *Doesn't he feel guilty for implicating so many people?*

Neither asked my crime, but I guessed everyone knew. The wall outside the cell door had mug shots of everyone with names, ages, and crimes.

❖

During rest time, I hatched a plot. When the hot water came on that afternoon and the first shower group came out, I made my move. I stripped, grabbed my soap and towel and rushed in with the second group, forcing one prisoner out of the queue. Embarrassed and humiliated hanging my underwear on the bars, I stood face-to-face with two men doing what I can only describe as an awkward bathroom dance. Despite trying to hold on, my soap slipped through my fingers and my shower-mates told me to reach in and retrieve it from the toilet. Instead I let that unpleasant reminder slip away and never bought Sulphur Soap again. As I scrambled into my underwear and rushed back to my cot, I realized I'd used my towel as a facecloth and had nothing to dry off with.

❖

On my fourth day in Cell 318 Guard Yang called Joe and me and took us to his office. Fear pounced. *Why us?* Joe climbed onto the desk and wrapped a black plastic bag over the wall camera. Joe was a computer whiz who could type for Guard Yang knew undetected with the camera covered. Guard Yang dyed his hair black to look younger. He was friendly so I liked him. His kind smile calmed me as he went through prison rules. "No hitting other prisoners. No swearing. Obey the guards. No stealing from other prisoners. If you try to escape, you will be executed." It wasn't thorough.

"Has anyone hit you? Has anyone sworn at you?"

"No, no," I answered, my mind fixed on the execution rule. *Harsh.* Joe typed everything then filed the report so the warden had proof of our meeting. Guard Yang nodded and Joe removed the plastic bag. Later, Joe told me he did all Guard Yang's reports.

❖

I couldn't call anyone in prison a friend at first but was glad to meet Wang Ting and Joe. In this community of criminals, I felt dirty, embarrassed, and ashamed. It terrified me that everyone looked so normal. After staring at the ceiling for more than an hour, I put my face in the pillow and cried hoping no one would see. Adjustment wasn't easy.

❖

Food orders were possible but complicated. Wang Ting took outside orders once a week. Prices were 20% lower than the prison store so despite having to buy in bulk, prisoners preferred it. Wang Ting explained, "Listed items may not be available so don't count on it. If you want something not listed, guess. It might come. Weekly lists rarely change so don't get your hopes up. Today we have peanuts, pre-cooked chicken heads, feet and legs (not wrapped), toilet paper, soap, toothpaste, drinks, instant noodles, cookies, water, socks, underwear, plastic slippers and a few snacks. Old Ding orders the communal stuff: garbage bags, laundry bars, dish cloths, and serving buckets. We pay a share. He also oversees prison store orders but there is no list so we guess. Only big orders are worthwhile. Guard Yang and Old Ding go together–one of his perks! Oh, and prisoners like you can make special orders for outside grocery items but they cost more and the duty guard does it as a special favour on his day off. That's about it." He grabbed his pen. "Do you want anything in this order?"

I chose water (24 bottles), peanuts, soap, yogurt, milk (16 bags), and toilet paper (12 rolls). Those were the minimums. Since soap doubled as shampoo, I ordered extra, mindful that I'd lost my first bar of soap to the *squatty*. Wang Ting copied orders twice. The combined order went on the front with individual orders on the back. "Prison forms can't have errors," he explained.

"When do we get the stuff?"

"It's random, starting on Mondays. Forms go in Thursday mornings and Thursday afternoons the guards swipe our stored value cards. If family or friends brings money to the prison gate, it's transferred to our cards. Prisoners without money depend on handouts from the rest of us. We stash our supplies under the cots. Pre-cooked meat orders come on Sunday because the kitchen is off duty. But it's fatty, unwrapped and there is no refrigeration." I decided not to order meat.

25

CRIMINAL DETENTION

A fox borrows the tiger's might.

—CHINESE PROVERB

—Julia—

The blue phone rang. It was Stephen.

"Tell Peter to take money to the prison gate for his father. He has none."

"How much?"

"We don't know. Give him what you can."

Peter rode his blue scooter out to the prison feeling awkward as a foreigner, dropping 700 RMB ($112) at a prison guard house by the front gate. He returned with a pink receipt unaware his Dad needed money for everything.

—Kevin—

I figured out the pecking order for showers. Old Ding went first, flaunting his position, ignoring the fact the water wasn't hot. I held my place in the second group because no one dared reassign me. The new guy in our cell stripped and waited naked for his turn in the last group.

"The cameras will see you and women monitor them!" laughed Old Ding, mocking and criticizing him.

"We did that in my other cell to be quicker. 28 of us in the same size cell," he answered pulling on his underwear.

❖

On Friday afternoon, Guard Yang tossed a bag filled with cards into the cell. Everyone grabbed their deck. Weekend poker matches continued from morning until night. Engrossed in playing, everyone stayed up until the 10 p.m. curfew and first thing Saturday morning after breakfast the games resumed. No one napped after lunch and this card frenzy continued all weekend. Inmates shouted and slapped cards on the cot, calling each other cheats and using snacks for wins. A few played alone but most joined bigger games. The cage stayed closed on weekends so games were a welcome break. The second weekend I ordered a deck and played Solitaire.

On Monday morning, Guard Yang collected all cards except mine, instructing me not to share or play with others on weekdays. My cellmates watched, telling me how to cheat when I was losing. Prisoners are a special breed. They celebrated my wins and felt frustrated when I lost. *I don't want to cheat and ruin the fun.* After a few days, uncomfortable with the special privilege, I controlled my urge to play and kept them under my cot until the weekend.

❖

On Monday mornings after breakfast, Old Ding took phone requests, listing numbers that had to be from memory. Only two messages could go out. *I need money. I want to speak to my lawyer.* I tried but Old Ding shook his head. Guard Yang explained my case was handled directly through the MSS. No calls for me.

❖

Old Ding was an easy puzzle to solve. Devious and proud, he refused to eat with a plastic spoon so made short chopsticks using small strips from the wooden board on his cot. He exploited Guard Yang's good nature by washing his uniform for rewards. Old Ding schemed and gloated over every pack of cigarettes or hair dye for his comb over. His antics were the cell's best entertainment!

He loved to admire himself. Since there were no mirrors in prison a recovering drug addict peeled off the thin tin foil inside wrappers from a few instant noodle packages, used water to stick them onto the glass bathroom wall, and smoothed out the creases with his stored value card. We all used the mirror but Old Ding was addicted. Once I counted how many times he checked his hair and lost track after 50. Hilarious but no one commented since he was cell leader. The mirror disappeared in time for a prison-wide inspection but an industrious cellmate fabricated a new one the minute it ended. We all tried to look good although I'm not sure why.

❖

On Wednesdays, between showering and dinner, the closed-circuit TV came on. I joined the pack and scurried to place my plastic stool in line with the rest and sat staring at a screenshot of an empty room with a bottle of water and microphone on a desk stand. The Chinese characters for *Dandong Detention Centre Broadcasting Centre* splashed on a red backdrop. For 15 minutes a tech team tried to fix the sound, shouting through cell intercoms. "Cell 311, do you hear us? Cell 319, do you hear us?" Joe rolled his eyes. After fidgeting on stools for nearly half an hour, the prison vice-warden flashed onto the screen. He placed a black book and thick stack of papers on the desk and adjusted the microphone. After a few announcements about Spring Festival Holiday, he explained new rules. No red underwear. No red socks. (Red is for good luck and prisoners can't be lucky!)

Next came a pep talk. "Don't whine and complain. You are in here for a reason so get over it and accept your punishment." He opened the thick black Criminal Code Law book and read detailed lists of crimes and punishments for 20 minutes. Finished, he thumped it down on the desk and snatched the top paper from the stack to give public readings of phone call results for the whole prison. "Cell 318, Zhou Ming, number disconnected. Cell 107, Li Hui, your message went through. Cell 206, Zhang Junshi, they say they don't know you. Cell 404, Sun Jiangzhen, no answer. Cell 238, Sun Hanyi, the number is not in service." His monotone voice filled the air for another 20 minutes.

Stop! What demeaning public shame. The demoralizing public proclamation *"your family says they don't know you"* horrified me. Prisoners had no choice. A call was the only way to get money or see a lawyer. Glancing at my cellmates, I realized they were desensitized.

Few messages succeeded. If families delivered money to the prison gate, Guard Yang brought receipts. No one knew about lawyer visits, trials, or transfers until guards came with handcuffs. Prisoners had no communication with family unless a lawyer passed a message along. Even that was rare.

I imagined the call I wanted to make. Today was my Dad's 80th birthday. I would have asked if he was going for his favourite seafood dinner or having homemade Italian pasta. Instead I prayed a blessing over him, put my stool back under the cot, and waited to see if dinner made it to our wing. *I hate what China is stealing from me.* Sadness formed a thick soup in my soul.

—*Julia*—

When Peter came home, I was gazing out the bedroom window.

"Mum, why do you always stay in the bedroom? Why not use the whole apartment–sit in the living room like you used to?"

"I don't know." I hadn't thought about it. It felt safe in the bedroom and was least likely to have cameras.

Instead of insisting I move, he brought another chair in and sat beside me. Then he carried in the landlord's television. The DVD player was gone, but smiling, Peter pulled out a tablet and cord, plugged it in and searched online. He had transferred his friend's internet to our house, so it worked. He'd won his tablet earning first prize in the university city-wide speech contest. I remembered Stephen passing on that message during isolation.

"You need to relax. You are so jumpy. Let's watch something together. Then we'll eat noodles." He found a popular British talent competition. My mind wandered. Everything seemed surreal. I was free to walk around the room, get a hairbrush or pour a drink of water without permission, but I didn't feel normal doing it. My brain had rewired over six months. The compressed nerves had packed together in survival mode and something inside me didn't want to let that go. In many ways, I couldn't. The world sped up, but I was still in slow motion.

"Mum, I set up a webcam app for you and put money on so you can call Hannah and Aunty Deborah and Granny and Grandpa."

"Am I allowed to call them?" I asked unsure of the parameters.

"Phone the investigator and make sure."

"Ok, we will," he answered calmly.

Reuniting with the children, grandchildren, and my sister through internet calls was overwhelming. Hannah burst into tears. Sarah, pregnant with our third grandchild shared the news she was having a boy. I talked to my amazing sister who said she had permission to visit and bring money. She relayed news from my Mum and Dad. I was so thankful everyone was ok. My sister Deborah called almost every night after that relaying messages from family and friends. She became a healing breath of daily hope and encouragement. Our conversations were recorded and we often heard breathing or street noise in the background. Sometimes they were cut off without warning or interference blocked our voices. But we knew the protocol and never alluded to the case.

❖

Peter had one semester of university left to graduate and I insisted he go back after the Chinese New Year break. He didn't want to leave me but we both decided it was best to keep things as normal as possible. Promising to return any time I needed him, he left on the five-hour bus trip to Dalian. The apartment was even emptier without him. My American friend Jean coaxed me out for noodles but surveillance cars followed and agents rode the bus with us. I hated it but Jean ignored them and continued to meet me once a week. An American teacher, Anna, and a wonderful Mongolian friend Sara who studied Chinese at the local university, invited me for wonton soup most Tuesdays at noon. We never discussed the case but getting together was a highlight.

The other person brave enough to spend time with me was my Chinese friend Lily. She brought cabbages and vegetables from her parent's farm and frozen seafood from her husband's company. We never discussed what happened but the concern and compassion in her eyes said enough. Once a week, she walked along the river with me after lunch when most people slept. I kept my head covered and Lily protected me if strangers, recognizing a foreigner, started conversations. She often stopped at two large metal drums, set up along the pathway as makeshift ovens, and treated me to fresh-baked sweet potatoes to munch as we strolled.

I had never realized how many cameras monitored the river. Now I noticed eyes everywhere and even though I was innocent, felt guilty and worried about Lily. "Is your husband ok with us meeting?"

"He says we are *small potatoes*. The surveillance agents won't care about us. He said, 'If Julia needs help, help her'."

Soon after, a letter appeared by my door. *We are so sorry for what happened to you. I hope in the future we can do healing prayer for you. We love you.* There was no signature but I knew who it was from.

❖

The worst moment each week was the dreaded phone call for a reporting session. When I heard the ring, I was back in the compound. My body shook and heart pounded as if the blood was in a panic. I never knew what they'd do or say and always worried I'd done something wrong.

The weekly meetings happened in the City Hotel complex, but in a run-down building with neglected ceilings and furniture. I went alone by local bus feeling like a criminal. I looked at every passenger as if we belonged to two different worlds. As I walked up the steep hill, with folded pieces of A4 paper itemizing my week, I rehearsed my words. The trepidation intensified with each step.

I buzzed. The door clicked open and they waited in a small room at the top of the stairs. I sat on a weathered black couch while Benji adjusted the camera on a tripod. When the light flashed on we started. I unfolded my paper and laid it on the table. They never looked at it then.

"Who did you meet this week?" Stephen started. I mentioned Jean and Lily. "Did you talk about the case?"

"No."

"Why is Jean in China?"

"She is retired and likes it here."

"Did you meet anyone new? Did you talk to any reporters?"

"No. No." Their questions took 30 minutes. At the end of each session they tucked my report into a black briefcase and gave me a paper to sign. Then I negotiated. I did nothing without permission. After six months, the unspoken rule was that if I helped them, they helped me. I asked to visit Kevin and tried to get my ID back. They never answered at once but passed my requests on. Few requests were granted but I always tried. They also gave me tasks. When I heard "Kevin needs two plain t-shirts" or "Kevin has run out of money" it was my proof that Kevin was alive.

❖

The MSS agreed that if we exchanged no money, I could tutor Danielle and a former university student in my apartment. Danielle and Simone's joyful personalities brought smiles and laughter and stories of daily life in Dandong. They brought snacks and flowers and their sensitivity, kindness and giggles helped undo a few knots in my heart. A few weeks later Danielle was fired. Her boss had been interrogated and didn't want trouble. When Danielle lost a second job because agents from Beijing phoned to *suggest* they not hire her to avoid putting the school under scrutiny, I was furious. *How unfair!* She applied to be an assistant in a school cafeteria! I complained at the next reporting session.

"We don't believe it. That doesn't happen in China. Your case has nothing to do with her," Stephen said.

Out on bail with restrictions made living in China so different than before. It was a longer leash than in isolation, but harder to figure out.

26

VISITORS

*There is no person that has 1000 good days in a row,
and no flower than stays red for 100 days.*

—CHINESE PROVERB

—Kevin—

Day 190 marked the day of my first consular visit since entering prison. Guard Yang brought handcuffs and led me through the prison maze into a room labeled *Foreign Meeting Room*. Two guards stood beside me as I waited at a huge boardroom table with plastic flowers down the middle reminding me of our first official meeting to discuss aid work in Pyongyang, DPRK. I waited with different anticipation today, fearful of doing or saying the wrong thing. Janine entered with Chief, Captain and the prison Vice-Warden. I felt relief Janine hadn't transferred yet.

With careful words, I praised the prison care even though I longed to scream, "Help, get me out of here!" Threats held my true feelings hostage. What is the answer to "How are you?" in such controlled monitored visits with an unspoken agenda?

"Ok I guess. Trying to get used to prison routines." I was barely coping, terrified of what might come, aware that 30 minutes was all I had. I sent messages to my family and asked about my father's health. "Are there any updates on the case?"

Janine smiled and reminded me the Canadian government continued to make the case a high priority and they hoped for progress on my status soon. She mentioned the family had deposited $100 for extras.

What extras? I pay for everything from rice to toilet paper. The prison was a business but I couldn't tell her that. She reiterated that the MSS assured them I had the best treatment available and there was no

charge for the upgrade to the medical room since they didn't classify
me as a medical patient. *Upgrade?* She made it sound like a hotel and I
realized she was cautious too. Janine spread out family pictures on the
table and I reached to grab them but handcuffs obstructed me.

"No, we will examine them," said the Vice-Warden scooping them
up. "You can see them later."

I panicked. *Will I?* I watched my connection to the outside world
stuffed into a plastic bag and whisked away.

"Time's up," the warden announced. Photos of my family's latest
adventures and encouraging stories of daily life went one way, and I
went back to the cell to survive the disappointment that nothing had
changed.

❖

Memorizing messages for the next visit and rehearsing questions I
wanted to ask helped pass time. Waiting was my work. *Will a lawyer
come? Will the meal cart have food? Will it be edible? Is the guard going
to give us cage time? Can we shave?* Answers to mundane questions
shaped our moods.

At first, I asked questions. *Why was that prisoner transferred? Why
is there no food today? Why doesn't the guard open the cage? I want fresh
air. Why do the hands on the cheap plastic clock make an annoying noise?
Why am I here?*

Wang Ting leaned towards me after ignoring many questions.
"Kevin, in prison there are no whys."

There was no legitimate reason for the lack of food except that the
prison focused on profit, making less than needed to sell everything.
Our cell often came last in the distribution line so as 10:30 a.m. approached, we predicted the daily dish was sold out. Rice, if available,
cost $10 for a large tray, enough for all of us so the whole cell had to
agree to buy it.

When it was my turn to pay, and the cart made it to our wing, I
grabbed a red plastic bowl and rushed to see if the dish was decent. If
it wasn't I let the cart go on and we felt disappointed. When a tolerable
dish came, I reached through the bars and signed for it, holding the
bowl for our group under the door slot. My favourite dish was *slivered*

meat with potatoes for $8 and I always asked the guard for extra meat. At first he added small shreds of fatty meat and my cellmates applauded. After two weeks of success, the guard laughed and gave me the usual scoop. Soon after, he died. Many Chinese are superstitious and word got around. *If the foreigner asks for more meat, give it to him.*

Wang Ting, Joe, and I ate from our communal bowl like caged animals with plastic spoons. Cellmates with contagious diseases ate alone along with a few loners. Leftovers went to prisoners without money. We were sad animals who said, "Oh! Looks pretty good!" when it wasn't because everyone wanted the joy of getting excited about the smallest thing. If there was no food everyone stopped talking.

I ordered little outside food. Always hoping I'd be out soon, I thought storing bulk food under my bed would be a waste. Soap, water and plain dry biscuits were my treats. I hoped $100 a month would last me but it disappeared in days and I had to request $500 a month. I hated putting that burden on Julia and my family but even toilet paper and water required money. The only thing to drink free was untreated ice-cold tap water. Inmates without money drank it.

❖

When my second sum of money arrived, I tried an outside grocery order. Guard Yang reminded me he had to do it on his day off so I took the hint and decided not to ask often. When the order of mini chocolates, bread, and cookies arrived, I stashed it under my cot with a plan. During afternoon rest period, I put a chocolate near each inmate's head. When they woke up and said, "Where did this come from?" others replied, "Kevin gave it to you," but I said in Chinese, "No, God gave it to you."

❖

On Day 200, Thursday February 19, 2015, after 17 days in the cell, a new guard appeared and handcuffed my hands behind my back. *What's happening?* At first the cuffs were in front but they'd changed the rule. If I tripped or slipped I had no way to brace my fall. It was hard to walk.

At the end of the main hallway we paused at the booth where escort guards sat on benches waiting for orders. Four sets of blue footprints faced the wall and I stood on them like a misbehaving child in the corner as the guard announced my arrival. The officer in the booth glanced at his list. *"Tíshěn liu* (Interrogation Room 6)". The prison wing door snapped shut and as we followed the tunnel to the administration building, a sudden rush of anticipation and excitement exploded in me. *I am getting out! The countries have solved it and will announce it in Room 6.* I got happier every step.

We climbed to the second floor lined with 18 doors. I counted. Each had two blue footprints painted on the floor facing the wall. I stood outside room 6, my flip flops filling most of the footprints as the guard unlocked the door. Expecting a clean room for Chief to announce my release, I entered a dingy one with a half wall and bars the rest of the way. The guard sat me in a metal prisoner high chair like I'd seen in Guard Yang's office. Dread filled me as he lifted my hands, folded the tray over my head, and latched my handcuffs to a chain on a hook in the middle so I couldn't move. I didn't have leg irons so thankfully he couldn't chain my feet to the chair bolted to the floor. Waves of nausea, fear and excruciating disappointment flooded me. I'd heard other prisoners call this the Tiger Chair. I wasn't sure which was worse, the humiliation or the horrible sinking feeling that this was not the end.

I stretched my foot, touching a wall covered in footprints and scuff marks; many had spent hours here. Cigarette butts scattered the floor and a garbage can with an empty plastic bag sat in the corner. Chief and Captain faced me through the bars. After shaking the handcuffs to ensure they were secured, the guard left. The door thudded shut.

Captain spoke first. "How are you?"

"Ok."

"What is your room like?"

"There are thirteen people right now."

"That's awful!" He showed great concern in my welfare.

"How is your health?"

"Ok."

"How are you feeling?"

"Trying to get used to it."

"Listen to the other prisoners. Try to get along. Watch and learn from everyone." Chief produced a list and photos that I'd seen in the interrogation. They been enlarged and printed on A4 paper. *What a waste of paper.* Chief tried to pass them through the bars but a desk impeded his reach. "You have to sign and fingerprint them to verify they are yours."

With handcuffs locked to the tray. grabbing them required skill and coordination. Spreading the photos on the tray with my fingers and straining for the pen and ink pad, I shuffled things into position. This illogical way to pass papers made me think other things I didn't voice.

Signing, dating and fingerprinting the photos was a feat of agility. Snapshots taken along the Dandong waterfront in public places, along the tourist route to Tiger Mountain, or on Chinese tour boats travelling the river between China and North Korea. A few showed North Korean farmers working in distant fields through border fences. I'd seen each photo multiple times during interrogation. *Can they execute me for photos?*

The long meeting gave the restraints ample time to pierce my skin. The loudspeaker called all prisoners back to their cells for lunch by 11 a.m. but I stayed. My back ached and the hard metal made sitting unbearable. Chief ran out and bought buns and water from a stall across from the prison.

"Let's have lunch." He passed a bun through the bars. My weak arms strained for it and we ate. The investigators, following orders from higher up, reminded me they were *small potatoes.* By 12:30 p.m. we'd rehashed everything but I stayed locked in agony with no comfortable way to shift my body for relief. We exchanged small talk and I asked about Julia. They said she was ok and her case was different. I imagined strolling by her side far from prison and fought back unwelcome tears.

At 1:30 p.m. Chief pressed the intercom button. "We're finished." The well-fed, well-rested guard sauntered in and undid the handcuffs but I couldn't stand. Every limb ached and pain shot through me. In four hours, I'd become an old man forcing himself to walk. Silent anger raged. *The photos aren't secret intelligence. What a waste of time, money and ink for colour photos.* I raged inside about the wastage so

I wouldn't lash out. *Someone is playing chess, and we are the easiest to take off the board.* The interrogators and interpreter were trapped too. China has a 99.9% conviction rate. Without a miracle, we were heading for conviction.

❖

When Wayne introduced himself as the consular affairs coordinator in Beijing, his title didn't matter as much as the chance to speak English with a man. "I came instead of Janine this month. How are you doing?"

I gave guarded answers. "I'm coping but things are incredibly hard. On March 5, the investigators presented an 8-page document detailing the conditions of arrest, but it was not the official arrest. What's going on?"

"The Department of Foreign Affairs, Trade & Development (DFATD) expects the Procuratorate to decide this week and then a lawyer will have access to you. The MSS has promised to expedite things. Then we move to the next phase. The Procuratorate reviews evidence and decides about taking it to trial. In most cases, China uses the maximums and they may send the case back to the investigators for clarification. We hope that won't happen."

"It is still a guessing game with no progress," I summarized.

"Try not to look at it that way. The good news is that the MSS has agreed to let Julia and Peter visit for 30 minutes right after I leave. Peter came back for the weekend to see you." I heard his words but couldn't believe them. *Really?*

I launched into memorized messages. "I'm outside twice a day if the weather cooperates. Shaving is twice a week. I have a deck of cards. My eyes and right leg are a problem. I try to pace in the aisle three or four times a day but never leave the room. I couldn't keep messages or pictures last month. I need more funds. Please give birthday greetings to Hannah (I love you so much and am so proud of you! I can't wait to see you again!) my Mom, my grandson Joey who turns two on April 1, and my brothers Jeff and Todd."

I wondered if I'd forgotten something as Wayne scribbled everything in the remaining few minutes.

❖

Wayne never heard the full story. The rule was no shaving in prison. Twice a week prisoners requested shaves and if Guard Yang agreed, he brought the bag of charged razors and opened the cage. The first time I saw my own razor in the bag and realized Chief brought it from isolation, I felt happy enough to hug him. The familiar razor comforted me. I picked it from the pile of cheap battery-operated ones sold by the prison and other inmate razors.

"Line up against the wall!" Old Ding barked, "Shaving is against the rules so you can't let the cameras see you." I rushed to the wall while prisoners without money rummaged for communal razors left by transferred inmates. No one had manual razors because of the blades. We stood in a tidy row. Without a mirror, we helped each other shave missed spots. Whiskers accumulated on the cement floor, with wisps blowing out through the bars. Finished, Old Ding collected the razors and rushed back to his office to charge them for our next shave. I couldn't tell Wayne the details.

❖

Julia and Peter walked in. "I love you," she said disturbed to see hand-cuffs. *She'll understand my unspoken story.* "I never gave up trying to see you. The Embassy said it was unlikely but I asked to come in their car even if it meant waiting outside. Last month I walked in with Janine and no one stopped me so I waited in reception, pacing, praying and hoping you might pass by the window.

As she talked tears trickled silently down my face. The table was too wide to reach across and touch her. The sadness in Peter's eyes met mine as he tried to cheer me up, talking about school and our friends. "Dad, everyone says hello and misses you."

"Peter." The words stuck in my throat and I fought back tears. "I love you. Tell everyone to keep praying. It's our only hope." I tried to draw strength from their faces as the warden rushed me away. *I will try to glimpse Julia once a month.* The thought renewed my determination to overcome even the darkest trials of this love journey. Every time the case tried to engulf me, the fire inside burned it away.

27

THE TIGER CHAIR

Paper can't wrap a fire.

—CHINESE IDIOM

—*Julia*—

That weekend Peter shared Stuart and Leslie's story. "The night you disappeared, two officers banged on their apartment door at midnight. They took Stuart to the coffee shop to witness them raid and confiscate anything resembling evidence since he was the acting manager. The MSS informed them they couldn't leave China while the investigation was ongoing, or reopen *Peter's*. Afraid and confused, they had to inform the staff they were jobless. Leslie kept teaching at the university until her contract ended five months later and Stuart hung out with friends and studied Chinese. In December, they contacted the MSS for clarification. With no reply, their parents purchased tickets to bring them home to Ireland. The airport check-in and bag check went well but they hit a roadblock at immigration.

"China had flagged their passports so they couldn't leave and had to turn back. The British Embassy couldn't help either. Apparently, China can refuse exit to foreigners who witness a crime or are connected to ongoing investigations. Shocked, they returned to Dandong. When you came out on bail, the MSS cleared them to exit China. It was super hard." My heart ached for them as Peter shared.

"Yeah Mum, for six months we all kept expecting we could open *Peter's* again. And one time the shop landlord brought thugs to intimidate me and extort money for storage. Thankfully I found a copy of the contract to prove the rent was paid in full for another seven months. And Dad sent me a message through the Embassy saying don't talk to the shop landlord."

❖

Peter returned to school after the weekend. Two days later someone banged on my door at 7 a.m. Expecting the MSS, I opened to the shop landlord and a hefty, scowling man. After barging into our building uninvited they demanded money. The landlord pulled out a camera. I panicked. *She wants to blackmail me.* "I can't help you now," I said shutting the door and calling Peter at university. I was shaking. Peter was furious and called the MSS. "The coffee house landlord is threatening my Mum!" Stephen promised to take care of it.

A few days later, an apology letter appeared under my apartment door saying we owed nothing and had until June to remove our items from her property. We never heard from her again. It was as if the MSS was saying, "These are our prisoners, you mess with them and you deal with us!"

The next weekend Peter returned to Dandong again to help me empty the coffee house. The local orphanage sent trucks, and we donated most things to help start a bakery to train their youth. We invited our former staff to choose items they could use. One former server saw me and burst out, "Now I really know there is a God!" As the coffee house emptied, we felt thankful everything found a new home. Our former barista took a start-up kit to open his own small coffee shop, and one server took the basics to start a convenience store. Peter wanted to keep the coffee machine for the day his dad came home so it came to our apartment by three-wheeled cart along with some *Peter's* logo signs. As the cart rolled down the back alley we noticed a neighbour had already recycled our thick foam-core sign as a pad for his bench!

The coffee machine had survived both a flood and abduction. In our apartment, it was a blessing. The apartment landlord and her husband appreciated lattes delivered to their door, and Jean and Anna enjoyed coffee too. I offered some to the investigators but after they declined I decided to bake for them. The next time my blue phone rang calling me to their black car for a meeting, I took three loaves of fresh-baked banana bread. They were shocked! I'd anticipated they had rules about gifts from prisoners, so had sliced it and ate a slice with them to prove it was safe. The smiles on their bewildered faces were worth it! I sat in the back seat answering the regular questions, handed them my notes outlining who I'd met and when and where, and then we ate banana bread together. When the meeting ended, they left with the rest of their loaves.

—Kevin—

The middle of the month between consular visits was toughest. The weight of group hopelessness and suffering inside the cell crushed me. My internal clock woke me at 3 a.m. without fail, to read and reflect before the prison loudspeaker woke everyone at 6 a.m. The first time I stood and paced at 3 a.m. a loud voice blared over the prison-wide loudspeaker, "Kevin Gao, get back to bed," which woke all the prisoners. Now guards and night monitors ignored my church of one. Morning readings began in Psalms where my desperate pleas for help found a friend. Next, I meditated on one Proverb for wisdom, then read portions of the New Testament and Old Testament in sequence. Hebrews was a favourite! At first I skipped Job and Revelation but later found Job refreshing and Revelation inspiring and encouraging. As John lifted the lid inviting me to glimpse heaven in fast-forward, the ride forced the daily grind of prison life to bump along behind. My final stop was the minor prophets with its reminders that the future unfolds with God's timeline.

Despite persisting with routines, at times I did not feel God for days. *Has he abandoned me? I know he answers prayers. Why not mine?* I begged and pleaded. *Not prison.* But he was silent. I knew he was there, but wanted more. I wanted the wind and earthquake and fire. I wanted the kind of God who would write things on the wall and miraculously open prison doors to set this captive free. I read the Bible, stopping at every miraculous deed. I underlined all the amazing things in Psalms. I didn't want to read or see things like "why have you forsaken me?" because I felt it. *Has God left me? Where are his whispers?*

❖

Henry Gao had been a friend since he discovered my name was Kevin Gao and had said, "We're brothers! We share the same last name." Henry always smiled and acted happy. Today he saw me suffering.

"Kevin, try to think of this as a long holiday." I couldn't. A week later, Henry woke while I was reading. "Kevin, I think God's giving you a chance to study." *Is he?* Slowly, I listened again. *Kevin, I am with you. You are my child. All things work together for good.*

❖

The next morning, forced back to the Tiger Chair, every muscle tightened and braced for the pain. Suffering wasn't a choice. *God, I can't go on.* The guard poised ready to bolt my cuffs to the tray when Chief interrupted.

"Can you leave them unbolted?" A tear formed in the corner of my eye at his kindness. My muscles relaxed, and I endured with new energy, able to lift the latch and stretch. I needed that pause. *Thank you, Chief.*

❖

A few days later I hoped for the same favour. Weak and achy from a sleepless night, the pain was immediate and cut into my skin as the guard locked me in tight. Chief's angry glares and hardened countenance suggested something had changed. *What have I done?* He held a thick stack of photos.

"The Shenyang Military Command has selected and classified these 23 photos as highly sensitive or sensitive," he said. He turned the first one to face me. "A military pontoon bridge. Highly sensitive!"

The authority assigned to this evidence alarmed me and my mind grasped for peace. The highly sensitive ones showed the Chinese military building pontoon bridges across to North Korea. In 2006, before our family moved to Dandong, Julia and I climbed a local piece of the Great Wall of China called Tiger Mountain. We hired a green taxi that drove along the banks of the scenic Yalu River to take us there. A commotion ahead blocked the road forcing us to stop in front of huge piles of dirt with angry protesting farmers standing on top. The driver told us to get out and wait on the bank while he negotiated. We guessed it was a land compensation dispute because this new highway along the river to beautiful tourist destinations cut through farmland. While the taxi driver explained to the farmers that it wouldn't look good for China if foreigners had no access to Chinese tourist sites, we snapped photos of our view from the embankment. Below were soldiers in bright orange life jackets building a pontoon bridge in sections. Fascinated, I got great shots. I never imagined ten years later I'd be facing allegations that these photos proved I was a spy.

The investigators insisted I purposely stopped to take photos for CSIS. They claimed both the taxi driver and Julia verified the story. Although the testimony proved my innocence, twisted another way it proved my guilt. No recording devices or surveillance equipment was found during the raids on our apartment and coffee house. There was nothing hidden in our walls, wall sockets, photo albums or picture frames–all examined. No data or classified information was found on our computers or devices. We had no high powered or hidden cameras. Even though my photos were discovered late in the interrogation period, they latched onto them to build a case.

"Police officers marching past Peter's coffee house. Sensitive!" Chief called out each classification in incriminating tones as the handcuffs cut into my wrists. "North Korean soldiers patrolling the border. Sensitive! A police jeep driving past *Peter's*. Sensitive! A fence separating China and North Korea close to town. Sensitive! Snapshots of the Friendship Bridge. Sensitive!"

My thoughts flashed back to Chinese photographers waiting by the bridge to earn extra cash snapping photos for tourists holding plastic flowers. "How can bridge photos be classified as sensitive?"

"It's the angles of the photos making them sensitive," Captain retorted. *The angles?*

The final classified photo was an old Chinese prison classified highly sensitive. A friend in another city had pointed it out as the place where North Korean refugees are kept before repatriation to North Korea. Interesting at the time, now I regretted that click of the camera.

The designations infuriated me. Similar photos were all over the internet. *Why prosecute me?* I didn't know what was worse, the Tiger

Chair or the scathing injustice. I kept my face down at the end of the session, dejected and weak. *Do I deserve this injustice?*

❖

Day 220. I missed my brother Jeff. Today, March 12, was his birthday. He often held parties in his log house on an acreage where we gathered to celebrate family events. We both liked photography. Lost in thought, I almost didn't hear the guard summon me.

The Tiger Chair again? I wallowed in the undertow of tension as I faced a camera on a tripod, on Chief's side of the bars. My precious camera had always been a source of joy, so unlike this sinister MSS camera. Chief clicked *start* and the red flashing light revived painful scenes of the isolation room and grueling interrogations.

"This is your formal arrest. You have to sign it!" Captain clutched two sets of papers.

Arrest? It feels like my death warrant! My anger boiled but I stayed in control and quieted the fire inside. "If I sign does it mean I agree to the charges?"

"No, it means you acknowledge notification of the formal arrest charging you with stealing state secrets and passing them on to foreign agents." Captain gave a rough English translation. My thoughts seethed. *With so many English speakers in China can't anyone provide written translations for an international case like this?* I fumbled to reach the paper, pen, and red inkpad through the bars. Sharp pains shot through my body. I signed to escape the chair. The second my fingerprint touched the page, cell phones appeared and both made calls. I froze. *What have I done? Who are they calling? What has my fingerprint put in motion?* I felt deceived but it was too late. Pain weakened me and the camera screamed guilt. Chief pressed the buzzer for the guard and clicked off the camera. The guard moved the handcuffs from front to back and shuffled me away. My cellmates announced the cart had run out of food leaving only steamed bread and watery cabbage soup. Most people hated it and refused to eat it because of the poor quality. I was too numb to care.

—*Julia*—

I hated seeing MSS agents outside our building. The new security camera installed above our apartment was identical to those at the compound, shooting arrows of fear into my heart. I had to pull them out one by one. I comforted myself. *This isn't the compound; it's my home.* But instead of Kevin, I had the blue phone by my side.

I paced back and forth to the window as if I had to spy on the MSS agents as much as they spied on me. At 10 p.m. each night I switched off the lights and stood by the glass in darkness watching until the cars left. It took 15 minutes most nights. I liked outwitting them, making them think I'd gone to sleep. Delightful moments of pure freedom ensued as I smiled at the stars twinkling over the river and the shimmering lights of the Friendship Bridge reflecting in the water. The sense of an ever-approaching storm raging in my soul diminished in those moments and peace tucked me in for the night.

❖

On Day 218 after five weeks on bail my sister Deborah arrived from Canada. Excited and terrified I welcomed her into my strange world and she brought hers to me. Joy overflowed as she unpacked cards, chocolate, books and messages. Her laughter brought back memories of childhood games, walks to pick blackcurrants and taking our bikes out in the spring before the snow melted. She reminded me of what was and was yet to come. My brave little sister.

We didn't mention my side of the case. Instead, Deborah gave me glimpses of a much larger story. "Family members and friends heard about your disappearance on the news and everyone united to help and pray. Canada arrested a Chinese spy five weeks before you disappeared and six days before, Canadian Foreign Minister John Baird accused China of hacking into and stealing data from the National Research Council. Everyone believed it was retaliation. Thousands wrote to the Canadian government on your behalf. Simeon protected Sarah, Hannah and the grandparents from reporters by having all calls directed to him. I met with Kevin's brothers often and we didn't do anything until we all agreed. I started a private Facebook page and posted a note every morning and an occasional photo to keep people praying. Many got involved. I held a candlelight vigil at Christmas, and made sure your children got to our home for Christmas. On your birthday, I hosted a prayer celebration in a beautiful atrium." I listened amazed. What a complex case. *A real spy? Hacking?* It all sounded surreal. And my family! What care and concern. *What an amazing sister I have.*

❖

Despite the joyous reunion the atmosphere remained strained. Two days after Deb's arrival the blue phone rang.

"Are you home? Stay put. We're coming," Stephen said. My heart lurched.

Deborah was on the balcony enjoying the river view and watching big blue trucks along the river picking up giant red lanterns. A white Land Cruiser drove into the complex and a father and son got out. "Nice," she called to me, "a family enjoying time together!"

The buzzer rang. That *father and son* were Stephen and Benji. They marched in, sat down on the couch, and pulled papers from a manila envelope. "These are Kevin's arrest papers," Benji announced. "Sign and fingerprint them!"

Deborah burst into tears.

"Don't cry," Stephen said turning to her, "Julia cried at first but now she's used to it." As I saw Deb reeling with the sudden shock and leaving the room to calm down, I realized Stephen was right. It was normal for me. After a rough translation, I signed the papers and asked for a copy.

As they left they called to my sister, "Have a nice time in Dandong." They meant it.

❖

Deb and I found joy despite constant surveillance and calls to report. We laughed, feasted on sweet and sour pork, and shared sister stories. Her husband Ed, set up a debit card so I could access money from family to pay for Kevin's prison fees, my rent, and living expenses. On the first trip to the bank ATM machine downtown, I felt like a criminal sneaking out for cash. Despite getting permission first, security agents boarded our bus and stood outside the bank overshadowing the joy of watching crisp red 100 RMB bills come out of the machine. Even our plan for a quiet picnic by the river was ruined by plain clothes agents standing behind nearby trees. We forged ahead with the final part of our plan. Thank you gifts for Deborah's friends. As she bought handmade pearl bracelets at a small pearl kiosk in the local indoor market, I noticed a towel kiosk displaying two bright red floral bathrobes. They made us laugh so much, we bought them and wore them every night after that.

The morning after our shopping spree, we awoke to rushing water. The living room pipes, installed in clear view after the original pipes malfunctioned, often gurgled as hot water came on twice daily and circulated to heat the apartment. Deb and I rushed from our bedrooms. The pipes were fine but the apartment was flooding. Locating the source, we found water leaking through the kitchen wall, filling the floor.

I climbed the stairs to notify the landlord. It still took courage to venture out alone, even for a moment. No answer. Soon water would be everywhere. Thankfully, her number had been added to my blue phone. In China things happen fast if there's trouble, and her husband and plumber friend arrived within minutes of my call. The door latch stuck and I jerked it. It was strange opening the door to let someone in.

"Blessing is coming!" said the landlord's husband when he saw the flood. "In China, when water bursts through the wall, it's a sign that blessing and good things are coming." Not the response I expected! Deb and I grabbed towels and rags. How gracious that he wasn't angry I'd interrupted his peaceful Sunday! The plumber cut out two huge slices of drywall, locating a broken tap connection. He promptly repaired the leak then asked for a thick roll of cellophane tape and to fix the drywall back into place. Renovations complete! I grinned, thanked them, and offered to make coffee.

❖

My investigators surprised me by allowing Deborah to attend one reporting session. Celina attended with the others and the video camera was noticeably absent. I handed in my reporting sheet and answered routine questions. Then Stephen and Celina chatted about Deb's stay in Dandong. Seeing the opportunity for a request, I asked if she could visit Kevin to take a message back to the family. Stephen said he'd ask and showed genuine concern. He picked up a brown envelope.

"We are returning things you had the first night that are no longer needed for our investigation," he said and poured my watch, earrings, wedding rings and 900 RMB ($145) onto a small table. I grabbed the rings which slipped on easily because I'd lost weight.

"Can I have my ID and credit cards back and the rest of our money?" I asked hopefully.

"No, but you can take this box home too," he added, lifting a box from behind the desk. Everything else is still part of the case."

The box had all the teaching supplies I had with me that first night. I wanted to laugh at the table mats, cutlery, markers, glue sticks and paper clips sitting in the evidence box, but said nothing. I stole a glance at Deborah and thanked them.

As we left with our strange loot Celina whispered, "I like your sister."

❖

Deborah's month was almost over when someone pounded on the door. Terrified and expecting the MSS, I opened to two local precinct officers asking to see Deborah's passport. "How long has she been in China? What's she doing here?" Deborah looked terrified. I took control, explaining in Chinese that she had MSS permission and we'd registered within 24 hours. They calmed down and left.

We sat down in shock and the blue phone rang. Stephen was coming. *Now what have we done?* The investigators appeared with several more boxes of confiscated goods. They piled books, a bin of children's knit hats, Hannah's music CD's, a bin of my winter clothes, and two safes from the coffee house, empty and without keys, on the living room floor.

Stephen turned to Deborah. "You can visit Kevin on your last day here. I hope you've had a great time with your sister." Despite everything, she had.

After the door closed, we rummaged through, laughing at the evidence. A recipe book, guitar chord sheets, and Hannah's teenage journal with the words *Confidential* on the inside cover. I called and offered the safes to Lily who said her parents could use them. Eager to take Deborah to the farm and to hug Lily's parents who I loved as family, we all piled into their car with the safes in the trunk. Suddenly two terrifying sirens startled us and we looked around for a police car, worried the MSS was chasing us. No car materialized and we realized in horror that a bump in the road had set off both safe alarms at once! We had to leave them blaring because there was no way to stop them without the keys. Lily's husband ignored it and kept driving. He was so wonderfully calm.

The next morning, Jean moved to a building in the complex beside mine. We met in the building lobby to help unload the truck. Squeezed into the loaded elevator with furniture and boxes, a stranger stepped in just before we pushed the button. He got out on Jean's floor and walked into the apartment uninvited, roaming from room to room as we unpacked. We ignored him once we guessed he was an MSS agent.

❖

On Deborah's final day we visited Kevin. A guard unlocked the series of doors. A large video camera just inside the final door pointed at us. We exchanged nervous glances as a man videoed Chief leading us to the meeting room. Janine, wearing a professional navy pantsuit, was on her way out. "Ignore the camera," she said.

Kevin sat in prison striped pajamas with a sweater on top. He looked pale and in pain. Benji held an IV bag up beside him and the tubing ran into Kevin's hand.

"I'm not doing well," he said. "There is a flu going around so most of us have it. I'm better than I was." He stopped talking and looked at the IV. It had backed up. Chief Wang ran over and yanked out the tube. Deb and I sat speechless but Kevin didn't flinch. Taking advantage of the lull, Deborah seized the opportunity to ask health and medical questions.

Kevin's pale face agonized as he spoke. "I can't hold a book or pace for long without my arms going numb. I have frequent sharp abdominal pains, headaches and radiating backaches. My heartbeat is irregular. This flu makes it worse. I can't hold on much longer."

Deb explained she was pushing for an outside medical check and hopeful a doctor visit would be approved. Kevin's desperate eyes cried *help* as he shifted in discomfort, straining to focus. I wanted to run and hug him. *Thirty minutes is a long time to sit in pain.* Chief turned to face the door as if the suffering bothered him too.

Deborah tried to cheer Kevin. "We sent a full bag of books through Janine, and family messages. Friends sent treats too but the prison refused them. Everyone sends their love."

"Messages keep me alive. Thank you. Tell everyone to keep praying. Hopefully they'll release me soon on humanitarian grounds."

The visit ended a few minutes early. Chief insisted Kevin get back to the cell for a hot lunch but I suspected it was for inspections. Kevin shuffled out in handcuffs with one last glance. As our eyes met I tried to receive some of his pain, mouthing *I love you.* The camera videoed us leaving through immaculate hallways. The prisoner holding cage was empty and I was certain we'd be part of the propaganda showing family visits. I didn't care. It was nice they let Deborah visit. We returned to town in the car Janine always booked for consular visits. Since it was my once a month ride in a decent car, I helped myself to the free water and offered Deborah a bottle.

Janine updated us. "Kevin kept track of the meals and 28.4% of the time food runs out before reaching his wing. He received an official arrest on March 12 and signed an eight-page document with a summarized statement of what he'd done before being taken into custody and the background to his actions. He can't see a lawyer and from our discussions with the Chinese Foreign Ministry (CFM) that's lawful given the specific charges. We told him Canada raised the case with the CFM and they promised to treat him in accordance with Chinese law. Kevin expressed appreciation for Canada's efforts and told us to keep hoping, trying, and pressing."

Janine transferred to Shanghai after that. Deborah returned to Canada. Watching her go without us was painful but she promised to rally family and friends to keep hoping, pressing and most of all praying.

28

THE ART OF RESILIENCE

I dreamed a thousand new paths.
I woke and walked my old one.

—*Chinese Proverb*

—*Kevin*—

273 days. The colourless cell smelled like a sweat-filled locker room. My eyes adjusted to muted shades of grey, navy and army green and no matter how hard we cleaned, the stench of fourteen sweaty bodies remained. Doctors and nurses passing by mentioned the stench but there was nothing we could do. Spring came outside, but inside there were no seasons. In favourable weather, if Guard Yang was amiable, he opened the exercise cage door and everyone able to walk shuffled into it. Those on IV, unhooked their bags from the wall and used plastic bags to tie them to the bars at the far end to breathe fresh air. The cement walls blocked the air flow everywhere else. Clouds drifted overhead as the sun cast bar-shaped shadows on the cement floor. I always looked up when I first stepped out to see a world bigger and better than prison. Those too weak to stand for 30 minutes, took stools. Sitting ten centimetres from the ground was unbearable so I tried to move around. We paced on the cement pad in small circles, one following the next. When our legs gave out we clung to the bars at the end or lined up our stools against the cement wall.

Banned activities like shaving or smoking happened there, out of view of the camera. On sunny mornings, we hung laundry on the bars or aired our bed covers, hoping to retrieve them before it rained. Since that depended on Guard Yang's mood, I seldom risked it. I dried clothes under my cot where I'd spread a few old *China Daily* newspapers the Embassy passed on. I shared extra pages with grateful cellmates.

Medical cells were exempt from prison work duty but during Chinese long bean season, everyone worked. Two or three large woven nylon sacks of long pale green string beans arrived from the kitchen. I pulled up a stool with my cellmates, as a prisoner dumped the beans in three piles on the floor. We broke and stringed them, often sickened to find small worms or insects inside. We worked as robots with little attention to end results. If the beans looked inedible, our group agreed in advance not to buy lunch the next day. We broke the monotony tossing the tips at someone sitting by another pile. It was a small victory to hit someone unnoticed.

We invested hours guessing sounds. The food cart? No, wrong wheels. It must be the delivery cart. Maybe it's our order from last week. No, wrong time. Oh, disappointment, it's only a doctor pushing a medical cart. We always hoped it was food. Once, a cake went by and we wondered who had that much power. We classified everything as good or bad. When we heard yelling we rushed to peer through the cell door. We couldn't see but always tried. Oh, a lawyer visit. Oh, good news. When someone returned from court, we tried to find out if we'd guessed right and get details. Guessing was like gambling for prisoners–the chance of a big win was always there. Being right helped us cope and feel in control. With physical strength stolen, knowledge was power.

If we glimpsed unusual things, the first to see it gloated.

"They're wheeling someone in on a gurney," Skinny announced with pride as we crammed over, craning our necks to see down the hallway. Stainless steel stretchers on wheels were a rare sighting. As guards carried a screaming prisoner into the next cell because gurneys couldn't fit through cell doors, we shouted guesses and discussed the victim's ailment. Knife wounds? Drug overdose? Botched surgery? Those were most common.

The biggest treat was trolleys with bananas or apples. Usually they sold out before reaching our wing so excitement mounted if a box or two remained. Once, raisins arrived in small bags and I bought six since I love them. I planned to buy more but they never came again.

—*Julia*—

After Jean moved, I could see her in the distance through my kitchen window, sitting by her apartment window in a red sweatshirt, reading early in the morning. Knowing she moved to be closer to me, calmed me. I watched her lights turn on and off. Each glimpse breathed life into my loneliness. And sometimes Jean used the back alley to come for coffee at 5 a.m. before the four *birds* (the name we gave agents who monitored the area) took up their posts and before my surveillance cars arrived at 6:30 a.m.

❖

Work was impossible with no visa, writing was too risky, and the orphanage was off limits. I longed to meet more friends but knew they'd be investigated. Instead, I painted. Unfolding the pain in my heart, it burst out in a splash of colour on canvas, in rushing waters and tumultuous seas. Sorrow, disappointment, and anguish seemed satisfied with its new spot raging on paper or canvas, and I felt lighter and freer.

I sketched portraits from family photos of people I longed to see. Isolated in my apartment I traced their faces with my fingers then translated that onto paper with full-length pencils. As their eyes appeared, their cheeks, and the lines on their faces filled a blank page with recognizable images, I had guests in my living room. The radiant and mischievous smiles of my grandchildren, Kiana and Joey, peeking into a fish tank. Little Lucas, who I'd never met, wrapped in a newborn blanket asleep. They appeared in my room with the caring touches of a pencil. These faces, soft and wrinkled, I sketched as gifts for future birthdays or holidays. They brought my family close enough to touch.

I got a notebook but threats stopped me from writing about the case. I noted who passed along the river under my balcony and stepped onto a cement pad with outdoor fitness equipment for public use. Everyone that walked there received prayer. I named it *The Mat*. Many came daily for prayers they never knew I spoke. The man with one leg who always carried a white bag. A group of men who stood every morning waiting for a work bus. The child who ran in circles around the poles while her mother stayed close. A group of grandmas stretching in unison. An elderly man who flung his suit jacket over a bar while he exercised. And agents who stepped on and off *The Mat* while on duty. They were my new community.

I would have joined them but seldom went outside where conversations lead to awkward questions like, "Where's your husband?"

—*Kevin*—

Listening to others discuss their crimes surprised me. Some denied them or felt they didn't deserve prison. Others accepted their punishment even if innocent. A few tried to fight the system. Everyone coped in different ways. Prison sobered us all since deep inside, we all were guilty of something.

Old Charles, a short well-fed policeman from a nearby county, cried for days after arriving in our cell. He begged and pleaded to see his daughter and family, not accepting the impossibility. I tried comforting him but rage controlled him. He'd believed in justice, never understanding how corrupt the system was until he became its victim. The longer Charles waited, the angrier he became. His leaders pilfered money yet he claimed to be the suffering scapegoat. Charles begged for a law book and out of pity, Guard Yang bought him one. Charles looked up every law applying to his case, writing copious letters the prison ignored. Frustrated without answers he prayed at the cell door, bowing his head at fixed times while performing rituals. Not getting results he changed locations, praying on his bed. I tried to talk to him but he brushed me off. His next desperate attempt was throwing fortune-telling coins smuggled in for him, hoping for a favourable reading. When nothing worked, Charles made two cardboard voodoo dolls of his bosses and stabbed them viciously with a pointy yogurt straw and then, in a fit of anger, stomped on them. I walked over to observe and when he saw me watching he stomped harder.

Charles got a 10-year sentence, reduced to 5 years after an appeal. The warden told him that was good. Furious, he had to feign happiness until his transfer. After he left, his popular law book circulated the cell and occasionally inmates getting an IV had a peek.

As I listened to cell chatter, I realized there were five former policemen in my cell! No one complained that former officers and privileged prisoners got special treatment. I never saw jealousy. Others accepted it because it was the same outside prison. Privileges varied from pen and paper, outside food, eye masks, to a chance to smoke in the guard's office or cage. I wanted a pen because I didn't trust the guard's records of my spending.

Old Zhang noticed and lent me his. After a few weeks, Old Ding gave me my own. Thrilled, I kept food statistics, recorded consular visits, books I read, quotes from books, and personal reflections. I documented each time we went into the outdoor cage–six of ten days. During morning readings, I wrote sermons. A school, a church, or people I knew came to mind and I crafted each one for that specific audience. I ended up with hundreds. After writing, I prayed the message would reach its destination even if I never did.

❖

"Henry Gao!" He ran to the cell door and grabbed a document an official handed through the bars. I sat up. He signed and handed it back, receiving a second paper. Too scared to look at the verdict, Henry stood by the bars in shock. He took a deep breath then flipped to the last page, fixated on the final paragraph which summarized the sentence. "Five years and a fine!" As the words came out, he shook and tossed the document onto a nearby cot. "I didn't know there were proper procedures or that reselling medical equipment to make extra money was illegal!" His shaking intensified and we tried to comfort him. *Is he innocent or guilty?* None of us knew.

"Henry," I said, "No matter what, you can pray and find hope in God."

He stopped shaking and looked at me. "I want to believe like you."

"Ask God for help to get through the sentence. Look for other Christians in the big prison. God will help, teach, and protect you. If you've done something wrong, tell God, and he will forgive you. And when you get out, you can tell your wife and teenage son and encourage them too.

"Yes, I will."

❖

We talked daily after that. On Henry's final morning, the escort guard's late arrival gave me one last chance to encourage him. "You are my friend. But most of all, you are God's friend and he is going with you. He has a plan for you and friends waiting wherever you go. You will find them."

"Thank you, Old Gao." His endearing term *Old Gao* touched me because it meant I was his friend. He picked up his small bundle, and stood in silence as the guard secured the handcuffs and led him away to join the busload of prisoners heading to *the big house*. I picked up the bookmark he left for me. *To Dear K.G., Good luck! Get well soon! Enjoy special long vacation. Can remember my friend. Yours sincerely. H.G. 2015.6.14.*

❖

The big house was a hot topic in the cell because most ended up there. Fresh news circulated because *the big house* couldn't house inmates with serious medical conditions so they came back to our wing. I absorbed every detail in case I went too.

"When I was in *the big house*," said a drug addict to another prisoner, "they forced us to make clothes and shoes in prison factories and bused us there and back. We ate in a cafeteria and slept in rooms with rows of bunk beds. At the beginning, you give five numbers to the guard and those are the numbers you can call when you aren't working. If you can't remember any then you can't call anyone. A few privileged prisoners get short family visits. Most people like me got none. It's better than here because work makes days go faster and you aren't confined to one room, but it's tough because the sentences are so long."

❖

God, please help Henry. My early morning prayer and reading routines helped me cope. I treasured every message, reading them many times to let each word rest in my heart. I examined every photo, even the tiniest details. This month's stash included a beautiful handwritten poem from Ma & Pa, and a photo of my new grandchild Lucas, born on May 1, lying in the arms of his proud big brother Joey and big sister Kiana. Lucas came into the world weeks before I got the news. In a cell with despair close enough to taste, when that first picture came I passed it from prisoner to prisoner. The beauty of new life revived us all! I shared his name, and they tried to say it but struggling with the 'L' sound, Lucas sounded more like Roocus. Reminding us of life outside bars and new beginnings, that tiny child wrapped in a blanket gave us courage. He was a promise. When life steps into darkness in even the tiniest ways, hope swallows suffering, joy swallows despair, and dreams revive. The day Lucas came to our cell we smiled.

Ordinary news of daily life beyond prison walls restored my soul. I read Sarah's comforting words, chuckled at Hannah's jokes, and stared at Uncle Phil's card with a silly dog in an inner tube. In June's books, I noticed *from the library of Fred Fulford* stamped inside each cover. Tears came as I turned the pages, inspired and honoured that the man who married us and gave wise counsel through the years, sent the best from his library without knowing if he'd ever get them back. *For me?* The books became gold in my hands, the daily bread that fed my soul in prison. I will never forget!

Julia wrote reassuring messages on blank business cards, one for each day in the month, all stacked in order in a soft plastic box. Each morning after breakfast I touched her handwriting as if she were with me and read one card. The cards were a treat and I never wanted to spoil the daily surprise.

❖

In July, Julia got bolder and wrote on both sides of the cards. One side was a diary of her life on bail and the other had a word of encouragement or promise. When I realized, I read them all at once as one story, then daily as usual. My cellmates liked Julia's cards even though they couldn't read English. They never complained and I shared all my news with them. The whole cell looked forward to my consular visits, hoping I'd return with magazines, photos and messages.

When new pictures arrived, they boasted, "Oh that's your eldest son, isn't it?" or "That's your Chinese daughter." Life flowed through messages. When a cotton undershirt arrived at the cell I didn't notice the tiny heart on the tag at first but when I did, I cried and never washed that shirt again. Julia occasionally drew miniature hearts in books the Embassy brought. I always searched. When I found one, it was as if we were together and each one was a kiss. Each tiny penciled heart made the hunt worthwhile.

Sometimes I circled letters or keywords in the table of contents writing cryptic love messages. *Will the Embassy give the books back to her? Will she notice?* I folded page corners with passages underlined to express my heartfelt agony and secret joys. I never stopped trying to communicate.

❖

Prison was better and worse than isolation. No pressure of daily interrogations or grueling assignments with my mind spinning through details unable to rest. No sudden fear and dread that latched on again and again during interrogation. In the cell, there was chatter and activity. Accomplishment meant getting a stool into position, folding a blanket like the others, or showering while the water was hot. In isolation, when interrogations ended for the day I was alone in silence, wrestling with meaning and trying to order my private world without community. In prison, I was one among many, juggling for my turn but belonging to a group. In isolation, the psychological suffering was intense and unrelenting. The pressure to complete impossible memory tasks and the daily failure to produce satisfactory confessions tied knots in my brain and brought insanity near. In prison, the deepest agony was sociological and physiological; men crammed together, suffering and experiencing the slow breakdown of our bodies through prolonged indefinite neglect.

29

THE LAWYER

You desire speed but cannot
reach your destination.

—CHINESE PROVERB

—*Kevin*—

I complained to Wang Ting. "No lawyer after eleven months!"
"Kevin, that's normal. Lawyer and family visits are complicated in China. You can't see a lawyer in a black jail because those jails don't exist. There are no lawyers during investigations because appointed interrogators are gathering evidence and testimony, and formal arrest when the case transfers to a prosecutor comes later. They don't want lawyers to interfere while they gather evidence, no matter how many extensions. Family visits are impossible until verdicts are finalized and then it's one chat for 20 minutes using wall telephones through glass walls. People with better relationships with the guards might get 40 minutes or an hour."

"That's unbearable." *It's insane and unreasonable!*

"Yes," he whispered so others wouldn't hear, "Wang Shu has not seen his wife and 12-year-old daughter for over 6 years and is still waiting for his final sentence."

Separation tortured many in my cell. Wealthy prisoners with status and the required permissions to hire and see lawyers could send occasional verbal messages to their families. Most had state-assigned lawyers. Few prisoners had even one family photo.

—*Julia*—

On Day 345, our Chinese lawyers arrived from Beijing and checked into the local 5-star hotel. Mine couldn't speak English so Peter came home to help translate. We met in their hotel room.

"Hello Mrs. Garratt and Peter. I'm Mr. Pan, Kevin's lawyer, and this is your lawyer Mr. Wang. I tried several times to see you but couldn't get access until now. I will leave you with Mr. Pan. Chinese law prevents me from listening to the testimony of connected cases."

"Thank you for coming."

Mr. Wang smiled. "Thank you for letting me take your case. Let's begin with your story." He scrawled on a notepad as I spoke. Peter sat on the hotel room bed and translated.

"I still don't know why they held me for six months and now I have many restrictions, can't work and have no ID or documents." With no concrete evidence connecting me to the charges, Mr. Wang had pieced my case together from bits and pieces he'd read and heard. Thirty minutes sped by without any clarity. I signed and fingerprinted his notes knowing they said nothing conclusive or helpful to my case. Mr. Wang's gentle manner impressed me but I sensed he didn't know what to do next. *There is no case. What a waste of money and time.*

Mr. Pan reappeared. "When are you meeting Kevin?" I asked.

"I'll review the case files tomorrow morning at the MSS office, see Kevin in the afternoon, and can meet you afterwards."

❖

The Canadian Embassy had asked our family to hire Chinese lawyers early on but I knew nothing about the process.

"With no idea how to find one," Peter explained, "Simeon's friend said he knew one but couldn't remember the name. After an internet search for prominent lawyers in Beijing, James Zimmerman's name came up. James (Jim) spent 17 years in China assisting many businesses involved in legal disputes. Simeon contacted him and heard back within minutes. James recommended Mr. Pan and Mr. Wang was another partner in the Beijing firm.

"Jim was incredible! He not only made the referrals but took a personal interest in our case, offering his services to our family as a consultant. I went to Beijing to meet him and later, when Simeon came in November expecting Prime Minister Harper to solve the case,

James sent a car to pick Simeon up. He stepped in when we had no idea what to do!"

This American *Good Samaritan* stepped into a role for two Canadian strangers with not only professional expertise, but with his heart. Unfamiliar as we were with law and the Chinese court system, his knowledge, skills, insight and assistance proved invaluable. His kind words of encouragement brought hope to a family grappling with unknowns. Behind the scenes, Jim pursued multiple options to keep the case on the table with both Canada and China. He wrote to top Chinese officials highlighting how our unusual case had grave implications for foreign small to medium sized business owners throughout China. He recommended proactive diplomatic solutions. He advised and consulted with our Chinese lawyers, standing in when we had no representation. His personal friendship with the Canadian Ambassador in Beijing, having met him at the Catholic Mass held in the Canadian Embassy, and his excellent relationship with top Chinese officials, paved the way for frank and ongoing dialogue on both sides of the case. God put Jim, our American *Good Samaritan* lawyer, in the right place at the right time.

—Kevin—

On Day 346, Tuesday, July 16, 2015 an escort guard arrived. *It's the wrong time for a consular visit.* Fastened into a Tiger Chair in an unfamiliar first-floor room, a stranger stared through the bars.

"I'm Mr. Pan, your lawyer. I work in a Beijing law firm and your family hired me to represent you. I came to Dandong 11 months ago but was refused access. Even now, I can't have the case files. The MSS allowed me to read unclassified files in their office this morning. Unfortunately, I couldn't copy or keep them. Please tell me your story."

His English was excellent and for the first time I felt hopeful. *I can talk to someone on my side.* Mr. Pan wanted to understand my perspective. I liked this 40-year-old man. *Maybe I can write Julia a message.*

"We came to help China and aren't spies. We did Christian non-profit work and ran a local coffee shop." I summarized 30 years in China and our recent work in Dandong and North Korea. "And as for the charges, the interrogators keep hinting there is something political and coach me before Embassy visits to push Canada harder. But I don't know what they are referring to. Our coffee shop had international, diplomatic, and NGO customers because of its proximity to North Korea and many were high profile to China, but I had no formal relationship with them. Most customers were locals."

Mr. Pan scribbled notes. Congenial and kind, he mentioned that since this was a state security case there were limitations but he, and his partner representing Julia, would do their best. Mr. Pan wasn't overly concerned with the serious charges and said the evidence was minimal. His professional tone calmed me. I signed and fingerprinted his handwritten notes with confidence even though I couldn't check the Chinese. *I can trust him.* Mr. Pan made me feel safe, renewed my hope and increased my determination to survive.

He couldn't discuss Julia's case but offered to transcribe a note.

"Can I write it myself?" After hesitating, he agreed. With hands clamped to the tray, I produced a shaky-looking note, imagining Julia's joy when she recognized the handwriting. At the bottom, I added a brief greeting for my mother. Despite feeling stiff and achy when the guard unlocked my handcuffs from the tray, my voice had been heard. Mr. Pan was excellent. *I won't be detained much longer.*

—Julia—

At 5 p.m. Mr. Pan accepted my invitation for noodles and handed me Kevin's note. His shaky handwriting disturbed me. *Why can't he write properly? Is he ill? On medication?* I tucked the note in my purse and read it again the minute I got home.

Julia, love and miss you so much. Not very nice here but I'm ok. Please send more books. I should get them, and one small comb. Nights are hardest. I'm looking up but it's hard. Love, love, love you. Miss the hearts in the snow. —Kevin.

—Kevin—

After meeting Mr. Pan, I expected progress but nothing changed. Summer was hectic in the prison and transfers more frequent. One stifling August morning, an extra cot arrived. The cell designed for ten cots now had 14 squeezed together. The newest inmate was a loan shark who talked like a Chinese mafia member. The guard put his cot in the best spot by the window. The prison capitalized on those who had power and lots of money to pay for extra privileges. He'd killed a man who refused to pay his debt, in a sword battle.

"He owed me money so I'm happy he's dead," he boasted. He only lasted two days in our cell and I didn't miss him. Inmates guessed he'd get 15 years for manslaughter.

Shazi (Crazy Fool), a disruptive drug addict took his cot. Recovering from stomach surgery, he screamed at night, pounding on the bars disturbing everyone and pleading for pain killers. Finally, a guard and night-duty doctor arrived to pacify him, but his persistent blood-curdling screams left me wondering if he'd survive. His pain rippled through all of us, disrupting our sleep. With a bandage wound around his entire stomach, he couldn't get up for inspection but no one bothered him. Nurses re-wrapped his blood-soaked bandages every few days, exposing his huge, rough wound without clear surgical lines. I wanted to comfort him but the suffering swallowed my words. *Jesus, the pain is too extreme.*

Shazi recovered from the surgery but his erratic behaviour continued. In desperation, he ripped pages from a magazine into shreds, ground them into small bits, and tried to sniff them to get a high from the ink. Arrogant and loud, my cellmates shunned him. I pitied him, a hopeless suffering man without friends. When another drug addict in the cell, saw me praying for Shazi he lifted his shirt revealing a stomach that looked like someone had scribbled. Shazi wasn't the only one suffering. *What kind of nightmarish surgery have these people had? Even if pain kills me I'm not opting for surgery.*

"It's common," Shazi explained, "to have poor care in hospital because criminals can't pay much. I couldn't pay anything."

The cell banter continued. "What goes on here or in local hospitals is nothing compared to black jails," said Big Boss, a convicted thief. "More than half the inmates in this prison have been in one. People disappear and weeks or months later, resurface here. Interrogators beat them, deny food, sleep, medication and much worse until they confess. We don't talk about it but we all know. One man who wouldn't give in was held six months until he broke. I got out after a few days." He looked down, avoiding details of his firsthand experience.

Big Boss and his accomplice in another cell, knew people. Since wealth and status gave him privileges, he wasn't afraid to talk. Every few weeks an unfamiliar guard dropped off treats like bread and cookies. A loner in the cell, he never shared or traded food with anyone but me.

"I'm sorry about your transfer. I will pray for you." I said before he left to serve five years. Despite his crimes, in a strange way Big Boss had become family. "

"Oh, it's like changing jobs. You change your jobs every five years or so. This is similar." He brushed it off and kept a cheerful face as they led him away.

A tall elderly cellmate took his cot the same day. Pointing to some small pieces of paper he whispered to me, "I'm writing my story of my 40 days in a black jail. About how they mistreated, beat me, and denied me food and insulin for periods of time, even though I'm diabetic. And now the court has given me 18 years but I'll smuggle these notes out before my transfer."

"What did you do?"

"Stole 1,000,000 RMB from a government department!"

❖

Sweltering heat is not good for criminals packed in cells like sardines. On Day 355, a sizzling hot Thursday afternoon, a fight erupted next door. Guards came running in response to yelling, screaming, cursing and banging. We heard something crash and break.

"Move him to Cell 318," a guard yelled and several guards dragged Pangzi (Fatty), the instigator, into our cell, chaining him to the only cot fitted for chains. With hands and feet bound, Pangzi sat with his legs straight in front. He could lie down but nothing else. When he calmed down, Pangzi told us the fight was over food. He was the size of a sumo wrestler so it didn't surprise us! After 36 hours shackled to the cot, they moved him beside me.

"Hi, do you want food?" I offered to make peace, scared he might roll over in the night and squash me since our cots were so close. He took the food and boasted he could do the splits.

"Ok then, do it." He went to the aisle and did the splits as we stared in disbelief! After four months in our cell because he'd stolen a motorcycle for drug money, the guard collecting him joked, "See you again next time!" as if he was a regular.

❖

Prison was one endless timeout. Our environment kept us weak and dependent. We weren't supposed to get strong. Chronic pain was normal and we suffered continuously. Chief noticed my deterioration month-by-month at consular visits, and after the family pushing for an assessment for months, Chief made special arrangements for an MRI and CT scan at a reputable hospital. His plans to bring me in and out incognito were disrupted after the CT scan. The MRI machine was broken. After frantic calls, we transferred to a less efficient hospital. Cellmate's hospital stories swirled in my head and the loud banging of the MRI machine terrified me. Lying immobile unable to speak, I wondered if I'd go home.

The prison doctor brought the results. "Extensive musculoskeletal and neurophysiological damage in your neck, back, and legs and the brain scan showed inconsistencies."

"What does that mean?"

"It's not life-threatening," he said. *Not yet!* He told me to endure and offered intermittent painkillers. Wondering what the real diagnosis was and coping with chronic pain consumed me, fueling recurring thoughts that dying would be preferable. I was not alone thinking this.

When Guard Yang announced a new rule that we must sleep with hands visible at night because another inmate had slit his wrists under the blanket, we all identified with the despair. Guard Yang removed the can lids we'd hidden behind a broken tile by the sink to use as knives for cutting food. He'd ignored them until now.

❖

On Day 360, after another full month in excruciating pain, I begged for help. After three days, guards took me for an in-house X-ray. In the hallway, a mentally and physically challenged man in his late 20s stumbled by, needing two inmates to help him walk. A guard spoke to him. *He can only moan and grunt to communicate.* Prison was no place for him. His hopeless condition distressed me. I overheard he was having his annual health check and X-ray. The prison forced inmates to pay once a year for a medical and everyone knew it was a money grab. *How many other prisoners are in such bad shape?* I prayed a desperate prayer and had my X-ray.

❖

I liked the cage at first with its rush of fresh air. Now when the cage door opened, I forced myself to go out. My hands hung limp beside me as my body struggled to push through 30 minutes. The short stool was worse than standing. *I hate this miserable endurance test.* On Day 365, the one-year anniversary of our disappearance, I dragged my aching body to the far end of the cage, trying to control my tears. Holding onto the bars I hid my face and cried. As I stared at the mounds of hard brown dirt between us and the next wing, poking through the dirt in front of me was a dandelion. *How amazing to see yellow! Did God put that dandelion there just for me?*

In the drab grey cell that dandelion renewed my hope that God was at work. The cell mood had been somber recently and many cellmates had silent days or cried with faces buried in the cot. The drug addicts exploded in rage, but most of us hid our pain and feelings unwilling to risk moving from our privileged cell. In this melancholy atmosphere, no one flinched when guards squeezed in another drug addict holding his stomach and writhing in pain. When we discovered this 20-year-old had feigned sickness to get in and was proud of it, anger erupted. Guard Yang heard the disturbance and lost it with this faker, putting a stool on his cot and sitting on it, mocking him as he groaned. The unexpected spectacle entertained us for over an hour but no one dared laugh or comment.

❖

Wisps of life before prison circulated the cell. We celebrated every fragment of outside news. Our stories wove together in moments of comfort and compassion that soothed the guilty and the innocent. And every day we hoped for kindness.

In late August, Guard Yang had health issues. A senior guard used to prisoners, replaced him. That afternoon Guard Chen announced we'd walk around the inner perimeter of the prison to collect garbage. *Beyond the cage?* Like school children preparing for a field trip we rushed into a line. Equipped with plastic garbage bags we stepped into the large dirt courtyard surrounded by its heavy prison wall. *There isn't any garbage,* He pointed to some edible weeds which inmates eagerly plucked from the ground to wash and eat later. We passed the prison kitchen and Guard Chen let us grab a few cucumbers from a storage unit. Later we broke the cucumbers into chunks and had a feast! Our first field trip was a success!

❖

Our joy dissipated two weeks later when Guard Chen burst in ready to beat us. "Traitors!" he yelled with fire in his eyes. "Everyone pack your things! You are leaving this cell. No one makes a fool of us! Joe and Old Ding smuggled messages out through their lawyers and we caught them. All of you will suffer for this!"

In a sudden panic, everyone stuffed their few possessions into small bins and rolled their cotton pads. I packed too, scooping a few spare clothes, photos, and dried food from weekly orders into my bin. I stacked my Bible, Rick Renner's *Sparkling Gems*, and Larry Crabb's *66 Love Letters* on top.

Guard Chen noticed. "Except you," he said softening his voice a notch, "only you can stay here."

I wasn't relieved. Everyone left, and I was alone. *I don't want new 'cellies'.* The thought scared me. When Guard Chen passed by later I asked, "Who will I talk with? Those were my friends."

"Don't worry. Some will return."

He was right. After lunch, Wang Ting, my pen and paper mate Old Zhang, and a few others returned. I felt better. From then on we were searched if we left the cell. I worried about Joe but no one dared mention *the incident.* But Old Zhang wasn't swayed. He paid a guard to smuggle messages tucked inside bananas, to his mistress in another cell, and succeeded in smuggling his black jail notes out to his son.

Old Ding disappeared but I saw Joe in an outdoor cage in the 200s wing across the courtyard. He yelled and waved, and I gave him a thumbs-up. I missed having him in our food group.

30

UNDERCOVER

The jail is closed day and night and always full;
temples are always open and still empty.

—CHINESE PROVERB

—Kevin—

I*'m here for a reason.* My story stepped into their stories of crime and guilt, of justice and injustice. I brought a message of hope and promise—a future beyond me that offered restoration, peace, and truth with nothing hidden—even for those facing long prison sentences or execution. China had watched us for 30 years, in seven different cities, but in the cell, it was intense and personal. Everyone noticed.

As I scrawled a note stating that 397 prison days passed slower than my 55 years put together, the big-boned female prison warden appeared. She'd shown concern for my international case, knowing she'd be responsible if anything bad happened. She seldom visited our wing, so I guessed she had important news. I heard my name and stood up.

"Kevin Gao, I see you reading your book every morning—the Bible." She paused. My heart leapt. *Will she take my Bible?* "That's good!" she said as if spitting the words to ground. Then she turned and walked off. Relieved, I smiled. *The prison warden has announced to everyone that reading the Bible is good!*

Word got around. On the way to the next consular visit my transfer guard said, "I see you reading the Bible every day. My wife and my daughter are Christians." *Is he a Christian too, but unable to tell me?* Elijah pursued by Jezebel, languishing in the desert complained to God he was alone but was reminded there were many like him. *I am not alone either!* There were always signs. Early on a man in street clothes had arrived at my cell door asking for me. Not a guard or inspector,

he showed genuine concern about my conditions and health. I asked
who he was but he only said, "A friend asked me to look in on you." I
guessed a well-connected friend sent him. *Or was he an angel?*

❖

On November 6, 2015, a chilly Friday morning and Simeon's birthday,
a female court official appeared at the cell. "Wang Ting!" I jumped
as he rushed over! I wanted to follow but didn't dare. Everyone sat
up straight listening as the woman handed papers through the bars.
"Sign and give them back." she said.

"What's my sentence?" He signed the first paper and clinging to the
bar with one hand, slid it back to her.

"I don't know." She slipped the second document between the bars.
Eerie silence filled the cell as we waited for the verdict.

Wang Ting turned to the back page. His face froze and he couldn't
speak. The official's footsteps faded away. Wang Ting sat on his cot and
buried his head in his hands, tossing the document onto the wooden
board. *God, help him.* Old Zhang walked over and picked it up. "They
denied the appeal. Wang Ting has to serve the full 5.5-year sentence."

Wang Ting's sobs burst into the room. We were *cellies* for ten
months. *What can I do? He is guilty.* Old Zhang circulated the document and everyone commented on their own cases and guessed their
verdicts. The conversation buzzed around me as I watched Wang Ting
suffer. I didn't dare talk while he was so distressed. His transfer would
take three to four weeks. When lunch arrived, I offered to share but
he refused. The warden pitied him and offered him a delay. "No." he
said, "I want to start the sentence because in *the big house* you get 20%
off for good behavior and I'm desperate to see my wife and daughter
as soon as possible."

The day before his transfer, I sat on his cot. A small red, white
and blue nylon woven bag held his thin cotton pad, plastic bowl and
spoon, and a change of clothes. He'd given away his tattered books and
leftover food. His freshly washed and folded prison uniform waited at
the end of his bed for reassignment. "If I can help your family any way,
let me know," I offered. His petrified gaze oozed sorrow and shame.

"The only hope you have is Jesus. Always remember you can call on him for help any time." He asked me to explain.

The next morning after corn congee and steamed bread, Wang Ting perched at the end of his cot waiting. His fear-filled eyes and worn pale face showed he'd aged in prison. He asked if God could help a criminal like him. I shared about my first encounter with God in the forest. "I needed that relationship to get through prison," I said.

He listened. "I'm always sad. Nothing makes me happy now. I can't bear this sentence but I must. My wife and daughter..."

"Tell me your wife's phone number. If I'm out before you I'll try to contact them and tell them how much you love them." He whispered the phone number and I wrote it three places in my Bible. The guard came 45 minutes late so we spent the whole time talking. His heart opened. I didn't want to say goodbye. It was a sad day, but he left hopeful.

❖

I missed Wang Ting. At least 60 prisoners had passed through the cell. New inmates tried to be macho and brave when they first arrived but some couldn't cope and cried. I listened and comforted them or invited them to my food group. Some shared, others stayed silent.

A prison cell is a society in miniature. Everyone has their role and status and must conform. There are rich and poor, powerful and weak. People without money are lowest on the pecking order. Some, like gang members and policemen, usurp the newcomer ranking because of status outside the prison and bribery. Some want friendships even with risks; others trust nobody.

Without choosing the role, I became the cell pastor people went to for hope. The guards were supposed to double as counselors but didn't take the role seriously and had no training. When prisoners got sentences, the duty guard took them into the hallway in handcuffs and they sat on stools chatting. If they cried or got emotional, he moved them to his office to calm down or encouraged them saying, "This sentence is not bad. Maybe I can call your family for you."

But many turned to me for comfort.

❖

One morning, staring through the cell door hoping to see Joe, I noticed a man in a bright neon yellow vest. "He's special," whispered a cellmate. "He embezzled money from his school." When an older gentleman in a yellow vest came in from the IV room after lunch, I was extra curious. Cellmates congregated in the cage to smoke and chat with him. He acted happy. "Young Jo," I asked, "Why the yellow vest?"

"The vests have different meanings. Purple for contagious diseases like AIDS. Orange and grey are regular. Red, blue and white striped uniforms are for inmates in the final months of sentences. They serve food, unload trucks, room together and get extra food. And," he paused and whispered, "yellow vests are for those facing execution. They stay in this prison until the last day."

I took a deep breath and eyed the man smoking in the cage. I'd never met someone facing execution.

"And he's happy," Young Jo said, "because he's pretending. Rumours say that those sentenced to execution get cigarettes and alcohol in their last weeks to relax them. He might have access to that. I'd need them too if I was a government official caught manufacturing drugs, and selling them from another location."

I watched him chatting but a fear in his hollow brown eyes told a darker story. *What a waste of a life.* Sickened, I paid more attention to the vests. No wonder cellmates tried to stop me from sharing food with inmates in purple vests. That night when I shut my eyes a yellow vest appeared. I shuddered. *Will I ever see the man in the yellow vest again?*

❖

Young Jo replaced Old Ding as the cell leader. We chatted and paced during the rest period when everyone else slept. He spoke English which was rare in prison. "The manager of the clinic where I worked cheated my father and I out of money. In retaliation, I broke a glass office door. A night security guard investigating, cut himself on the glass. I offered to pay for the window but the manager accused me of injuring the guard on purpose and put my father and I in prison. The manager is the guilty one! What did you do?"

Many prisoners had shared their stories with me, but he was the first who dared ask about mine.

"Nothing," I answered, "I'm falsely accused of spying. I've never worked for any government agency." I explained our work in China. "I took photos but nothing related to spying."

"Everyone who claims innocence is guilty of something," he said and not wanting to discuss it more, I changed topics. Young Jo had attended a house church in another city for two years but got disillusioned. We talked and he borrowed my Chinese Bible when I wasn't using it. Over time, our friendship grew as we grappled with faith in prison.

❖

At times, the Bible seemed to say everything. Now. Wait. Persevere. Trust. Sometimes my longing for miraculous deliverance created deep disappointment and I wondered if prison was my final earthly destination. I read…*An angel of the Lord appeared, and a light shone in the cell. He struck Peter on the side and woke him up. 'Quick, get up!' he said, and the chains fell off Peter's wrists (Acts 12:7 NIV).* "Yes, Lord!" I said excited, hoping this was for me. "God, this is easy for you. You've done it before!" But it wasn't my story.

I cried to God many times a day, often many times a minute. Every time peace came. Words, phrases or timely passages connected me to aspects of God's character and his larger story, helping me trust and manage the debilitating pain. Sometimes pain gripped so tight my whole body radiated pain in an all-encompassing ache as if my body would one day have enough and collapse. One evening deep despair set in. Overcome with constant waves of pain and unable to sleep, I hummed an old hymn and stopped after the first phrase. *Take my life, and let it be…* I wanted heaven to rescue me.

For days, my eyes couldn't focus. The varicose veins on my legs protruded and I avoided looking at them, afraid they would burst and I'd watch myself bleed to death. My hands lacked strength and after pacing, hung limp and numb at my side. If I held a book, they tingled until they lost all feeling. *Will anyone save me? Does Canada care?* My head throbbed and pain pierced my chest. My irregular heart rate spiked high and low. The prison doctor kept trying new medicines but nothing helped. The pain intensified until I couldn't walk or stand. It was hard to see goodness in the waiting.

Painkillers were sporadic in Chinese prison but after appendicitis and chronic dizziness was added to my list of ailments, the nurse hooked me up to an IV. The alien drugs dripping through IV lines into my body for 12 days, added terror to my pain. More poking and prodding ensued and the prison doctor added two inguinal hernias to my list, and one, he insisted, was pressing on my colon. Nothing made sense. Chief told me operations in China were too dangerous for me so they wouldn't do surgery. I agreed but my problems persisted. The language barrier meant frequent confusion and guards overruled prison doctors concerning medicine and treatment. I never felt safe. As my health deteriorated, the prison decided I had to pay $5 per day for the cot since I needed more medical support. I'd slept on it for nine months. *Why charge extra now?*

The doctors, nurses, guards, and warden watched my deterioration but prison rules were hard to bend without bribes or power. My 400-day wait lacked focus. Disappointments stacked up and each minute was a battle. Perhaps someone prayed or the prison called the MSS or both but suddenly a breakthrough came. Julia was allowed another visit. Struggling to sit in handcuffs, unable to stretch and relieve my aching back, Julia's face and uplifting words broke into my suffering with hope and courage. Love flowing from her renewed my despairing soul. She started to sing. *Great is Thy Faithfulness, Oh God my Father, there is no shadow of turning with Thee, all I have needed your hand has provided. Great is your faithfulness Lord unto me.* The familiar hymn filled the meeting room as the guards and warden fell silent. Three verses without interruption infused the room with hope. When she finished, no one spoke. Then the warden told Julia she could hug me. I shuffled back to my cell astonished, overjoyed and determined to persevere.

The excitement was too much. I fainted and Skinny caught me just before I hit the cement floor. Joy mixed with pain swirled inside.

I revived, but couldn't overcome the dizziness. New anxiety pushed hope into a back corner. *Was that Julia's parting song and final hug before I died? Is this my last day on earth?*

I reached for the box of daily notecards and slipped the stack into my palm. Tiny gold stars sprinkled out. Julia had tucked them between the cards. I tried to pick up and save every single one! I was a different man in prison. One who desperately rescues even the tiniest confetti-sized gold star that falls to the ground or onto the bed. A man who reads a family message at least 100 times and cries over every word. A man to whom one faint penciled heart is a survival kit. I held tight to every act of kindness and I wouldn't let go. Hope nestled in each star, encouraging me to live.

I still longed for heaven but focused on preparations for the next consular visit. It was the only thing dependable. I transferred what I'd forgotten to say to my list, choosing and memorizing verses, writing birthday greetings and other words of encouragement. As the visit approached I paced daily with my list and memorized everything in order, adding verses that stood out in morning readings. This month I had a word for the consular officer as well.

When Adele transcribed my messages, I mentioned I had one for her and the consular team. *If anyone gives a cup of water to…one who is my disciple, truly I tell you that person will not lose their reward (Matthew 10:42 NIV).* She thanked me.

❖

One dark day in early December, the escort guards ushered me into the last room in a row of 20 identical rooms filled with prisoners facing lawyers or prosecutors. Two youngsters sat across from me. A short pudgy one, his red T-shirt soaked with sweat, sat beside a tall thin casual-looking man in a baggy grey T-shirt and sweatpants. Benji stood behind them.

"They are the prosecutors,' he said as they fiddled with stacks of typed notes. *You must be kidding!* "Your case is transferred from the MSS to the Procuratorate. That is the body that prosecutes you once the case moves to the court." I struggled to take them seriously.

"We represent the Procuratorate," the pudgy one said. In an

unprofessional and disinterested manner, he and his co-worker asked brief questions from evidence received from the MSS. *I've waited months for this switch. These inexperienced young men are my prosecutors?*

31

SURPRISE

One joy scatters a hundred griefs.

—CHINESE PROVERB

—*Kevin*—

Day 507, Thursday, December 24, I awoke aching for my children. If only the grandchildren were coming for games and appetizers. Just one giggle would help or a little hand in mine with Joey's small voice saying, "Hi Gampa!" and a handmade card from Kiana given with her biggest smile. I fingered the Christmas family calendar tucked in my Bible. The children were meeting in Edmonton and Sarah was making dinner.

"*Shèngdànkuàilè!* (Merry Christmas!)" An escort guard stood at the cell door. "Put on the handcuffs, the MSS is waiting."

I rushed over. He led me to a meeting room without a Tiger Chair. Relieved and hopeful I'd see Julia, I sat at a tiny desk as Chief fiddled with a video camera in the corner. "Julia's on her way," he said smiling as if reading my thoughts.

The achiness and pain slipped behind a backdrop of anticipation. Julia entered with Stephen and two overflowing grocery bags. Chief insisted she spread everything out for the video so she draped a piece of tinsel around the desk and pulled beef jerky, chips, candy, crackers, processed cheese, grape juice and a small pizza from the bags. My eyes opened wide when four glass bottles of iced latte appeared but the guard grabbed them before I spoke.

"No glass," he said.

"Can you pour them into a cup?" I pleaded like a child.

"Maybe later," he answered putting them into a bag.

We had half an hour to celebrate, so I focused on the snacks.

"Let's eat the pizza," I began.

"Good idea," Julia answered sitting across a small desk from me and serving me a pepperoni-covered slice, "They called me this morning and told me to get money ready. Ten minutes later, Stephen picked me up, drove me to a shop to buy treats, encouraging me to buy as much as possible. Then Stephen carried the bags since I'm not permitted to bring food but they can. They even wanted me to buy a Christmas tree, but I convinced them tinsel was enough. Then Stephen stopped at the new mall for this pizza. The place wasn't open but we slid into a booth and waited."

She smiled as I ate and didn't complain when I talked with my mouthful. "I didn't expect anything," I said and looking straight at Chief added, "It's so kind. Thank you."

He said nothing but looked pleased. "You can send a message to your family," he said turning the video on.

"Hi everyone! I love you and miss you all tons. I love every message and card. Never stop sending them because they keep me going. I hope to be home soon. Keep praying. And thank everyone who is praying and tell them not to stop. Never forget God is the wonderful counsellor, prince of peace, everlasting father, and the government is on his shoulders," I said, trying to encourage my family.

❖

Thirty minutes gave me enough joy to unpack for days. Guards rationed the leftover treats but even the iced lattes were poured into my plastic cup. No one received the video but news of our Christmas encounter crossed continents and made my parents smile.

On Christmas Day guards appeared again. Another visit? Excitement soon dissipated when I ended up in the Tiger Chair facing Benji and a well-dressed official-looking man who introduced himself as Judge Ning. "Your case is transferred to the court," he announced, "I am the presiding judge who will handle things from now on. No more applications for family visits are possible. I will inform you of the trial date when I hear from Beijing."

No visits? No trial date? Christmas Day passed with longing looks at family photos and the New Year crept without fanfare into the small world of my cell. My cellmates started discussing Spring Festival. Crime always increases before Chinese New Year as people withdraw cash for gifts, and shop with cash, making them targets for thieves. Crackdowns, trials and sentencings intensify too. On January 16, Day 530, an emotional distraught young guy transferred into our cell with rectal hemorrhaging. He was from another province, arrested with a group of 20 who met to gamble online on NBA games. He lost it when other inmates guessed he'd get 3.5 years for gambling $5000. I invited him to my food group and he shared his story.

"I ran a tea business, drove a BMW and have two sons, 6 and 8. I wish I'd never come to this province. A friend convicted for a similar crime in my province got away with a fine."

Between meals I shared my family photos and later his lawyer smuggled him some. He gave me a peek when no one was watching.

❖

Repeat offenders weren't popular. Simple was one of them. His Chinese name meant *forever simple* so everyone called him Simple. Caught with a hand in a woman's purse on a bus, this angry diabetic with syphilis and hepatitis had to sleep between two cots squeezed together since there was no room for another cot. Simple was determined to get a message to his sister through the lawyer not to put money onto his card to force the prison to pay his medical expenses. A few days later, the nurse caught him pretending to inject himself with his diabetic needle. He intended to aggravate his condition to stay in our cell. They removed him at once and when he returned he had to stand on a stool at the cell door letting the nurse give him injections until his ten-month sentence ended.

Just days before Chinese New Year, theft hit our cell. When non-medical prisoners left to clean the hallway, I noticed a newcomer sitting by another inmate's cot. He reached an arm under, grabbed something, and slipped his loot under his pajama top. Surprised, I watched him return to his cot, bend over as if his stomach hurt and hide an 8-pack of yogurt under his own cot. The second time I told the cell leader who watched him. Caught stealing paper next, they transferred him within an hour. When I asked where he'd go, Young

Jo said, "Somewhere else." I'd heard there were solitary confinement cells in prison but had never seen one. There was zero tolerance for stealing among cellmates.

❖

At Chinese New Year, the year of the monkey in a Chinese traditional twelve-year cycle of animals, our interim guard left and Guard Wang, a former soldier with a reputation for drinking too much, took over. Since his arrival coincided with a mandate to enforce strict new rules, he banned pens, smoking, and outside underclothes.

I knew the protocol. When new rules came, cellmates strategized innovative ways to get around them and guards often helped in return for cooperation or a cut of the money. Guard Wang was no exception. The *no smoking* rule and *no shaving* rule were handled the same. Guard Wang purchased cigarettes for inmates who smoked in the outdoor cage out of view of the camera or gave prisoners extra cigarettes for nights. They appeared to be washing their hands or chatting while the other prisoner blocked the camera's view as they smoked. Although pens were banned there was no rule about pen refills so Guard Wang gave refills to prisoners with permission for pens. Even Young Jo had to use a pen refill to keep records and orders. I joined the few privileged ones and we rolled torn magazine pages and used tape from a cookie package to wind around the refills, making them easier to hold. Young Jin's persistent bleeding from a botched surgery just before he entered prison, meant soaked surgical bandages needing replacement every day. He offered me a roll of his medical tape, which made a more durable refill wrap. When I recycled it for the second refill, I felt even better!

❖

As the second Chinese New Year in prison approached, I surprised my cellmates with a gift. I'd requested bilingual books and Chinese car magazines through the consular official the previous month and Julia arranged it. Excited, we passed time discussing cars we might buy when released, cheering each other up. My cellmates passed around the news and stories, reading and analyzing every word.

During holidays, the cage stayed shut, and food was substandard except for a few overpriced festival options. Lawyer visits stopped, so no one left the room. The smell was so bad that the nurses criticized everyone when they came to hook up IV's.

On Chinese New Year's Eve, Day 554, the closed-circuit TV broadcast a video of women prisoners singing and dancing seductively to disco music in a prison karaoke room. The scene switched to another room where women did similar dances on a large Kang bed that ran the length of their cell. The prison rebroadcast the entertainment several times and my cellmates laughed it off. Shocked and disgusted I wondered what else happened to female prisoners behind closed doors. One guy announced that in *the big house* a guard got a prisoner pregnant. The prison freed her and fired him. In our prison with cameras everywhere it was unlikely, but after Joe and the black plastic bag I wasn't so sure. I later learned there were no cameras in the ICU room at the end of the corridor where Guard Wang kept his uniform and a night duty guard slept. Everyone knew that.

❖

On February 17, Day 562, the Spring Festival holiday ended and I returned to the Tiger Chair facing my lawyer. Mr. Pan had changed. *What's wrong? Did someone threaten him?* Earlier he thought the case would be easy to resolve and the trial and sentencing would happen the same day. This time there was no cheery disposition and he was guarded and careful. He announced matter-of-factly that Beijing rejected the first indictment and a new harsher one was in progress, causing more delays.

As my health deteriorated, the prison decided I had to pay $5 per day for the cot since I needed more medical support. I'd slept on it for nine months. Why charge extra now?

He informed me he'd try to help but I saw fear in his eyes. *I hope he's not being investigated for defending me?* Even under God's caring umbrella the prospect of going to *the big house* terrified me. Our meeting was brief. I couldn't write a note for Julia but he said he'd touch base with her. He buzzed for the guard and left me sitting in pain until the guard arrived to undo the latches.

Ten days later, fastened in a Tiger chair in an interrogation room, Court Judge Ning delivered the revised indictment. No wonder Mr. Pan was afraid. The new crimes listed lead to long prison sentences or execution. A pit of darkness swallowed me and pain worse than all the physical suffering. Anger didn't work. Patience didn't work. Truth didn't work. Interrogators, prosecutors, interpreters, and now even lawyers were on one side; I was on the other. Injustice had its own pathway and its own destination. The suffering I lived with day after day, gripped my soul and wouldn't let go. *I will die in prison.*

32

A LOUD CRY

Not the cry, but the flight of the wild duck,
leads the flock to fly and follow.

—CHINESE PROVERB

—*Kevin*—

B ack in the cell, struggling to breathe, I grabbed my Bible. I
plunged into Daniel chapter 9. *God, where are you? Even my
lawyer has abandoned me.* As I read my panicked breathing slowed.
Daniel's heartfelt prayer recounting God's incredible history with
His people and pleading for mercy echoed my desperate cry. *Lord,
hear and act! For your sake, do not delay, because your... people bear
your name* (*Daniel 9:18,19 NIV*) sunk into my soul, fueling my plea to
heaven. I paused on chapter 10, mingling Daniel's pain with mine and
longing for revelation of heaven's master plan in my suffering. Daniel's
response to eat *no choice food for three weeks* resonated with me.

My choice to fast for three weeks gave me purpose. I needed heaven's
perspective so my earthly perspective wouldn't crush me. This strategy
came just in time. I'd fasted for a few days here and there but never
this long. Determined to start on March 1, after skipping breakfast,
something nice came for lunch so I hesitated then ate it and postponed
my fast. Upset, this happened for three days, so I didn't start until
March 4th. Unknown to me, that was the day of a consular visit.

I sent a message through Adele, asking Julia to read Dan. 10:2-3,
so she'd know my plan. When Young Jo asked why I wasn't eating, I
explained fasting was a discipline. Puzzled, he said nothing. When the
doctor asked if I ate, he answered, "Yes, he had yogurt." The doctors
were annoyed. Fasting made them look bad. I explained I wasn't trying
to harm myself but stay stronger. They didn't understand.

The 12th day of my fast, I decided it would be ok to eat a boiled egg a day. Eggs were a special order to the kitchen through the guard. The whole cell had to agree to the order because the minimum order was 100, and if the guard cooperated and passed the message on, the kitchen had to be in the right mood to cook them. I wrestled with the temptation to suggest an egg order but decided against it. Despite this, God was at work. Within an hour the kitchen staff came by selling boiled eggs, two bags with 50 in each. I told my cellmates we should buy them and everyone agreed. We divided the eggs, tucking our stashes under our cots. I took ten, one a day for the rest of my fast. That was the first and last time boiled eggs came to our cell door!

—*Julia*—

When Adele mentioned Kevin had stopped eating, I panicked until I read Daniel. *I, Daniel, mourned for three weeks. I ate no choice food, no meat or wine touched my lips; and I used no lotions at all until the three weeks were over. (Daniel 10:2,3 NIV)* Kevin wasn't on a hunger strike, he was fasting. I still worried his body was too weak and Adele's concern fed my fears. Kevin's deterioration and the recent, more serious indictment and now this fast, could be too much for him.

After multiple requests for Kevin's medical records to get an outside assessment the MSS lent me the MRI and CT scan. I contacted an American English-speaking doctor in China at the time. I'd spoken to him several times on the phone and his kind compassionate voice had calmed and comforted me. His selfless offer to help reassured me.

Although his offer to visit Kevin in prison was rejected, I got MSS permission to borrow and show him the scans. He reviewed them but explained he couldn't do more than recommend vitamins without seeing Kevin. Then, the doctor knelt on the floor leaning his arms on the seat of his chair, and started to pray. Peace filled the room and tears streamed down my face. His humility and true compassion touched my broken heart and I will never forget those moments. When I left, I felt lighter.

I needed that prayer. After 19 months, the case had taken a turn for the worse with no trial in sight. Kevin's health was in crisis and in mid-March my rent ran out leaving me nowhere to live. Jean had returned to the U.S. the previous November, and Peter had returned to Canada in January. I asked if the Canadian Embassy had emergency housing or a part-time job in Beijing if I got permission to wait there. The consular officer said I could apply for a crisis loan for rent but unwilling to end up in debt to the Canadian government, I prayed for another option. Within a week one came.

I gave away everything left in our apartment that I couldn't cram into a taxi and bumped over dirt roads to a half-constructed complex of buildings near a natural hot spring in the countryside. Our former coffee house cook and her husband were fixing it for retirement. The cooking facilities weren't hooked up yet and dirt piles and dump trucks lined the small laneways, but it was ideal for me. I had an open invitation to stay. What a precious gift! It even had a tub and hot-spring water a few hours each day. The bed was a traditional Chinese Kang bed common in northern China.

I walked around smiling but saying little to avoid uncomfortable questions. A foreigner living in the countryside is very noticeable with MSS agent cars parking nearby at odd hours. I didn't miss internet or TV as I settled into another quiet waiting season. Deborah called from Canada most nights with updates and I transferred her news onto notecards stacked up for Kevin's next consular visit.

When the first Saturday morning arrived, I was jolted out of sleep at 6:15 a.m. with banging on the door. Fear seized me as I rushed to dress and answer the knocks. *MSS agents?* When I opened the door, five strangers walked in. I breathed a sigh of relief. It was our cooks' family coming for a bath! Her mother, sister, brother-in-law and nieces arrived with food, plastic basins, toiletries and scrub brushes and bathed two at a time, water splashing all over the floor. Those wonderful people livened up my weekend!

—*Kevin*—

On March 19, I woke up hungry. Determined to continue my fast I distracted myself with the Bible.

Blessed is he whose strength is in you. Who have set their hearts on pilgrimage. As they pass through the valley of Baca (weeping) they make it a place of springs. The autumn rains cover it with pools. They go from strength to strength until each appears before God in Zion. (Psalm 84:5-7 NIV)

The words spoke life as if springs of living water poured over me as I read. After breakfast, I read Julia's March 19 notecard. *Our friend Anna sends these words for you. Psalm 84:5-7. The same words!* She didn't know but God knew! I wrote a note beside those words in my Bible so I'd never forget.

Six days later, Day 600 and the final day of my fast, Mr. Pan returned. I braced myself. "The trial will be soon. It will be a closed trial so no family or Embassy officials can attend." My stomach churned as excitement mingled with fear. It was no accident the news came the day my fast ended. I had another surprise when Mr. Pan relayed a message from Julia. Today was Good Friday and she was standing outside.

How amazing I had postponed my fast four days, and because of that it ended on Good Friday, the pivotal day in history when Jesus died on a cross and was resurrected after three days, giving everyone a way to choose new life! The incredible and comforting timing assured me I wasn't alone. *If I can just see Julia!* As I passed the reception room window I strained to look out. Through three sets of glass windows with rooms in between, across a small parking lot, on a hill behind a wall, I saw her standing on the road! She couldn't see me, but I saw her face and whispered *I love you* to the air. A sign from our apartment flashed into my mind. *Remember the little things because one day you may look back and realize they were the big things.* Today, heaven's care package was perfect.

—Julia—

Standing outside the prison for two hours, I prayed and paced the length of the outer wall. A van pulled up and a lady whisked a newborn out of the prison and into the van and it drove away. *Is the mother a prisoner?* I ached for her and hoped the police van was taking the baby to relatives. *Were they?* Another lady sat sobbing in a parked car near the gate with a man comforting her as he stepped out. *Is her husband in prison?* The out-of-province license plate indicated they'd come a long way. The man pulled a wad of 100 RMB bills from his pocket and walked to the gate house. Prison for Kevin cost almost $500 a month which for many people in China is a month's wage. What was *their* story?

Pain everywhere. I chose three small stones from the ground commemorating the day and dropped them into my jeans pocket. For many years, I'd collected small stones as markers to remember places and significant events. I usually chose one stone, but today was Good Friday and I wanted three to remind myself a resurrection day was coming.

With the blue sky stretched out above me I asked God for a sign. *Can't heaven touch earth just for a moment?* As I gazed, a white cloud, high in the otherwise empty sky, drifted towards the prison. As the wind blew it closer, its gentle wisps spread out in two pieces like giant extended arms in white draped cloth reaching out over the whole prison. God whispered. *I am with Kevin. I am with everyone in there.* Peace flooded me as I witnessed this spectacular reminder. Where I couldn't go, he went. What I couldn't do, he did. I stood in awe, thanking him.

When Mr. Pan emerged through the gate with news that Kevin had seen me, my joy was complete. It was a Good Friday!

❖

That night, I took a 14-hour overnight train to Beijing by myself. Jim had encouraged me to meet the Canadian Ambassador face to face. In trepidation, I'd asked the MSS for permission and they returned my passport for travel only, warning me not to mention the case to anyone except my Embassy and to notify them and return my passport upon return to Dandong. After no response from the Canadian Embassy about accommodation, Jim invited me to stay with his family and relieved, I accepted his generous offer.

Leaving Dandong still under restrictions meant eyes watched around every corner and plain-clothes agents sat beside me on the train. Sounds made me jump and I looked at everyone except children with suspicion. Jim sent his own driver to meet the train in Beijing and shuttle me to his house. When two friendly dogs and his kind wife Ellen greeted me at the door, I entered another world. In the safety of the Zimmerman home, Jim suggested I wrote to Prime Minister Trudeau about the night of our capture and present desperate situation. I didn't dare use a computer so wrote it by hand. Safe in their home, my heart settled. The kindness of the Zimmerman family and a homemade dinner, filled me with joy.

Jim kept saying, "Hang in there. China won't let anything happen to Kevin. We have to keep pressing Canada and China to come up with a solution." Full of gratitude I lay on the four-poster traditional wooden carved bed in their Beijing courtyard style house. Jim truly was a *Good Samaritan* – he brought me into his house and cared for me during the worst time. Disappointed Canada couldn't offer more I realized sadly that government policies, rules, systems and budgets didn't include care plans for falsely accused spies' travel and accommodations.

On Easter Sunday, Jim invited me to a family dinner and Easter Mass in the Canadian Embassy. At the last minute, the mass was combined with mass in a Chinese government church so I couldn't go. Sensing my disappointment Jim offered to drop me at another church. Nervous to go alone, he promised to pick me up an hour later for the family lunch. I sat in the back listening to songs but struggling to sing. I was a stranger in the middle of a case while everyone else was free. Then something unexpected happened. I saw a friend I thought I'd have no chance of meeting! She was at that church on Easter Sunday morning! Unable to concentrate on the songs, we skipped the service and spent the hour chatting in the lobby. My heart filled with gratitude at God's detailed kindness!

❖

Monday morning, Jim and I passed through several layers of security into a soundproof room at the Canadian Embassy where the Canadian Ambassador Guy Saint-Jacques, Sean, the new Consular Affairs Coordinator, and Adele, waited across a large boardroom table. "I'm so sorry for your ordeal," the Ambassador started, "I know it's difficult for you and we are working hard towards a resolution." The gentle wrinkles on his face and his kind words and genuine concern made me like him from the start. He only had a few minutes but I appreciated him taking time to see me.

"Thank you for your efforts. I know lots goes on you can't tell me. I wrote to Prime Minister Trudeau sharing from my heart what happened and I hope he can help," I explained handing him my handwritten letter.

He took it. "I will make sure the Prime Minister gets it," he promised and passed it to Sean.

"Thank you."

"I'm so sorry I only had a few minutes." He stood and apologized he had other scheduled meetings.

"I understand. I really appreciate you meeting me." His kindness meant so much.

The thick, heavy door sealed shut behind him. "So, what's the plan now?" asked Jim getting right to the point.

"There isn't one," said Sean, "It's a waiting game. We keep raising the case at every opportunity and hope the trial will be soon." That annoyed me. *The Canadian government has no plan?*

"Let's push the humanitarian issues and try to get him out on that. If we're lucky, they'll do the trial soon and give him time served and deport him," Jim continued, asking for copies of previous direct requests for release on humanitarian grounds and medical grounds made to China by Canada.

"We will look for them," said Adele with hesitation, making me wonder if they existed. *Has Canada asked for humanitarian release multiple times?* I left with mixed feelings. Canada didn't know what to do. It frustrated Jim that Canada wasn't pushing harder and exasperated me that no one had a plan. This forced immersion politics experience was a nightmare. I walked out noticing the empty walls of the Embassy building. *I wonder why they don't have Canadian art on the walls?* There was lots of space and art would make the building look more interesting and cheerful instead of formal and grey.

❖

Later that afternoon, disappointed with the lack of progress on the case, I left for Dandong. A kindergarten-aged boy sitting beside me on the train, pointed to my blue phone. "What's that?"

"A phone."

He laughed. "That's not a phone!"

"It is," I said pointing to the numbers. He'd only seen smartphones and this wasn't even a flip phone.

"Then let me call my father on it," he insisted. His mother sat opposite us busy texting.

"Ok, you can." He dialed his father. Shocked when it worked he told his Dad, "I'm talking on a super funny phone." I grinned. We spent the rest of the trip drawing together. As we rolled into the station he handed me his motorcycle drawing with lines under the wheels to show it was moving quickly. I smiled as I thanked him and tucked it in my bag glad that something was moving fast!

I arrived back in the countryside just as a young couple who lived in a garage on the ground floor, fired up a Chinese-style coal barbeque. "Join us," they invited. Chinese are so hospitable. They insisted so I agreed, wondering if they noticed the agent's car appearing around the corner of the building a few minutes after I arrived. Making friends was awkward.

"Why do you live out here?" they asked.

"I'm a teacher between jobs and my friend lent me this place."

"That's nice. Where is your husband?"

"He's not here right now." *What could I say? He's in prison half an hour away?*

"Oh, a business man."

"Yes, and aid work." I tried my best to answer them.

"That's awesome! Well when he gets back, we'll have a barbeque together."

"Thank you," They knew I was alone and I didn't want to be rude. I ate, then excused myself wishing I had my old life back and could have invited them to the coffee house. This case had changed everything.

I returned my passport to the MSS the next day. They reminded me to keep my phone charged so they could reach me. They always said that, and I always did since batteries on old phones last for days. One week later, on Friday April 15, 2016, Day 621 of the case, they called me to their office. "The Procuratorate has decided your case won't go to trial. Kevin's will be Wednesday, April 20," Benji said.

"Do I get a paper saying I'm free to leave? And my passport back?" I wanted something on paper to be sure.

"No, you don't need a paper. And you can't leave because you're a witness and the case is still ongoing. Get clothes for Kevin to wear and drop them at the prison."

"But they don't permit outside clothes. New regulations were posted on the guard gate this March."

"We'll arrange it." He called later with a guard's number.

❖

Money was tight but came when needed. I clutched an envelope Lily had slipped me with money from a mutual friend. Perfect timing. Enough for a month of prison expenses and trial clothes. Knowing he'd lost weight and guessing the size I picked pants, a shirt, underwear, and socks. I hoped the slip-on leather shoes returned by the prison would still fit. After a bus took me part-way I flagged a taxi since no route went that far out of town.

"Dandong Detention Centre," I said, uncomfortable saying the words.

"Oh, I know the way. I spent two years in that prison for drugs. Why are you going?"

"To deliver clothes," I said taken off guard.

"Oh, you have a friend in there?"

"Yes." I gave as little information as possible.

"That prison changed me. Prison life wasn't easy. I had to get off drugs in a cell with 28 others. Crammed together in a row on one long wooden Kang bed! Most prisoners were *druggies*. My family was rich, so I had easy access to drugs and luxuries! It ruined me. After release, I refused family money. Now I have a wife and teenager and work hard like everyone else. And it's better. I won't ever go back to the way I was."

His deep regret for the pain he'd caused his family moved me. I admired him. "Can you wait here for me. I'll be quick." I pulled the paper from my pocket. The guard answered and two minutes later was at the gate. He shook my hand. *Is he expecting a bribe?*

"Here are clothes for Kevin's trial," I said handing him the bag. He rummaged through searching for contraband or hidden notes.

"Do you know the trial date?"

"April 20. Can you tell Kevin?"

"Yes." He smiled and shook my hand for ages. I felt sorry offering nothing and added, "Thank you for taking care of Kevin."

33

THE TRIAL

A gem cannot be polished without friction,
nor man perfected without trials.

—CHINESE PROVERB

—Kevin—

On Friday, April 15, Judge Ning came with the mandatory three working days' notice that my trial was Wednesday, April 20. On Saturday, the duty guard informed me Julia had sent trial clothes. I looked with longing at the bag, like a child hoping for candy.

"Can I have them?"

"Not now."

The weekend passed in slow motion. I wrote pages of notes planning my defense. My mind raced. I couldn't sleep. *God, help me.* While others enjoyed weekend poker games, I sat or paced. On Monday, I prayed and waited in silence. On Tuesday afternoon, handcuffed and locked into the Tiger Chair, I faced a worried lawyer. Mr. Pan spoke as if reading a to-do list. I asked to send Julia a note but he shook his head.

"You can explain your side at the trial. I'll try to help but this case pertains to national security," he said glancing both ways as if being watched. "You can't bring paper, pen or notes into the courtroom. Memorize your defense in advance. We will hope for the best."

After the short meeting, I felt worse. *How can I defend myself alone and memorize my notes in one night?* Luke 12 came to mind. *When you are brought before synagogue rulers and authorities, do not worry how you will defend yourself or what you will say. The Holy Spirit will teach you at that time what you should say. (Luke 12:11,12 NIV)* Peace tried to break in but the battle raged. I tossed and couldn't sleep.

—*Julia*—

I checked into the Life Hotel near the coffee shop where we often housed summer volunteers and guests. Within minutes my phone rang. The interrogators asked where I was. *I'm sure they know!* They instructed me to meet in ten minutes in a black sedan on the road beside the store across the street. My heart pounded. What have I done? *Will they take me away until the trial ends?* I'd heard of that. Two well-dressed North Korean businessmen wearing Kim Jong Un pins stood beside me in the elevator. *Can they hear my heart pounding? Sense my fear?* I forced a smile and they nodded in unison. A packed parking lot stood between me and the black car. Deep breaths filled me with courage that seeped out with each step. The dark tinted windows gave no warning of who was inside as I zigzagged across the street darting traffic. A door opened and I got in. Three men.

"*Hǎo xiāoxi!* (good outcome)" said one. I felt a wave of relief. *We can leave after the trial?* My mind raced through joyful scenarios. "If nothing goes wrong at the trial you can return to see your family for a short visit." He spoke as if delivering wonderful news. "But, we are trusting you. Make sure nothing goes wrong at the trial. No media frenzy, no demonstrations, no crowds, nothing." *What? How can I control the trial? Why this offer?*

"If everything goes well we'll call tomorrow night with our decision. Once you agree to our conditions, we'll return your passport to buy tickets. You can't talk to any media or be in public places while you are home. Visit your family then return to China or the outcome for Kevin will be terrible." Their threats overshadowed the offer. I was sure the Canadian Embassy wouldn't agree to the terms.

"This is a special privilege. You must follow our instructions!" I got out and stood stunned as the car sped away. *The trial isn't the end. I don't want to go home without Kevin.*

Back in the room I clicked the lock and called Adele. She asked for details and recommended I accept the home visit–for a change of scenery. *A change of scenery? Hide in Canada and the Embassy encouraging me to do it?* I hung up baffled and the phone rang again. My sister. I launched into a description of the offer and Canada's puzzling response. Global Affairs Canada had contacted her. *The Canadian Embassy knew? Why did Adele seem surprised?* This entangling web of politics exhausted me.

I gazed at the Yalu river in the distance to refocus. This tenth-floor room had a view of the river, city, and the Dandong Intermediate Court building's shiny dome. Watching lights sparkling over the city, I forced myself to zoom out. I belong to a bigger story–a city story, a nation story, a God story. *I can't drown now–Kevin needs me. God, help me!* I lay on the soft bed, and drifted in and out of sleep. Before I knew it, the sun rose on Wednesday, April 20. Day 626. Trial day.

—Kevin—

I woke up at 3 a.m. and crept to the bathroom, keeping the humiliation to a minimum. Next I flipped through notes scribbled in the margins and half-written sermons tucked into sections of my Bible for today's readings. Family photos bookmarked my starting points. *Even though I walk through the valley of the shadow of death, I will fear no evil, for you are with me. (Psalm 23:4 NIV)* Unexplainable peace flooded me. *I will walk into that valley in a few hours.* I turned to my devotional book, Sparkling Gems. My eyes landed on the title for April 20. *Not Guilty.* How amazing! *China will pronounce me guilty, but God has already pronounced me not guilty.* I needed those words! Only God knew when Rick Renner chose that title 13 years earlier for his vignette on the trial of Jesus, that I'd read it in prison on the morning of my trial in 2016. *Everything is connected!*

When my cellmates awoke, my trial was the topic. Young Jin encouraged me and Young Jo told me not to worry. At 8 a.m. I was still in striped prison pajamas. *Where are my trial clothes?* At 8:20 a.m. the duty guard arrived and I reminded him today was my trial. He rushed to get my clothes, tossing the bag through the hole in the door. A new blue shirt, a navy sweater, a new pair of pants and a pair of real shoes! I fought back tears as I slipped my feet into the familiar padded insoles of my well-worn brown, leather shoes.

"Kevin Gao," barked an escort guard, "Hurry!" Always a last-minute rush. Two guards handcuffed and led me out as others wished me luck. Cellmates tried to be positive when people left the cell. In the reception area, the escort guards switched my handcuffs to transport handcuffs and added leg irons. Ouch! In leg irons, each shuffled step was painful and awkward.

—Julia—

I drew the curtains to see the city and North Korea in silence across the river. The court building rose above the apartment buildings nearby with its dome roof glowing. The rising sun peeked through the clouds and shone directly on it. *God, shine on that court building today. Let everyone see you. Give Kevin courage and strength. Let the judges see his innocence.*

My goal was to stand where Kevin might pass by so he wouldn't feel alone. The sign *Life Hotel* at the entrance encouraged me as I walked two blocks to the 4-star hotel where Jim, Mr. Pan, Sean, the Consular Department Coordinator and Adele, the consular officer, stayed. Jim was in the restaurant and offered me coffee. He was always so thoughtful! Sipping warm coffee calmed me and Jim's support and willingness to attend the trial encouraged me. He treated me as family.

Mr. Pan arrived and exchanged words with Jim. Sean and Adele came soon after, and went straight to the breakfast buffet. I felt so different from them–so ordinary. Sean handed me a brown envelope. A signed letter from Prime Minister Trudeau offering his apologies for our *unjust detention and horrible ordeal*. He was right. I tucked the letter away, thankful my cry for help reached him and honoured he'd written back.

"This is a hard day for me," I said, tears close to the surface. Adele emphasized the government was raising the case at the highest levels. I burst into tears. Her official sounding response to my desperate plea for compassion and understanding was overwhelming. I needed coffee and comfort. I went to the bathroom to control my tears. When I returned, Adele apologized and everyone's tone softened. "This is a difficult day for me," I said again. It was hard to be strong.

Minutes later, we left for court. Determined to arrive 45 minutes early, I hoped to see Kevin arrive. Jim was a strong warrior by my side and my friend Anna met us there. Another sweet friend, Sara, walked back and forth along the river near the courthouse and prayed. I knew thousands of others were praying too.

—Kevin—

I sat on a bench seat in the back of the van with leg irons digging into my ankles. I watched for Julia, remembering other prisoners mention seeing family on the way to court. *She's there!* Beside her stood a man I guessed was James Zimmerman, the American lawyer I'd never met. Julia waved. Strengthened and knowing we faced the trial together gave me new courage. She couldn't see me through the tinted windows but I waved too.

The police van entered the courthouse gate. As guards shuffled me into an elevator, focusing on Julia helped me endure the pain as the leg irons cut into my flesh and every muscle ached. We entered a third floor holding area. I felt so embarrassed being treated like a common criminal. A guard released the handcuffs and leg-irons, locking me in one of ten little closet-sized cages. The others were empty. Standing in the tiny cage, I squirmed and shifted but nothing helped. *God help them see the truth. Help me be a witness here. Help me survive the day.*

—Julia—

A police van passed. *It's him!* I waved. Through the stone archway, I saw Kevin, frail and thin, shuffle out. My heart broke. I watched guards lead him off and wanted to shout out or run to him but couldn't. *Did he see me? God, stay close.*

We entered the main door of the court building with its huge cement pillars and sat in a sparse office as Sean negotiated for courtroom access. The bilateral agreement stated Canadians had the right to consular representation at trials but Chinese officials explained that in cases of national security, Chinese law superseded international law. Frustration mounted but the decision was final. Anna and I went outside to pray. Plain clothes agents stood nearby at intervals but I was relieved no cameras, crowds or media arrived.

—*Kevin*—

That cage, padded on three sides, made an hour feel like forever. I felt faint as two court guards in blue police uniforms unlocked the cage and put new handcuffs on. We took a well-worn elevator to an empty 7th floor courtroom in need of repairs. No one spoke or explained. Fifteen minutes later guards led me to a second threadbare courtroom, slightly better than the first. One handed me a bottle of water and unfastened the handcuffs. In the center of the room was a solitary prisoner chair. I sat there completely alone.

A large court desk with three chairs faced me on a raised platform. The guards sat two metres behind me, one on either side with two empty rows of seating for observers behind them. A camera man adjusted a video-camera near the platform to point straight at me. A door behind the platform creaked open and Judge Ning and two other judges, in long ceremonious black robes, took their seats with Judge Ning in the middle. Then my two prosecutors and the interpreter, entered and sat at a desk on the left. It surprised me to see them because at our meeting in prison, they seemed inexperienced. *Can they prosecute my case?* Benji was the court interpreter which wasn't good either since his English was limited.

Mr. Pan entered next and sat out of reach at a desk to my right. Everyone faced me and I faced the judges. I waited for the tiger to strike its prey. *God is with me.* The trial began but Judge Ning used technical words I couldn't decipher. The interpreter translated a word here and there, instructing me to stand up or sit down. Confused, I never knew if or when I could speak. Nothing included me and the process made no sense. I spoke to Mr. Pan, but Benji interrupted. "You can't consult your lawyer during a trial!" *Why not?* When I heard the word *zhàopiàn (*photos*)*, I guessed they were discussing evidence so I stood to defend myself. "No, sit down!" he said.

When Benji signaled, I tried again. "The pictures I took depicted daily life, not state secrets. No one tried to prevent me. Photography is my hobby. Many photos were on my computer for years." No one listened.

"Sit down!" Benji said. The session continued as if I wasn't there. *Is the trial already scripted and these are actors reading lines?* I heard reference to volumes of confessions but saw none. When Benji told me to speak again, I didn't know the topic so went through my own memorized scripts while everyone talked over me. The prosecution claimed I stole state secrets but nothing in their voices suggested it was serious. *They aren't prosecuting well. Perhaps they don't need to if the outcome doesn't depend on their expertise.*

It wasn't just me that felt chaos. No one listened when others spoke either. The lack of evidence should have proved my innocence but seemed irrelevant. *How can they give me a long prison sentence or execution after this sham trial?* Mr. Pan interjected a few times in Chinese.

"It's minor. It's obvious because he kept things on his computer for years and wasn't trying to hide or send them to foreign agencies." During the final summary, he asked the court to consider my bad health.

I hoped for freedom but lurking near was the thought God might need me in *the big house.* I felt thankful my fate did not rest in the hands of governments or courts or Judge Ning or these prosecutors. When I'd viewed court trials during the prison news broadcast, I'd always felt sick and hated watching. Solemn judges with harsh voices speaking to criminals in prison vests with a courtroom of people watching, had terrified me. My trial in this dated courtroom felt different. No prison vest, viewers, or carefully planned proceedings. Instead there was confusion and chaos. The outcome was out of my control. *And out of theirs too?*

Court broke for lunch which meant back to the holding cage with a Styrofoam box of tofu and rice and bottled water. I wished there were prisoners in the other cages to break the isolation. I tried to crouch but pain shot through me, forcing me to stand. The 90-minute break was torture. I envied Mr. Pan enjoying lunch and checking out of his 4-star hotel.

—Julia—

Mr. Pan couldn't discuss the case during lunch break. He said it would continue that afternoon and he hoped to be there until the end but had a train to catch. Jim had commitments too so I thanked him for coming. As court opened for afternoon business, the sky turned dark and rain pelted the streets. Heavy wind, too strong for umbrellas, blew violently as Sean, Anna and I crossed the street seeking shelter by standing against the court building. We stood waiting all afternoon, wondering when Kevin would come out.

—Kevin—

The chaos continued. I tried to speak again but Benji intervened. "No, you can't say that now." Nothing Julia or I said or wrote during six months of interrogation at the compound was admissible. The only evidence was the prosecutor's summaries. We'd only met twice and never with my lawyer present. Witnesses weren't permitted and my lawyer couldn't communicate with me even during lunch. Despite this I felt positive because the case lacked concrete evidence.

At 3:30 p.m. Judge Ning declared the trial over and the judges and prosecutors left. Mr. Pan's train to Beijing left at 6 p.m. so after skimming through 15 to 20 pages of Chinese court proceedings, he apologized for leaving me with Benji and two guards to finish the review.

"I expect the verdict will come in two to three weeks," he said. *I hope he's right.* Benji couldn't translate the full transcript so he summarized key points. I gave up trying to understand, frustrated my lawyer had left.

At 5 p.m. the court building emptied until we were the only ones inside. Exhausted but naively hopeful it would be impossible to prove my guilt given the evidence, I signed and fingerprinted the papers and returned to the police van still handcuffed and shackled. Every muscle ached and only a miracle kept me from passing out. I praised myself for surviving and wondered if Julia would be outside. She was!

Waving with wind and rain blowing around her, she looked frozen.

Did she stand there eight hours for me? I felt so grateful seeing Sean and Anna beside her and waved because I wanted to even though they couldn't see me.

The Cell 318 prisoners peppered me with questions. How did it go? Was anyone sitting in the back benches watching? Every detail mattered. When I told them the viewing area was empty, a former police officer said a closed trial was good luck and best for my case because it meant China wouldn't make a public spectacle of the trial on television. He said if they planned to, they would stage everything with a court full of people. His words gave me hope.

Despite the day's ordeal, God had pronounced me not guilty, and I'd survived. I'd been honest and truthful and seen Julia twice. I fell asleep exhausted but thankful.

—*Julia*—

Hoping Kevin saw my frantic wave, I thanked Sean and Anna and returned to the Life Hotel, grabbing fast food on the way. I'd seen no media or commotion. *Will the MSS call?* The moment I lay on the bed sleep swept me away. At 9 p.m. the blue phone jolted me awake.

"You did well," Chief said, "the trial had no disturbances. You can go home for a visit. Make plans and give us your travel details and contact information in Canada. Remember the restrictions. We've informed your country and they know the conditions too."

"Will you return our money? It's expensive to go back."

"No, the case is ongoing. We'll tell you where to meet to pick up your passport."

Probably a black car. I didn't want to go home alone. I wanted Kevin by my side. This wasn't good news.

—*Kevin*—

The day after I felt positive because the trial lacked evidence. Sean visited and seemed relieved. His next news shocked me. "Julia has permission for a family visit to Canada. She will return for the verdict." *What does that mean for me?* I'd imagined doing all the firsts together. Hugging the kids together. Picturing it made me sad. Nothing happened the way I hoped.

Sean left saying, "See you next month. Take care of yourself," and reminding me this special visit was not an indicator they would come more often. The disclaimers irritated me. I'd survived a trial. I missed Janine's *hope I don't see you next time* as I faced another open-ended wait.

The full impact of the trial hit me with a massive thud, and my body and mind screamed in unison. Julia's home visit was a final blow. *I will be the only Garratt left in China! Will they let Julia return? Why a trip now?* Nations never do anything without a reason.

34

HIDING IN CANADA

*An invisible red thread connects those
that are destined to meet, regardless of time,
place or circumstance. The thread
may stretch or tangle, but will never break.*

—CHINESE PROVERB

—Julia—

On Wednesday, April 27, I collected my passport from a black car and boarded a train to Beijing. Jim offered me his new apartment even though he and his family were in America. Finding the key as instructed, I entered a spacious spotless living room filled with artwork and carvings. I went straight to the window overlooking Beijing. *I love this city.* I reminisced for ages. Its historic charm, mouthwatering food, and fascinating people. The bell tower that used to be the city timekeeper. The traditional courtyard houses with carvings outside identifying the occupants' position in society. Our favourite inexpensive Beijing duck restaurant where we'd feasted many times on garlic spinach salad with peanuts and roast duck carved into 88 slices. So many joyful memories. *Will I ever be back?*

❖

The next morning, as if in a bizarre movie that might change course at any moment, I arrived at the airport. *Will anyone recognize me?* Nervous, I passed the checkpoints and boarded without incident. Seated between two strangers, I sat in silence. After 21 months held in China. I'd never pictured this secret and solitary return to Canada. Global Affairs Canada arranged with Canadian Border Security Agency (CBSA) to have two uniformed agents escort me from the gate in Toronto to an underground meeting room where my sister, Deborah, her husband, Ed, and a GAC official waited. The large empty underground boardroom was not the reunion setting I'd envisioned. As security pushed open the door, Deb and Ed stood up. Everything blurred. I heard voices but not words. I saw tears and knew some were mine as I scanned the secret welcome room. *Am I in Canada?* The CBSA officer told my brother-in-law there were 20 Chinese on the plane to watch me but they couldn't prevent it because they all had Canadian citizenship. *China sent people to monitor me in Canada?* It wasn't a comforting welcome home.

Two weeks rolled together in a tumult of sounds and foods and family. I can't remember when or where or what order the daily sequences unfolded. My parents arrived with a beautiful welcome home sign and Hannah and Sarah flew east with two bubbly excited grandchildren and a baby. I held our new grandson Lucas in my arms and watched Joey playing with super heroes while Kiana drew a cartoon dog. Tremendous joy mingled with the lingering awareness that I still wasn't free. Safe at my sister's house, I was a stranger hiding in my home country with only a passport. Suspicious cars sat by my sister's driveway and followed wherever we went. When I visited Kevin's family, a car was there too. Kevin's brother Jeff shared that someone had hacked his computer many times since our arrest and asked if I had anything from China with me. I had wedding rings and a watch. Tucked in the back of my watch was a miniature chip which they tossed into a pond. I was too scared to tell anyone this was happening in Canada since I wanted to obey the terms of my visit.

Only immediate family and a few trusted friends knew I was there. I kept silent about my 635-day ordeal to keep my promise to the MSS and ensure Kevin's safety. Surveillance cars plagued me and my family's phones, computers, documents and websites were compromised. Deborah said they'd been harassed since our disappearance.

I called Global Affairs Canada (GAC). I hoped they could facilitate a health check since our international medical insurance had expired during captivity. They explained health coverage was provincial not national so they'd try but couldn't guarantee anything. I asked about a driver's license and replacing documents. GAC noted my questions. An official was always available for phone calls but waited for questions before searching for solutions. Disappointed the government wasn't proactive during my two-week home visit, I realized how little they invested in cases like ours on the Canadian side. I recommended they take note of our challenges and prepare better for the next case. Canadian citizens trapped in international political disputes, who've lost everything, need support. Global Affairs Canada provided no debriefing, counsel, financial or re-entry assistance. Thankfully we have an amazing family!

Jeff and Todd shared how much time they'd spent with my sister petitioning the government and asking for interventions. From the start, they'd insisted GAC refer to us by name and never by case number. They'd rallied family and friends to help pay legal fees, travel, visas, and Kevin's prison expenses. And kept people praying. Now at home, they helped me navigate Canada with gentleness and care. When I went to get my new visa, I needed the help! The Chinese consular representative told me to apply elsewhere and refused to call GAC to verify their arrangement. My sister stepped out to call them since cell phones didn't work in the building, while I stood pleading my case. Suddenly a tall intimidating security officer approached.

"She has to leave," said the clerk.

"But Canada arranged this. Your government agreed. It's a...." Seeing the man about to grab me, I bolted for the door shaking and in tears. *This happened in Canada?* GAC lodged a complaint immediately. Thankfully the Chinese Consulate offered me a private appointment that afternoon and the woman who'd harassed me apologized. After I paid the fee, they issued a visa on the spot. My home visit was far from restful.

❖

On May 13, 2016, the night before my return flight to China, GAC informed me they'd secured provincial health insurance, retroactive to the day I landed. *It's too late! I leave tomorrow morning.* But another shock was coming. When I awoke the next morning, there was an email notifying me that Beijing had extended the verdict decision another three months! The news blindsided me. I flopped down on my sister's soft flowered couch to read the Bible and calm my soul. *Trust in the Lord with all your heart and lean not on your own understanding, in all your ways acknowledge him and he will direct your paths. (Proverbs 3:5 ESV)* I couldn't lean on my understanding. My sister, desperate to help, called Pastor Fred. It was 6 a.m. but he came at once.

"The word that came to me on the way," he said opening his Bible, "is Proverbs 3:5, Trust in the Lord with all your heart and lean not on your own understanding." *Astounding!* Courage returned and the weight of disappointment, although still there, loosened its tight grip. My weakened soul had to trust in God. Again.

❖

A CBSA van drove me directly to the airplane door to board the flight to Beijing. Kind, sympathetic officers said my case was rare, explaining they usually transported criminals. They smiled and said they hoped things went well for me. *Have I passed the test China set for me?* I sat on the plane alone holding the CBSA officer's kindness tight and told myself to be brave.

After 36 hours of travel, I lugged my suitcase to the third floor, flopped down on the countryside Kang bed and cried myself to sleep. Early the next morning, I walked a kilometre to register at the local police station, then called the MSS and returned my passport. Exhausted, I found my paints, watched a bird land on a branch outside the window, and painted it. The tiny brown bird emerging through watercolour brush strokes brought rest in my chaos.

❖

A week later Adele reported Kevin was in crisis. The little strength I had oozed out. His body had deteriorated and he sounded close to death. I begged the Embassy to do more and called Jim who promised to send an urgent letter to the Ministry of Foreign Affairs (MOFA) asking for humanitarian release on medical grounds.

A month passed in complete silence as I painted and wrote small notecards to Kevin, stacking them in a pile until the next consular visit. I peered through the window for hours at a time. On Day 672, I watched a lady fill a suitcase with dirt from the construction site and wheel it back to her home. On Day 673 a white balloon floated by and I rushed to the window. The sky was full of pink, white and mauve balloons blowing over the complex, scattering on the ground. *I want them!* Grabbing my key I rushed to collect balloons as if on a wild Easter egg hunt. I made three trips back to the flat, piling the balloons on the bed. For what? Perhaps, to catch some wedding celebration joy and bring it into the pain of my world. Perhaps, to be a child releasing the feelings of captivity and bringing freedom back. I'm sure the MSS agents in cars outside watching didn't know what to write in their reports that day.

❖

In June, not wanting to overstay my welcome in the countryside, and with no progress on the case, the MSS permitted me to return to Canada. Their warnings were softer but I knew I'd still be monitored. When dear friends Britt and Diethard offered me a peaceful basement suite to wait in, it was the perfect solution. With a huge comfy bed and a sitting room overlooking a spacious treed garden, I felt in the world but not of it. Every day I hoped for a call to return to China for the verdict. I joined the family for a trip to Ottawa to plead our case to Stéphane Dion and his Global Affairs team. Ottawa welcomed us, reiterated Canada's concern, and insisted they were doing all they could. *They want to wait it out with quiet diplomacy. But at what cost to us?*

❖

A terrifying message came out after the July consular visit. Adele relayed Kevin's words, "My next meal will either be with Julia or Jesus." He'd threatened to stop taking all medication. His cries hammered on my soul. Frustration with the whole diplomacy process surfaced. *He is dying. What's the point? Why can't I visit? God, please!*

The visa was delayed. There was no verdict date. Every day I called and heard disappointing news. A visit was approved but a visa wasn't. *God, please untangle this mess!* I sang and walked in the tree-filled garden behind the suite, enjoyed birds at the feeder or sat reading my Bible in a white wicker chair writing notecards for Kevin. Britt and

Diethard did all they could to make the suite cozy and comfortable. Their kindness stilled my soul. Britt, a sweet lady with a huge joyful smile, encouraged me. "When Kevin comes home, he'll love sitting here. When Kevin returns, we'll have the new fireplace and basement renovations ready." Her gentle words renewed hope that Kevin would survive when my heart wasn't sure.

❖

The visa came three days before the approved visit. On the plane, I rehearsed. *I'll wear my most colourful blouse and comfort him, encourage him, and tell him he is surrounded with love and should never give up.* Excited to be back in China near Kevin, I hoped China would deport him. Then my blue phone rang.

The visit was denied. Panic struck. Why? *Has he died? Will they tell me? Will I see the body?* I called Adele. The consular visit was going ahead. *Kevin's alive.* I passed on books and money for Kevin. As she gave an update my thoughts jumbled and words poured out. "We can't go on this way—without a home or job, isolated from everyone and everything, depending on others for money to live and to pay for prison. Can't Canada help? An innocent man is dying!" She listened patiently. The Canadian government was applying diplomatic high-level pressure but there was nothing else to say.

Waiting with no timeline, even for a day, is hard work. Throughout that lonely, hot, humid summer month, the dust swirled outside as if knowing my turmoil.

—*Kevin*—

August 4, 2016. Day 730. Two years in detention. My mind pushed through but my body dissented. Every position ached. The promise of a visit when Julia returned was a lie. I saw her signature on the deposit slip from the gate. She sent money. *Why not let her in? Why torture me? God, what is your plan?*

The 6 a.m. bell rang, and I wrote a sermon until I couldn't hold the pen any longer. Getting out of bed was a struggle. Every muscle throbbed. My voiceless scream for better care joined the silent refrain of complaint echoed by my cellmates. The minutes slowly ticked away another morning.

At 11 a.m. guards ushered in a man with a yellow vest fastened over his T-shirt. He came from the IV room, legs chained together cutting into his flesh as he shuffled past me in navy plastic flip flops. His youthful face and smile masked the terror lurking behind his eyes. He sat by the bathroom on a stool and a prisoner set his bowl on the bed. Three cellmates pulled stools over to chat. Everyone helped him and wanted news from other cells.

He stayed a few hours, chatting and acting happy, while I sat speechless as the weight of a life lost sunk deep into my soul. Young Jo sat beside me explaining. The 32-year old man had sold 23 kg of drugs. He'd never see his wife or young son again. What eternal consequences! I wanted to talk to him but cell gossip filled the air until guards returned and led him off leaving an icy chill in the room. Prison reality serves many horrible meals.

A few weeks later during rest period, we heard a strange sound. A thunderous engine and heavy wheels turning intruded into the stillness. I rushed over to the cell door. Craning my neck to look at an angle, through the hallway windows I saw a large green military transport truck. Everyone sat up. Young Jo and another man crammed beside me to get a look. I heard the uniform thumps of boots marching in the next wing and rushed to the opposite side of the cell. Eight to ten soldiers marched along the hallway with rifles, bayonets attached. After these loud unusual sounds came 15 minutes of complete silence. Then we heard chains dragged along the 400-wing floor. I asked Young Jo what it was but in my gut, I already knew. The final walk for the man in the yellow vest. His last hour. He shuffled along with his head bowed and soldiers on either side. The whole cell listened immobile to the horrifying steps. The transport truck's heavy door clanged shut, the engine revved and the ominous sound faded.

Fear crept in uninvited and in hushed tones, as if we would be next, the inmates discussed the off-site location where executions take place by firing squad or lethal injection. Some had lost cellmates. It was my first and I sat frozen in thought. *Where will he be tonight?* As if he stood there again like a ghost in our cell, I shivered and prayed. *Jesus, please find his wife and son and hold them tight. Let the man in the yellow vest cry out in his last breath to the one who loved him all his life.*

❖

The next morning, I read Julia's notecard for that day.

I went to the guard gate to check for mail since I'm living in the countryside but mail goes to our old address. There was a card from Hilda Weiss. I crossed the street and stood by the river. The tide was coming in as I opened it. Guess what the card said? 'The tide will turn.' Perfect timing. Kevin darling. It will! We will never give up hope. I can't wait to see you.

I read the message over and over teaching my soul to hope. Yes, the tide will turn. It must!

35

TWISTS & TURNS

Spring is sooner recognized
by plants than by people.

—CHINESE PROVERB

—Julia—

In the third week of August, Stephen called. I rushed to meet them, surprised they chose a tea house. Stephen and Chief ushered me into a private room. "You don't need a notebook," Chief said as I pulled one from my purse. "We'll just chat. Choose any tea you want." I remembered my prayer in isolation to have a meal with my captors before leaving China. *Is this my answer?*

"Go home and earn money for Kevin. He will adapt to the big prison. Don't worry."

"But his health is terrible! I'm afraid he'll die!"

"He won't die. Aches and pain are normal at these ages. He'll survive and you can visit when you like. He will be there a long time." *There hasn't even been a verdict.*

❖

August 25, 2016, I reluctantly took another solo flight to Canada. I hadn't seen Kevin since that April glimpse at the trial. Prime Minister Harper and Prime Minister Trudeau's interventions to date had failed. The court postponed the verdict another three months, until mid-October. *Will I see Kevin again? We aren't afraid to die but why this extended period of intense suffering? Do guards need Kevin there? Do cellmates need encouragement or a share of his food?*

While transiting in Beijing I looked for my gate and for agents. The square black bags strapped across their shoulders. Standing with legs apart like soldiers at attention. Cell phones held waist high recording.

256

Scanning the area for agents was normal. Idle conversations with strangers were no longer airport chitchat. Only babies were safe. I scanned the waiting room until I saw a little girl. We played peekaboo and she took steps towards me as the parents beamed. I smiled, opting to let them think I was a Beijing foreigner who hadn't bothered to learn the language so I wouldn't have to answer questions.

❖

On board, I sat beside a business woman and we both chose not to talk until the end of the flight.

"Are you going to Vancouver?" she asked.

"Yes, I have two sons there, and then I head to Edmonton to visit my daughters."

We exchanged trivialities and after telling me she worked in the technology field, she asked my occupation. "I'm between jobs." *I'm between everything.* My family, job, home, country, possessions–everything was in limbo. My passport labelled me Canadian but China was my home. I felt betrayed. The only consolation was that since China chose us, another Canadian couple was still free. And that couple might have had small children. Much worse.

My bags had little inside but my mind was packed full of Chinese memories. Hundreds of children running around laughing, then graduating from university instead of being marginalized for their orphan background. Students from not very famous schools believing in themselves and imagining bright futures. Families studying English together and having family fun. People who loved God as I did. Would I do it again if I knew about this ending? Yes. I would.

❖

Simeon met me in Vancouver and handed me a phone. Within 15 minutes a message filled the screen. *This phone has been compromised.* Simeon was furious and started calling friends. I told him I wasn't ready to have a phone and gave it back and went on to Edmonton the next day.

❖

On Monday, September 12, 2016, after a week reunited with my daughters and three grandchildren and avoiding the media, Global Affairs Canada called.

"Did something awful happen to Kevin?" I asked, an amber alert raised.

"No, no, and I am sorry we've been silent recently. We don't have answers but unlike other times in this case, I can tell you that China is engaging in ongoing talks, with nothing stalling them. One positive outcome is that the verdict hearing will be tomorrow at 4 p.m."

"What? I can't get there in time. I wanted to be there. Weren't they supposed to give three days' notice?"

"Yes, but they asked us to waive it. They want the verdict hearing as soon as possible. One representative from our office will attend. Jim and Kevin's Chinese lawyer will go too. We are sorry you can't get back in time."

You waived it without asking me? Why am I the last to hear? I longed to let Kevin glimpse me and be the first to see him if he was released. Now I'd miss that moment. *God, you knew this timing. Help him at the hearing. Please do a miracle and let him come home.*

❖

That night Kiana stayed over. Our friends were away on a cruise and had generously offered me their home. "Grandma, let's act out Grandpa coming home," she said knowing nothing of the upcoming verdict.

"Ok, what are you thinking?"

"Well, Grandma, you stand over there and be Grandpa and I will be you and stand here. Hold your arms out." She ran towards me smiling and jumped into my arms giving me a huge hug. "Now it's my turn to be Grandpa," Kiana said, and I laughed and told her I was sure me jumping into her arms wouldn't work too well. We laughed and went to watch a cooking show and draw pictures, our favourite Grandma/granddaughter activities.

—Kevin—

Day 773. A guard called through the cell door. "Kevin Gao, come with me."

"Why?"

"Your verdict hearing is today." He unlocked the door and put me in handcuffs and leg irons. Ouch. *Is this a trick? Hearings aren't in the afternoon.* "What's happening?"

"I don't know," he replied. I had no choice but to go with him. Thoughts stormed my brain. *Are they going to execute me?* This wasn't the protocol for that. *Are they shipping me to the big house?* I should have had warning. I expected Julia back for the verdict. The compartments of my brain flung open and a thorough search produced nothing. I shuffled along in leg irons with my heart pounding. Transport guards and the prison warden waited in the reception area. *I can't go to a hearing dressed in prison clothes and flip flops.* Something felt very wrong. "They didn't give me three days' notice," I said to the warden in desperation.

"It's ok," she said as if knowing something she couldn't tell me.

They locked me to bars in the back of the police van on a small, uncomfortable bench. *They didn't lock me back here last time.* Fear escalated. We pulled up at the court building and I got out in flip flops and prison clothes. I hated having no dignity, treated as a common criminal. Guards locked me in the holding cage briefly and then moved me on to a different courtroom than I'd been in for the trial. *This must be the verdict hearing.* The judges, prosecutors, and Mr. Pan were there, and I noticed Sean and another younger man I didn't recognize sitting in the front row of a three-row spectator section.

"I don't know what's going on," I said as they whisked me past to my chair. Behind them in the back corner was Chief by himself. My lawyer didn't speak as he took his place out of reach on my right. I tried to read his facial expressions but couldn't as I sat alone in the middle of the courtroom.

Judge Ning entered and court was in session. He read from a set of papers stapled together. The verdict. Nine pages. I only understood fragments. The judge said my defense and the lawyer's attempts to defend me or suggest mitigating circumstances were not valid. He said I lied about my crime during the trial but confessed it during interrogation. He read directly from the verdict papers as I listened in horror. "We found the defenses and defense opinion of the defendant (Kevin Garratt) and his attorney do not have factual or legal basis and therefore are not valid. (The People's Republic of China, Liaoning Dandong Intermediate People's Court, Kevin Garratt Criminal Verdict, p.7)" *Why had I hoped the court would find me innocent?*

Judge Ning continued, "Even if the defendant Kevin Garratt's act of providing information to the employee of Canadian Security Intelligence Service (CSIS) constitutes espionage crime, the relevant circumstances are not severe. We found upon review that the facts and circumstances described above are true and accept the defense opinions provided herein. (p.8)" Good, they considered Mr. Pan's plea for leniency. *I hope that spares me from execution.*

The judge turned the page. He paused before listing various *Articles of the Criminal Law of the People's Republic of China.* I felt emptiness in the room as if the air had drained out and gathered to return in a mighty gust. Judge Ning took a deep breath and read as if I was one criminal in a long list of criminals who had received sentences in his courtroom. *Here it comes.*

Judge Ning's wrinkles gathered around his lips as he spoke in a loud, strong voice, enunciating each word, "Kevin Garratt is guilty of the crime of stealing and illegally providing state secrets to overseas (organization/individual) and is subject to the following penalties: five years' imprisonment, confiscation of personal property and deportation." He took a deep breath then continued, "Kevin Garratt is guilty of the crime of espionage and subject to the following penalties: three years' imprisonment, confiscation of personal property and deportation. (p.9)"

Eight years and then deportation? *I won't survive.* My head spun and the proceedings became a blur of standing, sitting, and following protocol until court was adjourned. The judges left, followed by the prosecution. As Chief Wang and Mr. Pan left, Benji let me talk to Sean. I couldn't comprehend what had just happened.

"Kevin, it's ok," Sean said, "the important word is deportation. We have a meeting tonight and we'll talk to you tomorrow." I wanted clarification but the guards hurried me to the van. *What can I believe?* I returned to my cell in leg irons and handcuffs. *God, is it true I will be deported? When?* I dared not entertain the thought as the cell door locked behind me and I flopped onto my cot. I'd missed dinner.

My cellmates had many questions, but I lacked energy to answer. I needed space. The whirlwind day, the sentence, and Sean's words replayed in my head. An enemy lurked nearby trying to overrule any traces of hope. I ached for Julia and the kids. *Is this one more disappointment to add to the others?* A conviction for collecting political, economic, military, and other information and providing it to a CSIS agent? How did life segue without warning into this? A man who loves China as his own family sentenced to eight years in prison as a spy? Julia as the only witness against me? Photos taken in public places along tourist routes classified as military secrets by the Army Political Office of the Chinese People's Liberation Army? I drifted in and out of sleep that night with the verdict roaming through my consciousness. With no English copy my brain concocted its own fragmented version.

The next morning, a guard led me to a meeting room. Sean was there. "There was a meeting last night, separate from the court," he said, "And I heard deportation could happen as early as Thursday or Friday. We won't be sure until you're on the plane. They'll probably ask you to sign some papers. I can't tell you what to do, but I recommend you sign them."

The meeting was short, but promising. Back in the cell, a guard instructed me to pack my box and leave it on the bed. My Bible went in first, then sermon notes, family photos, my favourite devotional books, and a few clothes. The rest I left to divide as spoil among the inmates. I'd seen many times how the minute someone left, the others rushed to grab what loot they could. Most inmates left with nothing so I was glad they let me keep a box. The signs were positive, but my heart remained fragile.

As I ate lunch with my group, I realized my body wasn't aching. In fact, I'd noticed it getting better in recent weeks. *Is God healing me?* At first I was upset because I'd hoped to get humanitarian release on medical grounds. *Is God preparing my body for freedom?* Still contemplating the mystery while swallowing a final bite, I heard my name. *Three meetings in two days?* MSS officials waited in a new room usually reserved for guard and officer meetings. Chief explained I needed to write and sign a few conditions of release and handed me pen and paper. Sean's recommendation to sign documents if asked, rung in my ears so I wrote each dictated sentence:

> *I will not appeal the sentence. I will not talk to the media. I will pay all the fines, including the fee for the investigation period. I will pay the fee for my medical care in the detention centre. I will pay the fine that goes with my sentence.*

I signed my note and they tucked it into an envelope. Then someone walked in with a bag of my sermons and notes. "They're Bible study notes and personal thoughts. They're not dangerous," I explained as my heart sank into the pit of my stomach. They ignored me.

"Follow all the conditions. Julia was good when she went home. You need to be too. The media is not your friend. Don't talk to them. You can come back to China later. I'll take you on a tour." Chief went on like this for at least an hour.

When I returned to the cell, my box was empty. I knew they'd taken my notes but my Bible and family photos were gone too. Panic seized me. I questioned everything. *Is it a trick? Am I going to the big house?* Tears trickled out as I stared at the empty box under my bed. Family photos, my Bible and notes had been my companions for 19 months. *How can I get up in the morning without my Bible?* The tears wouldn't stop. Pieces of me had left in a plastic bag and I wanted them back. I collected the few remaining food items under my bed and gave them away.

Despite the signs, I tossed and worried throughout the night that deportation was a lie.

36

HUGGING THE BEARDED MAN

The time to publish joy is now.

—JULIA GARRATT

—*Julia*—

I shuttled Kiana to school Wednesday morning and dashed back to meet Gerry and Karen Johnson who I'd invited for a visit. With the coffee pot plug in my hand, the phone rang. It was Randall from GAC. *Kevin's dead.*

"The hearing is done. The court handed Kevin an eight-year sentence but at a meeting separate from the court, the MSS discussed deportation. We don't know for sure but Kevin could arrive in Vancouver as soon as Thursday. He must sign away his rights to appeal, accept a fine and agree to several other conditions."

I was relieved but not sure he'd comply. He'd never admit to being a spy and I didn't want him to. *God give Kevin wisdom. We want him home but your plan not ours.* Still in shock, the doorbell interrupted my thoughts. Karen and Gerry appeared smiling and I apologized for not having coffee ready, launching into an explanation. "Kevin got an eight-year sentence but I just heard there's a remote possibility of deportation soon." *Can Kevin bear an eight-year sentence?*

The phone rang again. It was my Aunt Janelle and she sounded excited. "Julia, I had to call. As Amanda (her granddaughter) got out of the car for school this morning, we prayed for you and Kevin. She yelled, 'God, enough! Let him out!' It was powerful!"

Since Aunt Janelle knew the Johnsons, I put her on speaker phone, marveling at the timing and shared my latest news. "I knew it! God is on the move and change is coming!"

The next few hours I hovered near the phone. Randall finally called, apologizing he had no updates. "Should I book tickets to Vancouver or wait?" I was desperate for guidance.

"We can't tell you what to do, but it might be wise," he said. When government representatives say "we can't tell you what to do, but...," what follows the "but" is important.

"Ok. I will go." I scrambled to contact Sarah and Hannah asking if they could come. Both said Thursday worked but Friday they had important commitments. *God, please let it be Thursday!* I booked tickets for the girls and grandchildren and within hours my good friend Kathy shuttled me to the airport. My last-minute flight had a stopover in Calgary. Waiting to board the second flight, my phone rang. An Ottawa number. Loud construction noise in the temporary waiting room made it impossible to hear so I clicked speaker phone.

"Hello, Mrs. Garratt? This is Prime Minister Justin Trudeau's office." People standing nearby stood stunned and leaned in as I switched the speaker off, wedging against the retainer wall to listen. "We want to ask if the Prime Minister can phone you this evening. He wants to be the first person to tell you when Kevin is on the plane and out of Chinese airspace."

"Yes, that's fine," I answered confirming my number. My thoughts raced. *This is happening! Kevin's coming home!*

—*Kevin*—

September 15, 2016, our daughter Sarah's birthday, I got up at my usual time of 3 a.m. It was agony to miss my morning Bible and reading routine. I prayed but struggled for words. At 5:30 a.m. guards appeared. The morning bell hadn't gone off and the prison was silent. *God, help me. Whatever comes.*

My mind wandered back to soldiers marching and chains dragging along the ground attached to the man in the yellow vest. I shuddered. *That could have been me!* Instead I dared to hope I was being deported. Leaving my cellmates behind awaiting unknown fates was bittersweet. I was eager to go but sad I couldn't help them. Even Wang Ting's scrawled number to call his family was in the Bible I didn't have. I glanced at each one lying on their cots. A few stirred and said goodbye. "I won't forget you," I promised. Nor would I forget the unbearable isolation from family and long and painful waits confined in one room. This could have been my execution day but instead my imminent departure was an unfolding miracle. I asked God to reveal himself to each cellmate and give each one the grace for their stories—whatever they were.

The guards rushed me through a blood pressure check and ECG. *No handcuffs or leg irons?* I felt human again. Women sobbing in the next wing filled my ears as I took my final prison walk. Passing guards and TV monitors without handcuffs was strange. It was as if I had changed sides and joined the guards who marched beside me. As doors clicked and bolted behind us, the taste of release intensified. We climbed into the administration building, stopping at the revolving gate while a guard fumbled to unlock it. I stepped though.

Chief and four Dandong MSS agents greeted me in the reception room. A van and two unmarked cars waited by the door. *Will this be the happiest day of my life?* A guard handed Chief a carryon suitcase. It was mine. *Was it here the whole time?*

As we stepped outside, I noticed the license plates of all three waiting vehicles started with FB and remembered that first night when they'd told me they were the Chinese equivalent of the FBI. An agent opened the door for me as if I was a hotel guest getting into a chauffeured car. The clean, tan interior smiled at me. No bars on the windows. No restraints. No sirens. I moved to the back seat and stretched my legs out in comfort. The agent passed me a bottle of water as I buckled my own seatbelt. *That was fun!* I glanced back at the thick dark prison walls shrouded in morning mist. Everything was surreal as the prison faded into a dot on the horizon behind us. I was in a convoy of cars so different from the midnight procession that led me captive to the raid. I felt honoured. *All this for me?*

We drove three hours to Shenyang, the provincial capital. I hardly dared trust my eyes. The airport came closer and closer. My body ached after two sleepless nights, and my mind was a cushion full of stuffing, unsorted and hidden behind a shell of skin and bones. *Is it a trick? A carrot before we turn and drive towards the big house to serve my eight-year sentence with 5,000 others, learning the prison rules and receiving my work assignment?* My mind raced as the car stopped outside the terminal. Eight plain clothes security officers rushed me through airport procedures and into a private waiting room.

At least 12 officers including airport security, stayed with me. "You leave on the first flight out of China this morning," one said, "It goes to Japan." *Japan?* not Canada? Overwhelmed and confused I wondered how I'd get home from Japan with no credit card or money. An hour ticked by and officers announced the other passengers had boarded. The officers led me to the gate, arguing with the airline staff. They wanted to seat me on the plane but the airline policy meant no one got on without a ticket. Defeated, they walked me along the air bridge to the plane door. Chief handed me the carryon, asking me to turn and pose for a picture. The final proof this convicted spy was exiting China. They always needed proof. I smiled.

As I stepped onto the plane I heard a cheer. Jim and Sean were on board! I found my seat beside Jim. Sean was across the aisle. Business class. *Nice of China to deport me in style.* I looked around in shock and disbelief. My thoughts jumbled as if someone had cut the puppet's strings expecting it to function without direction. I lifted my bag into the overhead compartment with a rush of strength and sank into the spacious seat. My choice. I buckled my seatbelt. My choice. No officers, no handcuffs, no leg irons, and no cellmates. Only seats, stewards, and ordinary people.

Tears formed. Not from exhaustion, loneliness or plaguing physical pain. These were good tears. Tears of release. I'd waited 775 days for those wonderful tears!

"Welcome Kevin," Sean said as Jim reached over and handed me a box of maple cream cookies. I smiled through my thick beard and had my first look at this hero dubbed the *Good Samaritan* by my family. He smiled and offered me his tablet. *tablet?* I hadn't seen or held technology for two years. I beamed as he scrolled to downloaded messages from Julia and the family. The screen filled with notes welcoming me home and I feasted on drawings from my granddaughter Kiana showing me on a plane waving goodbye to China and another with me holding a huge hamburger in my hands. *Is this real?*

The wheels left the runway. *Goodbye China.* I looked around surrounded by colour. The fuzzy images in my brain focused one by one like puzzle pieces on a blank surface next to a box showing the whole picture. The flight to Japan was three hours and five minutes. As the plane left the runway, intense joy filled me, as if someone scrambled to complete the puzzle all at once before my eyes creating the most magnificent picture ever seen. I couldn't believe it was true. Sean informed me he'd notified Canada and once we were out of Chinese airspace, Prime Minister Trudeau would call Julia to confirm I was on the plane. I couldn't focus even with my eyes wide open so I asked the flight attendant for a cup of coffee.

"Milk and sugar?" she asked smiling.

Does she know who I am? "Yes please." I was so thankful to choose. Holding the warm cup in my hands, I sipped to everyone and everything. A dream coming true. Scenes from the last two days flashed through my mind. The hearing which came out of nowhere–the conviction–an eight-year sentence–Sean's comforting words–my life belongings disappearing without warning–the ache at leaving my Bible and special books with their margins full of tiny precious notes. I comforted myself. My prized possessions were gone, but I was heading home to my family.

I asked for more coffee. *Why not?* I chatted with Jim and Sean but as each sentence ended it disappeared into an abyss. Each moment was so significant I was fully consumed trying to live it. Words floated and people moved like figures in a story I had not been part of for so long. I was in my own world–coming out of something yet not quite out.

I got up to use the toilet and opened and closed the door myself. The private cubicle had no glass walls, cameras, or cellmate stares. I was alone and liked it. Back in my comfortable seat, I drank one cup of coffee after another. The flight attendant kept offering, and I kept accepting–because I could! When the airplane meal tray arrived, I turned to Jim and said,

"This is absolutely the best meal ever!"

—Julia—

Pastor Fred and Micki, who propelled our whole journey years before, picked me up in Abbotsford and prepared a wonderful dinner. They stayed up with me waiting for the phone call. Well after midnight, while joking that maybe Trudeau fell asleep reading bedtime stories to his children, the phone rang. I jumped.

"Hello."

"Is this Mrs. Garratt?"

"Yes."

"This is Justin Trudeau. I wanted to be the first to tell you your husband is on the plane on his way to Japan."

"Oh, I'm so excited. Thank you so much for calling me."

"We are so thankful and have been working hard for this day and doing everything we could to bring him safely home."

"Is he ok?"

"Well, he lifted his own bag into the luggage compartment and said 'yes' to a cup of coffee."

"Thank you so much for all you've done."

"You are welcome," he replied, "Enjoy your reunion. Is it ok if I call again tomorrow night to speak to Kevin?"

"Sure!"

"What time works best?"

"Any time after 5 p.m. works, since the rest of the family leaves at 4:30 p.m."

"Great. I'll call again tomorrow. Nice talking to you Mrs. Garratt. Goodbye."

"Thank you for calling. Have a good sleep."

Kevin is coming home!

—Kevin—

In Japan, I had my first private shower in the airport business lounge. Pure joy. Hot water flowed, and no one watched. I think I stayed for a full 30 minutes wondering how I ever shared that time and space with twelve others. As I flew on Air Canada from Tokyo to

Vancouver, I drank more coffee and wondered why I'd ever thought airplane food wasn't good. It was amazing! I ate everything, and the hours spun forward. Time moved so much faster in freedom than in prison.

—Julia—

Thursday morning, Day 775, border security ushered us into a private meeting room behind the luggage carousels in the international section of Vancouver airport. Sarah, and our three grandchildren, Kiana, Joey and Lucas flew in with Hannah that morning and Simeon and Peter arrived by sky train. Pastor Fred and Micki waited with us. An unexpected bonus included a CBSA sniffer dog brought in to entertain the children while we waited. We got updates when the plane landed and unloaded. The anticipation and emotion in the room intensified along with the grandchildren's giggles and laughter as they petted the dog.

—Kevin—

No one met us at the gate. Just before immigration, two border security agents knew who we were and greeted us. They took our passports and led us to a side room away from others going through customs. They pointed to a door in the distance and I didn't know what to expect. I imagined Sean and Jim walking in with me but they held back, letting me go first. The door was open a crack. Sarah! She was sitting at a large table. I hesitated. *Am I dreaming?* I took a final step and reached out my hand, pushed open the door, and walked into a room filled with my family!

—Julia—

The door opened. Kevin walked in with a huge beard and a massive smile and we rushed into his arms. It was one giant hug. We were so happy and so thankful! We never wanted that moment to end!

—Kevin—

I saw Julia and my children and grandchildren–the whole family surrounded and wrapped me in love. I held Lucas, my new grandson, for the first time. Kiana and Joey left a CBSA dog they were playing with, and ran into my arms. Overwhelmed with joy, I couldn't believe I was back. Everyone whipped out their phones and took pictures. I realized I didn't have one.

Simeon's phone kept buzzing with media requests asking if I was back. That surprised me. Jim and Simeon prepared a statement. As they talked, I was in a bubble and the conversation was beyond me. *Why is the media a big deal? Why do we need an official statement?* I overheard a call with consular affairs–something about leaking my arrival to the media. Not understanding the commotion, I held Lucas and made him giggle as a statement and two photos went out.

"Well, I came the furthest to celebrate your birthday, Sarah!" I said smiling, "And I bought a gift too, thanks to Jim giving me some money in Tokyo."

She hugged me and I took a photo with each of the children. I thanked Sean before he left for a return flight to Beijing and CBSA led us through a secure exit. James mentioned he had an ongoing flight to San Diego and wished us all the best. Our Good Samaritan lawyer had walked with us every step of the journey until we were safely home! We thanked him and said farewell. As our entourage rushed to a car, I realized sadly that I'd left my new sweatshirt, my first piece of clothing outside prison, in the meeting room.

Fred and Micki drove us to the hotel room provided by friends. I entered the lobby amazed! We entered a clean cozy suite and I stretched out on the soft couch in awe. The grandchildren piled on top of me tugging my coarse beard and giggling. Every moment was pure joy! When Julia suggested we go to a nearby park I realized I could go anywhere now. Outside was fantastic–a pond and ducks and pathways. Everything delighted me. The children ran free, and I scooped Lucas up and took him to see the ducks. I chatted with our kids freely, loving the sound of their voices and the expressions on their faces. The hours flashed forward in a marvelous dream. I had hoped for so long and without warning release came. I could do things I wanted. The opposite of everything I was used to in the cell.

My mind jumped into freedom with a marvelous splash. Without a phone, I borrowed Julia's. Even dialing was fun. In the lobby and outside, I wondered if people recognized me. At 4:30 p.m. after a laughter-filled family picnic in the room, the kids and grandkids left and Julia and I were alone. What joy to be alone without agents or interrogators or pressure to confess! An hour later, her phone rang.

"It's the Prime Minister," Julia said handing me the phone as I lay beside her on the comfortable bed.

I felt honoured that he called. I knew he received reports but it never occurred to me how many people had heard our story. He welcomed me back and said everyone in Ottawa celebrated my reunion with family. I thanked him. "Maybe we can have coffee one day," I suggested as he explained how hard they'd worked to bring me home.

"Bless you," I said still overwhelmed I was free.

"Yes, God bless you," he replied. I fell asleep smiling.

❖

The next morning, I woke wanting a shave and realizing I could! I was on jet lag and excited! My full beard had been a protest because shaving was so hard and unpredictable in prison. Since the shops didn't open so early we went for coffee. I ordered, then realized I didn't have money. I hadn't touched money for two years. While Julia paid, I grabbed a newspaper from the rack. The front-page spread was a picture of us hugging. I held coffee in one hand and the paper in the other and asked Julia to take a picture. At nine, I bought a razor from the drug store and at the checkout saw a stack of newspapers. The whole front page was me on the airplane holding maple cookies. I bought one and folded it over to avoid being recognized by the cashier. My first strange yet joyful normal morning!

A few friends dropped in to see me. When Phil rode over on his shiny blue motorcycle, I sat on it for a picture. We met Simeon for hot-pot in Richmond. My head spun doing normal things.

On Saturday, we flew to Ontario and my brother Jeff met us at the airport. Emotion overwhelmed me as we hugged and drove to meet the rest of our family at Britt and Diethards', where we'd stay while we transitioned. I got out of the car and took Julia's hand, so aware we were together. With each step, I anticipated the reunion. Aniela and Tristan, my niece and nephew, stood at the door holding welcome signs with my brother Todd, and his wife Natalie behind them. My mother rushed into my arms as everyone crowded into the front hall. My Dad and his wife Angie, my Aunt Renee and Uncle Ken, Julia's parents and her sister and family. Safe and loved I sat in the comfy cushioned living room chair in a fog—a good fog. Everyone had questions as we celebrated freedom with food and balloons and smiles.

When everyone left, Julia and I went downstairs to the bedroom.

"It's too dark," I said turning on the lights. I'd slept with lights on for 775 days. Julia understood. The ordeal was over and whatever we did next we'd do together. We smiled and went to bed with the lights shining around us. There were no tears on the window that night.

Epilogue

Our joy-filled freedom is mingled with tears that we have left the country and so many wonderful, kind and precious Chinese people we love as family. We already experienced one miracle of kindness when, one year after our deportation, the Dandong MSS returned Kevin's Bible, notes and some personal valuables via our son. We hope one day an invitation to return will come and we can put the past to rest in a new and wonderful embrace of friendship.

Until then, we wake up every morning thankful: for life, for friends, for family, for freedom, and for thousands of tiny things we'll never overlook again. Rediscovering freedom after losing it is a journey of its own. Every choice we make is an incredible victory. The world is big again and we treasure the simplest things—the open skies, the exquisite flavours of food, and marvelous giggles and joy on our grandchildren's joy-filled faces. Reacclimatizing and catching up on two years of our children's lives takes time and we still find gaps. Each of our children has their own extraordinary 775-day story!

The partnership of human resilience, prayer, and God's personal involvement in our stories is a mystery and a miracle! It's also a daily choice. We know for certain that in every situation God is always at work, always present and always has a bigger plan than we can see. We step forward with joy into a future designed just for us and hope many others will be encouraged, impacted and blessed by *Two Tears on the Window*.

ACKNOWLEDGMENTS

Two Tears on the Window comes from hours of piecing together our two years apart, and setting it in the context of 30 years of work in China. Learning of the incredible partnership of family, government, friends and the Christian community around the world that persevered in prayer and quiet action, continues to amaze us. Many times, we reflect. *People did all this for us?* We feel unworthy of such care but deeply appreciative. First, we are thankful to God who was a true, caring and comforting father, staying by our side every moment of the ordeal. We are thankful to Canadian Prime Minister Trudeau, former Prime Minister Harper, and M.P.s from all parties who kept raising our case and pressing for solutions. The commitment and coordinated efforts of Stephane Dion, Randall and the Global Affairs Canada team, Canadian Ambassador Guy St. Jacques and Sean Robertson's Beijing Embassy consular team was invaluable. James Zimmerman, our American lawyer, deserves more than a thank you. He is a true hero who dedicated endless hours as a consultant and committed friend, advising, navigating, encouraging, and giving legal and practical counsel and support to our family and our Chinese lawyers.

To our family and friends, who encouraged, prayed for, invested in and kept us writing this book, we are so very thankful: our children Simeon, Sarah, Peter, and Hannah, Claude & Monica Gidman, Jo Decarie, Ross and Angie Garratt, Deborah and Ed Bergman, Jeff Garratt, Todd and Natalie Garratt, Don and Dorothy Robinson, Gary & MaryEllen Hartmann, Janelle Thomas, Britt and Diethard Boettcher, Fred and Micki Fulford, Gerry and Karen Johnson, Paul and Heidi Hughes and the River community, Kathy and Perry Zelmann, David Wells, Murray Cornelius and the PAOC family, Jordan and Sonya Tetley, Sue Keddy, Carol Olson, Mike and Olga Spino, Don and Hilda Weiss and the MGT community, Simon and Gloria So, Doreen McIntyre and girls, Nathan and A.J. Rooke and the Three Hills community, Dave and Lise Ash, our Vancouver home community and many others who collected articles, sent stories, and prayed throughout this time.

To those who provided quiet spots for writing: Elizabeth Walker and Katherine Thompson, Laurie and Lily Wallace, Gary and Penny Culverson, and Tony and Annette Chia. Thank you for your generosity. To our former co-workers and aid partners around the globe, what an honour to serve with you. Thank you for your encouraging notes, visits, and prayers.

To our close Chinese friends who cared for us throughout the ordeal, giving practical assistance to our children, a listening ear, and keeping joy alive on our darkest days – fēicháng gǎnxiè nǐmen (heartfelt thanks)! To China for giving us 30 amazing years and a safe and nurturing place to raise our children and work and live alongside wonderful business associates, teachers, students, and neighbours. Thank you for the wisdom, joy, laughter, food, and hospitality! Those years we would never trade!

To those who offered insight, wisdom, editorial advice, and fact-checking, we are very thankful. Ruth Thielke, who spent hours editing the early and final manuscript versions, Gina Chiarelli and Laurie Tetarenko who edited the final manuscript, and Sarah Garratt, Deborah Bergman and James Zimmerman, who reviewed the manuscript and gave valuable feedback. Thank you for your encouragement and invaluable contributions.